Defending Democracy

To defeat demagogues like Donald Trump, citizens must vote to defend democracy, otherwise it will not be there to defend them. Taking off from Max Weber's "Vocation Lectures," David Ricci's *Defending Democracy* explores the idea of "citizenship as a vocation," which is a commitment to defending democracy by supporting leaders who will govern according to the Declaration of Independence's self-evident truths rather than animosity and polarizations. He examines the condition of democracy in states where it is endangered and where modern technology – television, internet, smartphones, social media, and so on – provides so much information and disinformation that we sometimes lack the common sense to reject candidates who have no business in politics. Arguing for the practice of good citizenship, Ricci observes that as citizens we have become the rulers of modern societies, in which case we have to fulfill our democratic responsibilities if society is to prosper.

David M. Ricci was a fellow at the Institute for Advanced Study in Princeton, the Woodrow Wilson International Center for Scholars in Washington, DC, and the Brookings Institution in Washington. He was the Chair of the Hebrew University Department of American Studies and the Department of Political Science. He is the author of eight scholarly books including *The Tragedy of Political Science* (1984), *The Transformation of American Politics* (1993), *Good Citizenship in America* (2004), *Politics without Stories* (2016), and *Post-Truth American Politics* (2023).

Defending Democracy
Citizenship as a Vocation

David M. Ricci
Hebrew University of Jerusalem

CAMBRIDGE
UNIVERSITY PRESS

Shaftesbury Road, Cambridge CB2 8EA, United Kingdom

One Liberty Plaza, 20th Floor, New York, NY 10006, USA

477 Williamstown Road, Port Melbourne, VIC 3207, Australia

314–321, 3rd Floor, Plot 3, Splendor Forum, Jasola District Centre, New Delhi – 110025, India

Cambridge University Press is part of Cambridge University Press & Assessment, a department of the University of Cambridge.

We share the University's mission to contribute to society through the pursuit of education, learning and research at the highest international levels of excellence.

www.cambridge.org
Information on this title: www.cambridge.org/9781009731584
DOI: 10.1017/9781009731614

© David M. Ricci 2026

This publication is in copyright. Subject to statutory exception and to the provisions of relevant collective licensing agreements, no reproduction of any part may take place without the written permission of Cambridge University Press & Assessment.

When citing this work, please include a reference to the DOI 10.1017/9781009731614

First published 2026

A catalogue record for this publication is available from the British Library

A Cataloging-in-Publication data record for this book is available from the Library of Congress

ISBN 978-1-009-73168-3 Hardback
ISBN 978-1-009-73158-4 Paperback

Cambridge University Press & Assessment has no responsibility for the persistence or accuracy of URLs for external or third-party internet websites referred to in this publication and does not guarantee that any content on such websites is, or will remain, accurate or appropriate.

For EU product safety concerns, contact us at Calle de José Abascal, 56, 1°, 28003 Madrid, Spain, or email eugpsr@cambridge.org.

For the members of my
Thursday morning
breakfast "parliament"

Contents

Introduction *page* 1

1 Crisis 8

2 Enlightenment 22

3 Vocations 36

4 Democracy 53

5 Muddling 77

6 Information 108

7 Dysfunction 132

8 Common Sense 153

9 Fixing the Phones 181

Index 196

INTRODUCTION

Donald Trump is a crook. He was convicted in May 2024 of financial fraud. He is not the victim of some "deep state" plot but a flat-out criminal tried in court and condemned by a jury of twelve fellow citizens in the State of New York.[1]

Nevertheless, in November 2024, 77 million Americans voluntarily and enthusiastically elected Donald Trump to be president of the United States for a second time. In shock, many other millions of American politicians, pundits, activists, and ordinary citizens have been grieving and arguing non-stop about how that could have happened.

For the anguished, Trump's behavior since entering the White House in January 2025 has only made things worse. Some of them believe that, unlike earlier presidents, Trump regards his victory as a mandate for disrupting government agencies and practices. They fear that he will shatter some of both, thereby undermining safety nets and environmental protection, and they are sure that he will misuse and corrupt others, promoting autocracy and maybe even fascism, at home and abroad.

Moreover, they see that, by firing thousands of federal employees and impounding enormous budgets approved by Congress, he plans to eliminate parts or all of government offices such as the National Institutes of Health, the Agency for International Development, the

[1] http://bit.ly/4bCt4sQ.

Environmental Protection Agency, the Food and Drug Administration, the National Labor Relations Board, the Consumer Financial Protection Bureau, and the Department of Education. All of these were created by Acts of Congress that have not been repealed or amended by majority votes as constitutionally required in both Houses on Capitol Hill.[2]

In other words, if Trump will ignore those Acts and their intent, which add up to properly enacted laws of the land, he will coldly violate the separation of powers that the Founders built into the Constitution between the Executive and Legislative Branches of government.[3] On that score, the Constitution assigns to Congress the power to legislate in various areas of public need and policy,[4] whereas the president's signature designation is as the administrator ("Executive") of decisions and apparatus created by Congress.[5]

Transfixed by such a gloomy analysis, anxious critics mainly blame Trump's victory in 2024 on the Democratic Party for failing to inspire enough Americans to vote against him. That party's leaders, they say – from former President Joe Biden, to former Vice President Kamala Harris, to former Majority Leader Senator Chuck Schumer, and to former Speaker of the House Congresswoman Nancy Pelosi – were out of touch with ordinary folks. Moreover, in public life, they did not fight as aggressively as MAGA (Make America Great Again) Republicans like Governor Ron DeSantis (R-FL), Senator Mitch McConnell (R-KY), Senator Lindsay Graham (R-SC), and then-Senator J. D. Vance (R-OH) were willing to do.

---

[2] As a candidate, Donald Trump did not issue a platform, so we have no clear understanding of what he is aiming to do. But we can speculate that some of his intentions resemble recommendations which appear in the 920 pages of a Heritage Foundation report entitled *Mandate for Leadership: The Conservative Promise, 2025* (Washington, DC: The Heritage Foundation, 2023). For some time, the Heritage webpage of publications showed *Mandate for Leadership* as "sold out," but it was even then available at www.documentcloud.org/documents/24088042-project-2025s-mandate-for-leadership-the-conservative-promise/.

[3] Readers should not be misled by Trumpian claims that he and his loyalists (like Elon Musk) are promoting "efficiency" as if that is, obviously, an admirable goal. Founders like James Madison inserted separation of powers, and checks and balances – that is, complications – into the Constitution precisely because they thought that some measure of *inefficiency* would be valuable for preventing ambitious people from establishing tyranny. Fascists like Mussolini are always promising to get our trains to run on time. We must never forget that such achievements may cost more than they are worth.

[4] Article I, Section 8.

[5] Article II, Section 2.

Common Sense

This book takes a different approach to where America is now. Instead of attacking Trump as a flagship of disaster – which I believe he is – I will argue that things shifted in America to make it possible, or even inevitable, for a politician to behave like Donald Trump to begin with. That is, I will explain how American society, especially in recent decades, opened a place in its thinking and acting for a demagogue like Donald Trump to take center stage in public life and get away with it.

My aim, then, is to explain that what dropped America into a democracy pothole was a shortage of "common sense," which too few voters exercised on Election Day. In Chapter 8, "Common Sense," I will discuss why not enough of this political resource is available now. When I get to that, I will not accuse anyone in particular. The point is not that some Americans are born stupid and lacking in common sense,[6] but that many of us, in all walks of life, lack some measure of common sense *because* modern information instruments – including radios, movies, televisions, computers, and smartphones – together muddle our thinking and confuse our consciences.

On my way to saying that, I will assume that readers already know how important common sense has been in American history, because they know that vital expressions of it informed the Founders' devotion to "self-evident" truths enshrined in the Declaration of Independence. Wherefore, on the basis of that dedication to straight and accurate thinking about what they regarded as obvious truths, in the Constitutional Convention, the Founders set up an astonishingly successful republican form of government almost two hundred and fifty years ago.

The new government, whose historical foundations I will discuss, and which many Americans and Europeans immediately admired, was a matter of separating powers, setting up checks and balances, and safeguarding fundamental civil rights. It was based on ideas endorsed by Thomas Jefferson, Benjamin Franklin, George Washington, John Adams, James Madison, Alexander Hamilton, Patrick Henry, and many

---

[6] My friend and former neighbor, Professor Danny Kahneman, of the Hebrew University, and later of Princeton University, came close to saying that, in more elegant language, and received for his thesis the 2002 Nobel Prize in Economics. See his *Thinking, Fast and Slow* (New York: Macmillan, 2011).

of their colleagues, the best of which, as long-term insights and convictions, are still sensible and capable of serving the country well today.

Of course, what the Founders wrought, and what the erratic tantrums and toxic prejudices of people like Donald Trump may undo, was, and still is, a collection of institutions and practices that were never perfect. For example, many Americans now confess that the Founders' original creation shamefully excluded from political participation almost all women, Blacks, and Native Americans.

Fortunately, however, that system underwent several crucial upgrades enshrined in constitutional Amendments like Thirteen to Fifteen, Nineteen, and Twenty-Six. It therefore fostered, over time, increasing levels of equality for many men and women who were previously excluded.

On the other hand, in recent years the Constitution has been flagrantly misinterpreted by Supreme Court justices like Clarence Thomas, John Roberts, Samuel Alito, Brett Kavanaugh, Neil Gorsuch, and Amy Barrett. Such judges, who are all later-day Republicans, have issued retrograde decisions such as those which legalized unlimited campaign contributions, which discontinued federal supervision over states that still underwrite racism, which authorized personal acts of discrimination in public accommodations, and which revoked a nationwide women's right to abortion.

All of this backsliding indicates that American public life needs some serious upgrading now. Instead, the country got Trump again, who more and more resembles a rogue president.

Democracy

I won't summarize *Defending Democracy* in this "Introduction" but will let it speak for itself in coming chapters. I will only insist here that scholars should maintain a special consideration for democracy, because to write plain-spoken books and articles about its potential demise under the leadership of someone like Donald Trump is one way to help all of us to pitch in together and avoid the political disasters that devastated rank-and-file Europeans only three generations ago.

On that score, as historians grimly explained after World War II, many Europeans did not dissent strongly enough in the 1920s and

1930s to prevent the rise of terrible political regimes – fascism, communism, and totalitarianism – in Western society.

The moral of their story, delivered especially by people who survived unspeakable tyranny in Hitler's Third Reich, was straightforward. History shows us that some people are capable of every sort of atrocity. But we must not let abominable aspects of history repeat themselves. We must not yield an inch to political poison. Every occasion calls on us to promote civility and mutual respect. And every event demands that we will shun bigotry and brutality.

Ergo, ordinary people, across the board, must permanently hold democracy in mind. And while we do that, we must lobby for, organize for, demonstrate for, vote for, and pay for only candidates to public office who will support democracy wherever possible.

Such imperatives do not assume that democracy is flawless. No system of government is. But every day challenges us to defend that system wisely, deliberately, unswervingly, and tirelessly, else in difficult times, it will not be available to defend us.

The Mission

To that end, starting in Chapter 1, "Crisis," I will explain how we can avoid repeating Europe's twentieth-century disasters by putting up a strong defense, which means by sensibly exercising our citizenship rights. The good news is that we have it in our power to save ourselves. The more challenging news is that a great many of us must accept that mission before it is too late.

Moreover, we must not slacken. Donald Trump and his loyalists are not going to start behaving better, as we shall see. Therefore, we must be in this for the long haul. Free-riding is out of the question when a hooligan like Trump holds the national scepter and the biggest megaphone. In words of one syllable, if we don't do what needs to be done, no one else will do it for us.

Reports and Essays

Before starting to discuss where we are and how we got there, I should arrange some technical matters. I am an academic. I want to explain at the outset, therefore, that this book is not what scholars call a "research report." That is, I have not selected, say, a political issue, or a contested election, or a legislative face-off, or a confrontation between ideologies, and then studied it intensively by collecting data or conducting experiments in order to report what I found.

This book is, instead, an "essay." Essays deal with general matters that cannot be represented by specific events, or practices, or ideas, or institutions, as if something exactly there, at that spot or moment, is the main point and can be interpreted usefully if investigated with techniques such as conducting surveys, comparing committee votes, ranking policy preferences, checking documents, and interviewing protagonists.

Essays are in fact like mosaics, containing many pieces which, when seen together, offer a special picture, or a sort of gestalt, for our consideration. In this case, with Trump always, figuratively, in the room, I will comment on ideas and events that relate to American democracy – which is a very large and complex enterprise – and I will illuminate those items by reference to the views of impressive thinkers who have studied major aspects of democracy very seriously.[7]

This means that I am not proposing in this book what scholars sometimes call a "theory" – that is, a systematic but compact explanation – about what such items mean. I am, instead, offering a wide-ranging survey which incorporates some "terms" that together, I hope, will help us to think sensibly about the present condition of American politics.

Footnotes

I should explain here also a further technical point, about footnotes, because we live in an era where partisan language and intense reporting create an enormous and confusing flood of information and disinformation. Footnotes in this essay direct readers toward relevant sources

---

[7] On writing an essay, see Daniel J. Boorstin, *The Image: A Guide to Pseudo-Events in America* (New York: Harper & Row, 1961), which is about "how we hide reality from ourselves." Therefore, p. iii: "This is a large subject for a small book. Yet it is [also] too large for a big book. If I pretend in this volume to survey or comprehend all the bewitching unrealities of American life in the twentieth century, I would misrepresent the vastness of the subject. The task of ... [comprehension] is finally not the writer's but the reader's. The complete survey must be made intimately by each American for himself."

but, because many pieces of the mosaic I am assembling are themselves contested at great length – especially between what we call the Right and the Left – such footnotes cannot possibly cite all the sources which discuss those items.

For example, Chapter 4, footnote 1 refers to recent books which consider how "populism," generated by social and economic grievances, may bear on the current crisis of democracy. The books offered in that footnote are a sample of relevant thinking, no more. Even together they do not demonstrate conclusive understandings – that is, certainty – on this particular matter, which is populism, in a marketplace for ideas that, as we shall see in Chapter 6, "Information" and Chapter 7, "Dysfunction," backs up every idea, including some that are quite false, with books, newspaper editorials, op-ed articles, think tank reports, blogs, talk radio, television chatter, podcasts, and social media excitement.

Put it this way. I am not using footnotes to "prove" the matters I discuss, as if this book were a research report on whether corona vaccines work or don't. I am simply presenting many points of fact and judgment which together, and while supported by some thinkers who I believe are serious, offer what I regard as a sensible argument – especially about democracy and citizenship – for readers to see and consider.

Bear with me, then, as I start this essay with the federal election of 2020, which Trump claimed then, and still claims now, that he won.

1 CRISIS

In 2020, Republican Donald Trump lost the presidential election to Democratic Joe Biden.[1] By modern standards, it wasn't even close, because Trump got only 48% of the votes. Afterwards, he denied that he had lost, tried to persuade Vice President Mike Pence (R-OH) to ignore some of the state-certified electoral ballots, and encouraged his fans in January 2021 to storm the Capitol Building in Washington, DC.

Thereafter, Trump's behavior got worse. Still, almost 50% of American voters decided to support him in 2024. This time, everyone knew he was a crook, having been convicted in a New York State Supreme Court of felonious activity by falsifying financial records regarding hush-money payments made to a movie actress named Stormy Daniels.[2] On Election Day, he had not yet been sentenced. But he was eligible for years of imprisonment, and additional cases were pending in other jurisdictions.

---

[1] Biden's colleagues call themselves the "Democratic Party." Since the 1940s and 1950s, many Republican and/or right-wing opponents of Biden et al., have referred to the New Deal's political heirs as the "Democrat Party." This is a snarky way of intimating that that party should not be permitted to suggest or imply, by use of an adjective, that it is especially committed to democracy. I will discuss this sort of ideological polarization in Chapter 5, "Muddling." For an example, see Mark R. Levin, *The Democrat Party Hates America* (New York: Threshold Editions, 2023).

[2] https://bit.ly/4pJpRLr. See also www.nytimes.com/live/2024/05/30/nyregion/trump-trial-verdict.

Nevertheless, because Democratic presidential candidate Kamala Harris (D-CA) received in 2024 about six million votes *fewer* than she and Joe Biden had received in 2020, Trump won the election. Therefore, regardless of his criminal record, Donald Trump would take office in 2025 as the 47th president of the United States of America.

Many millions of Americans, who did not vote for Trump, believe that his most recent triumphs, first in dominating the Republican Party and then in capturing the presidency, are generating a national crisis. Maybe they are comparing his first steps in office, this time around, to those of previous Republican presidents, such as Abraham Lincoln, Theodore Roosevelt, and Dwight D. Eisenhower. Whatever, I believe they are right.

However, the crisis now unfolding is *not* the crisis I will explore in this book. Before we obsess on where the country is today, we should try to understand how, even before Trump was first elected in 2016, America prepared a political space for someone like him to act – often impulsively and inconsistently, sometimes ignorantly and illegally – as he does.

Eventually we will see how, by moving into that space, Donald Trump became a symptom rather than the cause of America's plight. Unfortunately, however, hard political times will live on after him, based on trends already existing.

It is that situation which suggested to me, and I am not alone, that American democracy may be falling apart. Therefore, I decided to write this essay in response to where the country is now, which sometimes looks to me like Wile E. Coyote running off a cliff and standing, although not for long, on thin air.

Citizenship

Let us begin at the beginning, then, even before Trump introduced himself to Americans as a candidate for the presidency by riding, with his wife Melania, down the golden – well, brass – escalator in the atrium of Trump Tower in Manhattan on June 16, 2015.[3]

---

[3] It is a little noted fact that, despite Trump's incessant slurs against legal and illegal immigrants, he is married to one. Maybe he is a fan of Ralph Waldo Emerson, who observed that consistency is the hobgoblin of small minds. On the hobgoblin thesis, see Emerson's essay

To explain the escalator event, and to dip into other, related events, the main aim of this book is to explore the nature of "citizenship" and especially the version of it that I will call "good citizenship." Thus, the subtitle of this book is "Citizenship as a Vocation."

The context for this emphasis is clear: Tens of millions of Americans in 2016, 2020, and again in 2024, failed to exercise their citizenship properly. That is, they failed to do it *well* – in the form of practicing "good citizenship" – when, as we shall see, they elected Donald Trump to the White House, not once but twice.

Citizenship and Democracy

For our purposes, it is useful to consider the entire matter of citizenship, good and bad, within a framework of understandings first promoted by the great German sociologist Max Weber. Therefore, I will introduce him to readers of this book starting in Chapter 3, "Vocations."

In just a few words now, however, let us note that such citizenship is a matter – of practice and ideal – which is admired by political societies known as "democracies." That is, since the more or less formal end of the Enlightenment in the late 1700s, many Europeans, and after them Americans, have believed that most residents in modern countries should enjoy the status of citizen and possess the rights and obligations of democracy's smallest public office.

In this sense, citizenship since the Enlightenment is a singular possession (1) which entails the right of "political equality" – that is, the right of each citizen to participate in choosing public officials and to hold public office if elected – and (2) which we regard as the hallmark of democratic life. Accordingly, we believe that citizens who enjoy that sort of equality should use it so well that we will succeed in living together safely and prosperously.

Our Target

The overall problem is this: on behalf of what they regarded as good government and common decency, but not perfection, Americans decided

on "Self-Reliance" (1841) at https://nationalhumanitiescenter.org/pds/triumphnationalism/cman/text8/selfreliance.pdf.

about 250 years ago to become, roughly speaking, a democracy. This they did even though there were respectable ideas and experiences in circulation at that time warning that democracies – ruled by many citizens possessing equal rights – can easily deteriorate into unmanageable regimes while no one knows how to define good citizenship in them as the right way of participating in public life under all circumstances.[4]

So, there is what puzzles me. In fact, the Founders who promoted democracy, no matter how inadequate by today's standards, were thereby committing themselves, as I will show, to something which they did not entirely understand.[5] And we have recently realized that enabling many approximately equal citizens to act through the institutions of democracy – for example, through free speech, frequent elections, fair trials, and freedom of religion – will not necessarily produce desirable results such as domestic peace and prosperity.

The Trump Shock

So where are we in all of this today? Many impressive thinkers – among them scholars, journalists, activists, and politicians – now believe that the practice of American citizenship is deeply in trouble. Therefore, let

---

[4] For our purposes, I am simplifying the story of what happened. For more details, some of the many and sometimes conflicting ideas that underpinned the move of Americans toward democracy are described and explained in Jonathan I. Israel, *Democratic Enlightenment: Philosophy, Revolution, and Human Rights, 1750–1790* (New York: Oxford University Press, 2011), *passim*, but esp. pp. 443–479. See also Michael Schudson, *The Good Citizen: A History of American Civic Life* (Cambridge, MA: Harvard University Press, 1998), *passim*. Schudson describes how the Founders feared some aspects of democracy as it was understood then. But he also explains how they believed in trying to maintain it within constructive limitations (such as less-than-universal suffrage and indirect election of senators) and informed by schools and newspapers.

[5] Certainly, the original concept was imperfect by today's standards. The United States did not immediately establish democracy for everyone but excluded most African Americans, most Native Americans, and most women. But no other countries in those days made much democratic room for such people, either, so we can leave that discussion for elsewhere and regard American democracy as an imperfect project that has, fortunately, undergone several serious upgrades, none of them arriving as quickly as we now think they should have. On one of those upgrades, better late than never, see Noah Feldman, *The Broken Constitution: Lincoln, Slavery, and the Refounding of America* (New York: Farrar, Straus, and Giroux, 2021). On the Nineteenth Amendment, an upgrade that assured women's suffrage, see www.neh.gov/article/winning-vote-divided-movement-brought-about-nineteenth-amendment.

us begin by noting some of their observations. With the qualification, of course, that there are so many worriers, sometimes from the Right and sometimes from the Left, that we can cite only a few of them and their ideas here.

* * *

Act I in this play started in 1789, when elections according to the Constitution were first held. Since then, as we shall see, exactly how to practice citizenship well has been debated and no consensus among thinkers has emerged. However, even where no consensus reigned on how citizens should behave, it was obvious all along that there were some things that good citizens should never, ever, do.

Accordingly, many Americans were thoroughly shocked in 2016 when, as described by Steven Levitsky and Daniel Ziblatt, "for the first time in U.S. history, a man with no experience in public office, little observable commitment to constitutional rights, and clear authoritarian tendencies was elected president."[6] Senator Ted Cruz (R-TX), a graduate of Princeton and Harvard universities, who was one of that man's opponents in the 2016 Republican primary elections, put the matter even more starkly. Trump, said Cruz, is "a pathological liar … utterly immoral … and a narcissist at a level I don't think this country's ever seen."[7]

According to Levitsky and Ziblatt, the 2016 election elevated a "demagogue" to the presidency. We will return to that momentous term. Let us note here only that, at that time, Donald Trump, who was the demagogue in this case, had never held public office, was most famous for bombastically hosting a television "reality" show (which, of course, was not at all real), and had displayed (a) an exciting rhetorical flair that was accompanied by (b) zero regard for truth.[8] Nevertheless, with all of these characteristics fully on display, Trump

---

[6] Steven Levitsky and Daniel Ziblatt, *How Democracies Die* (New York: Crown, 2023), p. 2.
[7] Quoted in Ezra Klein, *Why We're Polarized* (New York: Avid Reader Press, 2020), p. 177.
[8] Journalists have for years variously described Trump's disregard for truth. For example, a newspaper article before the 2024 election dismissed him as "a political candidate known for improvisational departures." See www.nytimes.com/2024/10/14/us/politics/trump-town-hall-dj-music.html.

in 2016 obtained the voluntary support of 61,985,106 voting citizens and won the election.

In other words – and here was the shock – in 2016 almost 62 million adult Americans decided, of their own free will, that they wanted as president of their country a man who had no experience managing any public enterprise, and who was therefore patently unqualified to run the Executive Branch of America's government, whose four million or so employees, including massive armed forces, are responsible for dealing with national defense, environmental protection, currency regulation, diplomacy, food and drug safety, national forests, agricultural subsidies, workers' safety, industrial pollution, strategic intelligence, scientific research, educational standards, social security, health insurance, border patrolling, and more.

After 2016, I thought that some of those pro-Trump citizens should be forgiven because they knew little about how public policies are made and administered in the nation's capital, and therefore they did not know in advance how badly Trump would perform while in office.[9] But I am less forgiving of citizens who, unrepentantly, voted for him again in 2020 and 2024.

In 2020, there were 74 million of those unapologetic Americans, and they endorsed Trump after seeing, if they had watched him from 2017 to 2020, what a disaster he was in the White House. In 2024, there were 77 million such voters, even though, in the interval, Trump had revealed no new talent for the job. In which case, the second-time shock of his winning was even bigger than the first time around.

---

[9] His supporters should have read some of his critics. For instance, John Bellamy Foster, *Trump in the White House: Tragedy and Farce* (New York: Monthly Review Press, 2017), p. 12: "By any independent account, Trump is a lazy, ignorant, unreflective, and unprincipled sociopath, a blowhard and a dangerous moron – a person who lies so routinely it appears he is incapable of even understanding the idea of truth or falsity." Or, Mark Thompson, *Enough Said: What's Gone Wrong with the Language of Politics?* (New York: St. Martin's Griffin, 2017), p. 92: "Donald Trump seems to have attained a unique Zen state in which random and rambling invention is truth, and the actual truth is a litany of lies cooked up by the pygmies who oppose him." See also The Fact Checker Staff of the Washington Post, *Donald Trump and His Assault on Truth: The President's Falsehoods, Misleading Claims, and Flat-Out Lies* (New York: Scribner, 2020). In Trump's first three years in office, the Fact Checkers logged over 16,000 "false or misleading" statements.

Populism

Trump is obviously a striking example of nationwide democratic strain. There have been many other strains, accumulating for years, and we will look at some of them later. Here, let us consider that scholars and pundits who currently fear for the survival of modern democracy have described that regime as suffering from a political malady which they call "populism."

There has never been a conclusive, uncontested definition of this disorder, but several components of it have often appeared. One is that someone very articulate will offer to rule on behalf of "the people" as if "the people" are entitled to throw off oppression by "elites."[10] The assumption, usually on the Right, is that such a candidate will attract support because many of "the people" are angry from being exploited, to the point where they will vote for candidates like Donald Trump in America, or Viktor Orban in Hungary, or Marine Le Pen in France, from a sense of "resentment" over their social and economic rank in society.[11]

---

[10] A leader who claimed that he would rule on behalf of "the great majority of Americans, the forgotten Americans, the non-shouters, [and] the non-demonstrators," appeared when Richard Nixon accepted the Republican nomination for president in 1968. This was later broadened when he claimed to speak, in 1969 while president, for "the silent majority" of Americans who had been abandoned by various elites but were patriotic citizens opposed to the anti-Vietnam War movement, which Nixon described as more of a threat to America than the country's enemies abroad. On Nixon's populism, see Joseph E. Lowndes, *From the New Deal to the New Right: Race and the Southern Origins of Modern Conservatism* (New Haven: Yale University Press, 2007), pp. 106–139. Then came Donald Trump, who declared that he would speak and act on behalf of all "the people" to put "America first." See his 2017 Inaugural Address at https://trumpwhitehouse.archives.gov/briefings-statements/the-inaugural-address/.

[11] Resentment is often described as stemming from inequality felt within the modern American economy, and that inequality is often charged with especially afflicting people who regard themselves as middle class. These are important talking points on the American Left, approximately speaking. Thus, Jeffrey Madrick, *The End of Affluence: The Causes and Consequences of America's Economic Dilemma* (New York: Random House, 1995); Barry Bluestone and Bennett Harrison, *Growing Prosperity: The Battle for Growth with Equity in the 21st Century* (Berkeley: University of California Press, 2000); Louis Uchitelle, *The Disposable American: Layoffs and Their Consequences* (New York: Knopf, 2006); Robert Kuttner, *The Squandering of America: How the Failure of Our Politics Undermines Our Prosperity* (New York: Vintage, 2008); Donald L. Bartlett and James B. Steele, *The Betrayal of the American Dream* (New York: Public Affairs, 2012); Hedrick Smith, *Who Stole the American Dream* (New York: Random House, 2012); Jeff Faux, *The Servant Economy: Where America's Elite is Sending the Middle Class*

On this score, some thinkers more on the Left understand populism to be a form of "anti-pluralism," where populist voters regard themselves as "the real people" while other countrymen, of various sizes, shapes, colors, origins, sexes, genders, convictions, talents, and preferences, are somehow outsiders.

Jan-Werner Muller made this point in classical terms. Candidates promising to serve the Roman "plebs," he said, were representing "the people" properly. However, if candidates regarded the plebs, and no other classes, as the sole "authentic people" of Rome, they were unforgivably assigning moral weight to only part of the Roman population.[12] And that, although Muller did not say so but I will add, would be like during the McCarthy Era (roughly 1947–1954). At that time, some Americans, including the film star Ronald Reagan, who was president of the Hollywood Screen Actors Guild from 1947 to 1952, scorned many other Americans – like Arthur Miller, who was a leading playwright and husband of the popular actress Marilyn Monroe – as "un-American."

Neoliberalism

Various thinkers have highlighted additional populist practices promoted by candidates and voters, leaders and followers. Many of those people, say the critics, are inspired by modern economic theories – a

---

(New York: Wiley, 2012); Robert D. Putnam, *Our Kids: The American Dream in Crisis* (New York: Simon & Schuster, 2015); and John Ehrenreich, *Third Wave Capitalism: How Money, Power, and the Pursuit of Self-interest Have Imperiled the American Dream* (Ithaca, NY: Cornell University Press, 2016). Concern for the American Dream and middle-class troubles also animate the American Right. They usually blame government policies (liberalism) and personal irresponsibility rather than the modern economy (neoliberalism) for hardships felt by Americans. Thus, William J. Quirk and R. Randall Bridwell, *Abandoned: The Betrayal of the American Middle Class since World War II* (New York: Madison Books, 1992); James Bovard, *Freedom in Chains: The Rise of the State and the Demise of the Citizen* (New York: St. Martin's Press, 1999); Wayne Allyn Root, *The Murder of the Middle Class: How to Save Yourself and Your Family from the Criminal Conspiracy of the Century* (Washington, DC: Regnery, 2014); and Governor Ron DeSantis (R-FL), *The Courage to be Free: Florida's Blueprint for America's Revival* (New York: Broadside, 2023).

[12] Jan-Werner Muller, *What Is Populism?* (Philadelphia: University of Pennsylvania Press, 2016), pp. 1–40, but esp. pp. 22–23. On the idea that populism fosters the legitimacy of some people over others, see Nadia Urbinati, *Me the People: How Populism Transforms Democracy* (Cambridge, MA: Harvard University Press, 2019).

sort of Friedrich Hayek, Milton Friedman, Robert Lucas, and Greg Mankiw worldview writ large – which extol and recommend a later-day form of capitalism recently labeled "neoliberalism."[13]

Again, there has never been an uncontested definition of neoliberalism. But Wendy Brown, for example, describes it as "licensing capital, leashing labor, demonizing the social [which is identity politics] ... and the political [thus respecting economic markets more than the state and other communities], attacking equality, [and] promulgating freedom ['against state solutions to economic and social problems']."[14]

In other words, as Brown and other critics understand neoliberalism, (1) it dismantles the existing society, in the sense of not insisting on some measure of equality whereby citizens can, by acting as an empowered *demos*, maintain a democratic regime. Moreover, (2) it dethrones politics, in the sense that it recommends that some fateful statewide decisions should be made not by politicians and their loyalists but by commercial actors – here, think Bill Gates, Jeff Bezos, Elon Musk, and Mark Zuckerberg – in a so-called "free" and "rational" marketplace.[15]

And (3) it extends the personal rather than the social sphere, which invites religious zealots to impose their sectarian beliefs on other members of the community.[16] This, in effect, downgrades the community as a whole, which consists of all its citizens together – secular and devout – because some religious people claim, against the community's

---

[13] I have discussed the characteristics of neoliberalism in David Ricci, *A Political Science Manifesto for the Age of Populism* (New York: Cambridge University Press, 2020), esp. pp. 61–91.

[14] Wendy Brown, *In the Ruins of Neoliberalism: The Rise of Antidemocratic Politics in the West* (New York: Columbia University Press, 2019), p. 2.

[15] The relationship between capitalist philanthropy and democratic policy-making is fraught. For example, see Daniel M. West, *Billionaires: Reflections on the Upper Crust* (Washington, DC: The Brookings Institution, 2014); Linsey McGoey, *No Such Thing as a Free Gift: The Gates Foundation and the Price of Philanthropy* (London: Verso, 2015); and David Callahan, *The Givers: Wealth, Power, and Philanthropy in a New Gilded Age* (New York: Knopf, 2017).

[16] Thus *Masterpiece Cakeshop v. Colorado Civil Rights Commission* (2018), where the Supreme Court allowed a baker, licensed to serve the public, not to bake a wedding cake for a gay couple because he, the baker, being constitutionally free to believe in his religion, believed that their, the couple's, lifestyle violated God's commands. See the decision at www.oyez.org/cases/2017/16-111.

neutral stance, that their principles, known by faith, are divinely inspired and therefore possess superior moral validity.[17]

All these acts and practices together, Brown said, create conditions of life which are so stressful, especially for many traditional white men, that they will enthusiastically vote for someone like Trump because he promises to punish those whom they "hold responsible for their suffering."[18]

Imbalance

Populism and neoliberalism are abstract analytical concepts, but concrete institutional arrangements also affect American public life. Thus, in constantly changing configurations and alignments, through small and large groups and organizations, via modest campaign contributions of ordinary people and huge financial interventions of megadonors like the Koch brothers, Miriam Adelson, Michael Bloomberg, Elon Musk, Richard and Elizabeth Uihlein, Kenneth Griffin, and Timothy Mellon, the preferences and aspirations of democratic citizens come to bear in complicated ways on how elected officials make decisions.[19]

Who gets a tariff? Who gets appointed to the Second Circuit Court of Appeals? Who gets an air pollution ban? Who gets a Cabinet seat? Who gets mortgage relief? Who gets a public park? Who gets a NASA contract to build a moon rocket? Who gets a soil bank? Who gets a new subway? Who gets a presidential pardon? Who gets to drill for oil in the Arctic National Wildlife Refuge? Who gets to hear Pablo Casals play his cello in a White House concert? Who gets to sleep in the Lincoln bedroom?

---

[17] Brown, *In the Ruins of Neoliberalism*, pp. 23–122.
[18] Ibid., p. 179. An earlier version of some of this analysis, framed in different terms, appeared in Thomas Frank, *What's the Matter with Kansas: How Conservatives Won the Heart of America* (New York: Metropolitan Books, 2004).
[19] See Larry M. Bartels, *Unequal Democracy: The Political Economy of the New Gilded Age* (Princeton: Princeton University Press, 2008), and Christopher H. Achen and Larry M. Bartels, *Democracy for Realists: Why Elections Do Not Produce Responsive Government* (Princeton: Princeton University Press, 2016). On mega-donors, see Jane Mayer, *Dark Money: The Hidden History of the Billionaires behind the Rise of the Radical Right* (New York: Doubleday, 2016), and Nancy MacLean, *Democracy in Chains: The Deep History of Radical Right's Stealth Plan for America* (New York: Penguin, 2018).

Scholars have long studied such political pay-offs, and pro-democracy thinkers are especially worried about them. They worry, for example, that polarization and gridlock flowing from antagonism cultivated by populistic leaders and their followers can produce undesirable budgetary jackpots by bypassing longstanding checks and balances upon which liberal democracy rests.[20]

Thus, Levitsky and Ziblatt explained how, in forums like the Senate, the Electoral College, and the Supreme Court, passionate Republicans, representing low popular-vote counts, mostly in "red" rather than "blue" states, often prevent popular Democratic majorities from making great national decisions and vital judgments, especially about who gets what, in budgetary allocations and legislative resolutions, which can extend to personal issues, such as misogyny, racism, and abortion.[21]

This situation amounts to a triumph of minority over majority rule, to which we will return. Where it obtains, it violates one of democracy's basic procedural axioms, which says that, apart from occasionally exercising momentary power, a minority cannot continually and legitimately represent the self-governing will of most of the people.[22]

---

[20] See James A. Thurber and Antoine Yoshinaka (eds.), *American Gridlock: The Sources, Character, and Impact of Political Polarization* (New York: Cambridge University Press, 2015).

[21] Steven Levitsky and Daniel Ziblatt, *Tyranny of the Minority: Why American Democracy Reached the Breaking Point* (New York: Crown, 2023). We will later discuss how, in the marketplace of ideas today, most ideas are denied, rejected, or discounted by their opposites. In this case, an argument with considerable supporting evidence, which claims that left-wing minority-espoused ideas deny various majority-espoused principles related to housing, health, transportation, and more, is available at www.nationalaffairs.com/publications/detail/minoritarianism-is-everywhere.

[22] A clear statement of this rule came from Abraham Lincoln in his First Inaugural Address: "A majority held in restraint by constitutional checks and limitations, and always changing easily with deliberate changes of popular opinions and sentiments, is the only true sovereign of a free people. Whoever rejects it does of necessity fly to anarchy or to despotism." See the address at https://avalon.law.yale.edu/19th_century/lincoln1.asp. Books that discuss institutional imbalance, which amounts to minority rule, include Jacob S. Hacker and Paul Pierson, *Off Center: The Republican Revolution & the Erosion of American Democracy* (New Haven: Yale University Press, 2005); Thomas E. Mann and Norman J. Orenstein, *It's Even Worse Than It Looks: How the American Constitutional System Collided with the New Politics of Extremism* (New York: Basic Books, 2012); and David M. Ricci, *Post-Truth American Politics: False Stories and Current Crises* (New York: Cambridge University Press, 2023). Some Americans, who fear what they call the

Democracy and Citizenship

Enough for the moment. These are matters that concern sensible thinkers who worry about democracy today. We will return to some of their worries later, but now we need only to note that the *talk* is about democracy, but the *problem* is citizenship.

Here is a crucial takeoff point for my analysis. For almost a decade, grim thinkers have cited Trump's effect on American democracy as evidence that the problem is not abstract and theoretical but concrete and dangerous in the real world. However, in a way, the problem is not really democracy in the sense of a collection of roles, agencies, and procedures, but the fact that these things are in the hands of people who look like they may not do all that needs doing to preserve liberal government.[23]

That is, an impressive collection of writers suggest that citizens, including all of us, should do their job better than they are doing it now. The analytical assumption on this score is that, as we have seen, citizens occupy "the smallest public office" in democracies because, together, citizens choose the men and women who represent "the people" in the halls of government and should therefore promote prudence and decency in the conduct of public life.[24]

So in a way – and I will have more to say about this – while citizens are small cogs in the democratic political system, they are also, as a sector, the designated rulers of most modern societies, whereupon they must do their work *well* – via good citizenship – for those societies to prosper.

"tyranny of the majority," believe that virtuous minorities are morally entitled to thwart, say, wicked majorities. This sort of approval for the filibuster and Electoral College may be linked, as in the case of many evangelical Christians, to the notion of virtue flowing from the observance of tradition, where "tradition" is regarded as "something fixed and unchanging, a pure spring that issues into a polluted river." That is, in this view, if the Counterculture people wanted to create some new traditions, they had no moral right to do so. See the quotation in Philip Gorski, *American Covenant: A History of Civil Religion from the Puritans to the Present* (Princeton: Princeton University Press, 2019), p. 202.

[23] See Michael Walzer, *The Struggle for a Decent Politics: On Liberal as an Adjective* (New Haven: Yale University Press, 2023).

[24] On the duties of citizens, see Joseph Tussman, *Obligation and the Body Politic* (New York: Oxford University Press, 1960), and David Shelbourne, *The Principle of Duty: An Essay on the Foundations of the Civic Order* (London: Sinclair Stevenson, 1994).

Defending Democracy

That is why this book is entitled *Defending Democracy*. I will return to that point later but, for now, in plain language, (1) it is citizens who must defend democracy, because, (2) if they don't do that, democracy will not be in town to defend them.

For instance, they must believe, not partly but fully, in democratic principles and act to uphold them in political institutions.[25] To this end, they must not vote for candidates like Donald Trump, who they can see will do nothing to maintain self-government.[26] And if some local governments use police powers to trample civil rights, as in the Minneapolis murder of George Floyd in 2020, citizens must act to assert reasonable control over those police. And if some judges, as in the Supreme Court case of *Citizens United v. Federal Election Commission* (2010), authorize unlimited spending by anyone, like Elon Musk, who spent $270 million in 2024 aiming to buy Republican electoral success and policy dominance, citizens must support candidates who, if elected, will appoint new judges to replace those set on issuing decisions that permit such behavior.[27]

In short, and we will come back to this, there are things that citizens should do to preserve democracy. Therefore, the cardinal political problem is how to produce good citizenship rather than how to preserve democracy. If "the people" will achieve the former, the latter will be there for them to enjoy.

Terms

But if that is the goal, what should be done? What are modern citizens capable of? What are they disposed to do? And what can we expect from them today?

---

[25] See, especially, Timothy Snyder, *The Road to Unfreedom: Russia, Europe, America* (New York: Tim Duggan Books, 2018), and Anne Applebaum, *Twilight of Democracy: The Seductive Lure of Authoritarianism* (New York: Doubleday, 2020).

[26] Alan Wolfe makes this one of his "lessons for the future" in *The Politics of Petulance: America in an Age of Immaturity* (Chicago: University of Chicago Press, 2018), p. 179: "Treat every vote as if the future of democracy depends on it."

[27] The size of Musk's contribution is so unusual as to warrant demonstrating it by citing a right-wing rather than left-wing source. So here is the *Wall Street Journal* at www.wsj.com/politics/elections/elon-musk-trump-republican-super-pac-investment-78a725cb.

As I noted earlier, I will address questions like these in the following pages in an essay which incorporates useful terms that I hope will permit us to think sensibly about the present condition of modern democratic politics. These terms will include some of those I already highlighted, such as good citizen, democracy, political equality, demagogue, populism, the people, elites, anti-pluralism, resentment, neoliberalism, minority rule, majority rule, and democracy's smallest public office.[28]

---

[28] Here is an observation more fit for a footnote than for the main text. Any book like this, about politics and democracy, will make its argument by using common words such as democracy, justice, equality, pluralism, populism, federalism, rights, dignity, decency, and more. That is appropriate. But, because these are *concepts* rather than *entities*, readers will tend to understand them differently. Not like when we discuss, say, dogs or eclipses. On dogs and eclipses, most readers will accept the opinion of experts (veterinarians, astronomers) and agree. But let's say we confront even a higher-than-usual degree of shared understanding over what is written in a particular political text. So the text uses a word – for example, the word "party" – and two readers say that they agree 90% on the meaning of that word. That may be unusual but welcome, given that parties are really complicated entities and not all the same. Then the text moves on to another word, like "neoliberalism," and the same two readers again agree on that word's meaning at the rate of 90%, which is a lot better than they would if, say, one was from Seattle and the other was from Detroit. It takes only a simple mathematical calculation to see that the actual amount of agreement between the two readers is now down to 81%, that is, 90% × 90%. Add a few more contestable words, and one sees that any text with more such words brings the area of agreement steadily down, multiplying it by 90% repeatedly, so that, in the presence of eight or ten such words, it quickly reaches 30–40% and less. Therefore, it is because political language inevitably and inexorably works this way that I am trying in this book to explain my terms at the outset so that readers can follow later what I mean to say. They may still disagree with me. But my collection of terms, defined in advance, will at least draw readers in the direction I have in mind, to be persuaded or not about whether I am correct.

2 ENLIGHTENMENT

From Enlightenment thinkers who lived mainly during the seventeenth and eighteenth centuries, European civilization inherited a vocabulary of public life including words such as "politics," "monarchy," "democracy," and "citizen." These terms came to them from studying classical languages, especially Latin and less so Greek, which became hallmark accomplishments of people who were especially trained in church schools and fledgling universities to work as lawyers, doctors, and priests or ministers.

What they learned constituted a framework of understandings that is still important today because it provided a context within which most political thought in Europe evolved and eventually reached America. The point here is that democracy as we know it arose within a collection of political ideas which informed European thinkers during the Enlightenment, therefore it is important for us to know something of those ideas, which many Americans admired, if we are to understand the concept of mixed-government democracy which some of those Enlightenment thinkers bequeathed to America's Founders.

I will simplify while explaining these European understandings, of course, which were based on two thousand years of study and acquaintance with early sources such as Herodotus' *Histories* (c. 430 BC), Thucydides' *History of the Peloponnesian War* (c. 411 BC), Plato's

Republic (c. 375 BC), Aristotle's *Politics* (c. 350 BC), and Polybius' *The Histories* (mid second century BC). Following which came later items like Niccolò Machiavelli, *The Prince* (1532), King James I, *The Divine Right of Kings* (1610), John Locke, *The Second Treatise on Government* (1690), the Baron de Montesquieu, *The Spirit of the Laws* (1748), and James Madison, Alexander Hamilton, and John Jay, *The Federalist* (1788). All of these, and others, have produced an enormous number of learned commentaries projecting an endless variety of opinions concerning how such materials were related and what they really meant.

Cyclical History

I will begin my analysis by noting a fundamental assumption made by classical thinkers, which was that history is "cyclical," or circular. That is, in commonplace language, what goes up must come down, or what goes around must come around.

Thus Herodotus described Croesus warning the Persian king Cyrus: "Human life is like a revolving wheel (*kyklos*) and never allows the same people to continue long in prosperity."[1] And Thucydides portrayed the drawn-out Peloponnesian War, the subject of his great history book, as a disaster for Greek cities such as Sparta, Athens, Corinth, Thebes, and Argos, which fought that war and consequently lost much of the prosperity which they had acquired after defeating Persia in earlier battles such as Thermopylae, Marathon, and Platea.

More formally, in the classical context, if an existing political regime – say a monarchy or an aristocracy – is doing a good job representing the interests of all classes of people in the state, then, most likely, through character flaws of the ruler or rulers, that good regime will, sooner or later, deteriorate into a bad regime acting selfishly on behalf of only its own members and interests.

Thus every good monarchy will eventually turn into a tyranny, which enriches mainly its single bad ruler, and every good aristocracy will turn into an oligarchy, which profits especially its few bad rulers, and every good democracy run by the many will dissolve into anarchy,

---

[1] Herodotus, *Histories*, Book 1, section 207, 1.

which will confiscate properties belonging to wealthier citizens and disintegrate into mob rule.

The upside of such predictions was that Greek thinkers also thought that every bad regime will eventually be overthrown by the citizens it oppresses and then replaced by a good regime, say when a tyrant is dethroned and supplanted by a few aristocrats, who will rule on behalf of the entire population.

Six Boxes

We can make these permutations easier to remember by arranging them in a matrix of boxes, with good and bad regimes, and their offspring, shown together.

GOOD REGIMES (ruling for all)	BAD REGIMES (ruling selfishly)
Monarchy (rule by one)	Tyranny (rule by one)
Aristocracy (rule by few)	Oligarchy (rule by few)
Democracy (rule by many)	Democracy (anarchy)[2]

This chart does not appear in early Greek writings because I made it up for our analytical convenience.[3] Nevertheless, they worried about the three undesirable possibilities so much that they envisioned an ideal form of government which they hoped would restrain everyone – the king, the aristocrats, and the *demos* – from turning into bad people and exploiting other citizens.

Aristotle especially recommended this "mixed" regime and argued that, by incorporating into it an element of monarchy, an element of aristocracy, and an element of democracy, different class

---

[2] Or "mob rule." Hannah Arendt, having in mind Franz Kafka's chilling novels – such as *The Castle* (1925) and *The Trial* (1926) – added to this typography what she called "Bureaucracy," which she characterized as "rule by Nobody." Hannah Arendt, *On Violence* (New York: Harcourt Brace Jovanovich, 1970), p. 81.

[3] It is based on Polybius' writing much later while living in Rome. See his *Histories*, Book 6.

interests would be represented. In which case, their spokespeople would have to compromise among those interests to run the state. None of the sectors would get everything they might want. But they would accept compromises because they would all know that any other regime was sure to deteriorate disastrously, sooner or later.

Demagogues

Modern political conversations retain two further classical terms worth keeping in mind.

The first is "demagogue." Rabble-rousers were regarded as especially dangerous in democracies by thinkers like Plato and his student Aristotle, because the city's ordinary citizens might be swayed by unreasonable pitches made to them by slick orators who, when they behaved badly, the Greeks called demagogues. That is, even if a democratic regime is ruling the city well, there always exists the possibility that an exceptionally talented speaker may come forward and, like a Pied Piper, lead the local crowd to where it should not go.

Such a demagogue was immortalized by Thucydides when he described Alcibiades, who helped to convince the Athenian Assembly around 415 BC to send the city's army and navy to besiege Syracuse. When that venture failed miserably, Thucydides reported that 40,000 Athenian soldiers and sailors never came home.[4]

Republics

The second term is "republic." Polybius, who was a Greek writing in Rome during the mid second century BC, used this Latin term to describe a mixed Roman government that existed before it deteriorated into the Roman Empire ruled by single men who, after Augustus, called themselves Caesars. In Polybius' analysis, the Roman republic was a mixed government where its consuls ruled like a king, the senate represented its aristocrats, and its tribunes spoke for the people.[5]

---

[4] If demagogues were dangerous for many centuries, we may regard them as equally so today, in an era that invites widespread indifference to climate change, environmental destruction, and nuclear stand-offs.

[5] See Polybius, *The Histories*, Book 6.

Very importantly, for later generations, Polybius highlighted how, in a republic, the existing governmental elements interact fruitfully with one another and therefore constitute an early example of what, later in Europe and America, became known as constitutional checks and balances. No less important, however, was his attributing to this interaction a capacity for inspiring Romans to act nobly on behalf of the state.

Thus Polybius and later thinkers infused the model of "mixed government" with a quality of encouraging ethical excellence rather than, as previously, only pursuing useful prudence. He thus conveyed to future generations the hope that mixed government could translate public spiritedness into a practice of "republican virtue," which was appropriate because the term "republic" (in Latin, *res publica*) meant "the public thing" which its citizens were, hopefully, devoted to serving together and well.

Rule-by-One

After Constantine the Great converted to Christianity in AD 312, the followers of Jesus came to dominate most of Europe. Which meant that Christian savants replaced the original Greek and Roman thinkers, who were all pagans, until the Enlightenment, when atheism became possible though not mainstream.

Early generations of these new thinkers, largely in response to existing power arrangements on the continent in their times, admired strong men who would fit well into the matrix box of rule-by-one. Thus Dante Alighieri, in *De Monarchia* (1213), recommended a good emperor for all of Europe. And Thomas Aquinas, later in the thirteenth century, building on Aristotle's concept of natural law, favored kingship and warned against tyranny.[6] And Niccolò Machiavelli, in *The Prince* (1532), offered political advice, much of it cautionary, to lesser but usually single rulers in Northern Italy.[7]

---

[6] See A. P. D'Entreves (ed.), *Aquinas: Selected Political Writings* (Oxford: Basil Blackwell, 1959).

[7] In his *Discourses on Livy* (1531), Niccolò Machiavelli also praised republics for promoting valor and virtue.

The chorus of praise for single rulers continued with, for example, Jean Bodin, in *Six Books of the Republic* (1576), who called for the acceptance of a "sovereign" power in war-torn France – that is, an all-powerful ruler – especially to prevent civil strife from arising among antagonistic Christian sects during the Reformation. Later, James I, king of England and Scotland, buttressed such arguments with *The Divine Right of Kings* (1610), in which he declared that not only was a monarchical sovereign excellent for maintaining law and order but that God himself had sanctified that arrangement as the appropriate political regime for mankind.

The Social Contract

However, alongside these praises for one-and-only-one rulers, a different concept arose, praising limited rule. And more and more thinkers promoted this concept as the Enlightenment unfolded between, roughly, 1600 and 1800.

What happened was that forward-looking Europeans suggested that even a government led by a powerful king should rest upon what came to be called a "social contract." Thomas Hobbes promoted this idea in *Leviathan* (1652), which argued in favor of a sovereign who, while Europe was riven by catastrophic religious wars within and between countries, would promise the people in his community to maintain peace between rival sects and factions but could be replaced by his subjects if he failed.[8]

John Locke broadened the social contract argument in his *Second Treatise on Government* (1689) by making it more social, by saying that the best regime will divide up governmental powers, while not necessarily excluding a king, in order to protect men's natural rights to "life, liberty, and property." Then Jean-Jacques Rousseau took this idea a step further with *The Social Contract* (1762), wherein he argued that government should somehow represent "the general will" of citizens who, by common consent, would shun "chains" and pursue "freedom."[9]

---

[8] Thomas Hobbes, *Leviathan* (1651), did not say point blank that the sovereign had to be a single person. But his book was widely interpreted as if that was what he had in mind.
[9] Jean-Jacques Rousseau, *The Social Contract* (1762).

The French Revolution

Such notions fueled what Jonathan Israel called the "Radical Enlightenment."[10] And they reached a sort of climax when revolutions against monarchies took place first in America and soon afterwards in France.[11]

The French Revolution came second in this sequence but was, for our purposes, important to explain first. It started, more or less, when, in *The Declaration of the Rights of Man and the Citizen* (1789), the Estates General declared that the French "nation" was entitled to replace the French "monarch" as the "sovereign" of the state. In that sense the French rebels endorsed a concept of "popular sovereignty."

Which means that, in principle, they assumed that the regime became a social contract entity between the people and themselves, somewhat in line with what Rousseau had in mind. But, just like Rousseau ignored nuts and bolts, the National Assembly, which grew out of the Estates General, did not create a set of institutions capable of translating popular sovereignty into sensible administration and policies.[12]

We can attribute this to, if nothing else, the French people being constantly engaged in warfare, because powerful allies of the French monarchy, some from neighboring kingdoms and empires, but others from the French aristocracy and Catholic clergy, regarded the new regime as dangerous and opposed it violently as soon as it appeared.[13]

---

[10] Jonathan Israel, *A Revolution of the Mind: Radical Enlightenment and the Intellectual Origins of Modern Democracy* (Princeton: Princeton University Press, 2010).

[11] The point here refers to what we now call the liberal part of the Enlightenment. There were also Romantic opponents, mainly promoting what we call nationalism but also thinkers opposed to the separation of church and state. For surveys of the full story, see Jonathan I. Israel, *Democratic Enlightenment: Philosophy, Revolution, and Human Rights, 1750–1790* (New York: Oxford University Press, 2011) and Jonathan Israel, *Enlightenment Contested: Philosophy, Modernity, and the Emancipation of Man, 1670–1752* (New York: Oxford University Press, 2006). For why I am focusing on liberal aspects of the Enlightenment, see Anthony Pagden, *The Enlightenment: And Why It Still Matters* (New York: Random House, 2013). On the opponents of Enlightenment radicalism, see Corey Robin, *The Reactionary Mind: Conservatism from Edmund Burke to Donald Trump*, 2nd ed. (New York: Oxford University Press, 2018).

[12] Jews as a political community in modern Israel have the same problem. The Old Testament *Book of Exodus* explains how they emerged from Pharaonic Egypt to freedom but says nothing about how to build institutions to preserve that freedom. See Michael Walzer, *Exodus and Revolution* (New York: Basic Books, 1985).

[13] Simon Schama, *Citizens: A Chronicle of the French Revolution* (New York: Random House, 1989). Schama describes how the universalist principles of the Revolution – liberty, equality,

Consequently, under extraordinary pressure, France descended into a disastrous civil war known as the Terror, from which the charismatic but dictatorial leader Napoleon eventually emerged. Greek thinkers would have said that what happened was an obvious turn of the wheel, whereby rule-by-one was replaced by rule-by-many, after which that was replaced by rule-by-one.

And that is the point at which we need to observe here no more about the French Revolution because what happened in that country is not really relevant to our story of democracy in America. Let us note, however, before we go on to America, that Napoleon was not overthrown by the French nation. That is, the tyrant was not rejected by oppressed democrats, and they quickly reenlisted when he came back from exile in Elba. He was, however, defeated in the battle of Waterloo, while opposed by armies led by the English Duke of Wellington and fielded on behalf of European monarchies, princes, and emperors.[14]

With Napoleon gone, those one-man regimes placed the family of Louis XVI back on the throne. In later years, additional ups and downs, or turns of the wheel, have brought us to the present situation, where President Emmanuel Macron of France is operating under the fifth French constitution.

The American Revolution

Fortunately for what became the United States, its efforts to build a stable and effective political regime succeeded more than those of France. Much of that success emerged from how the British colonies in North America revolted against their imperial masters within a historical situation very different from that which obtained in France a few years later.

---

fraternity – amplified by the *Declaration of the Rights of Man and the Citizen*, aroused enormous opposition from counter-revolutionary forces from inside and outside of France, even as a new sense of citizenship adding up to nationality arose and provided the charismatic General Napoleon Bonaparte with the massive armies and solidarity that enabled him to conquer much of Europe until the battles of Leipzig (1813) and Waterloo (1814).

[14] The point is worth remembering today because Hitler (a tyrant) arose in twentieth-century Germany and, like Napoleon, was not overthrown by local democrats but defeated by outside military forces. Which suggests the possibility that American democrats may not be able, for various reasons, to prevent Trump and his ilk from hollowing out democracy in America. But if that happens, where is the outside force that will come to save the American democrats of both parties?

The Americans in fact rebelled in a delayed response to what was known in Europe as the Seven Years War and in America as the French and Indian War. In that war, the British fought in North America against French troops and Native American allies, to the point of taking Canada from the French and adding it to the British Empire.

Next, and not surprisingly, members of England's parliament, which wealthy aristocrats controlled, argued that the war had protected American colonists, and therefore the MPs fashioned means, including new taxes, to force the colonists to help England pay for the war. Against this annoyance, and inspired by slogans like "No Taxation without Representation," the Americans resisted in places like Lexington, Concord, and Boston, and then in New York City, Princeton, and Trenton.

In the circumstances, colonists who were loyal to Great Britain mostly kept a low profile or left for British lands. That is, they didn't make much trouble. Plus, the rebels received military and financial aid from France, whose monarch was pleased to help them undermine his country's perennial enemies in England. This he did even to the point of (a) sending a French fleet to prevent the British navy from rescuing Lord Charles Cornwallis' army at Yorktown in Virginia and thereby (b) forcing the British government to cut its losses and permit the Americans to leave the empire.

Born Free

Several notable factors influenced the course of the war regardless of battlefield events, and here the terms we have already used show up again as cardinally relevant. One of these factors, as Louis Hartz pointed out in what he called the "storybook" version of American history, was that the colonists came to America, mostly from northern Europe, but the feudal system did not come with them.

As Hartz put it, "America was settled by men who fled from the feudal and clerical oppressions of the Old World."[15] In this view, people who were comfortable in Europe were not likely to abandon their

---

[15] Louis Hartz, *The Liberal Tradition in America: An Interpretation of American Political Thought since the Revolution* (New York: Harcourt, Brace & World, 1955), p. 3.

advantages and migrate to the wilderness. As a result, there were almost no rich and powerful aristocratic landowners in the English colonies, and entrenched and wealthy state churches did not exist there either.

Consequently, in the absence of fierce resistance to the revolution arising from leftover feudal establishments which were not there, the American rebels were more at liberty than the French were to build for themselves new political institutions. The French nation, taking over from the king, in conditions beyond its control, was immediately attacked and distracted by European monarchs, by many French aristocrats, and by local Catholic clergymen, all of whom aimed to return Louis XVI or his heirs to the throne.[16]

The Liberal Tradition

Another factor which crucially facilitated political success in North America was that the Americans managed to work out new arrangements by paying attention mainly to what Hartz called "the liberal tradition." He used this phrase to refer to moderate political ideas which were strongly promoted by some leading Enlightenment thinkers, such as John Locke and Baron de Montesquieu, whom Hartz described as spokespeople for middle, more than upper or lower, class interests.[17]

Many historians today, inspired by modern standards, regard Hartz's liberal tradition as seriously flawed, with little or no political room for at least Black Americans, women, and Native Americans. Nevertheless, for those times, having decided that states in the United States would be democratic if not perfectly so, the Founders put their decision into effect by fashioning institutions designed to make sure that what Alexis de Tocqueville later called "democracy in America" would not lapse into either anarchy or mob rule. And to make those institutions sound even more attractive, writers like James Madison described the final product as more "republican" than "democratic,"

---

[16] Hartz pointed out that de Tocqueville had already written that Americans were "born free" because there were no feudal constraints in their society.

[17] See John Locke, *Second Treatise on Government* (1690), especially books (actually, sections) within it on natural rights and the separations of powers, and Baron de Montesquieu, *Spirit of the Laws* (1748), especially books (sections) on the separation of powers in England and the ability of republican governments to inspire virtue.

thus imputing to it the sort of virtue that Polybius had introduced to European political thought almost 2,000 years earlier.[18]

In terms we have already noted, the American decision was to update ideas going back to the Greek and Roman ideal of "mixed government." To this end, delegates from most of the former colonies met in Philadelphia in 1787 and in four months at the Constitutional Convention drafted a founding document that proposed adopting federalism between a nationwide government and the existing state governments, separating the executive, judicial, and legislative powers in the national government, and creating checks and balances between and within those three branches of governmental power and authority.

The original Constitution was ratified by the American states in 1788, and its mix of governmental institutions, procedures, practices, and safeguards started working in 1789 with unanimous support in the "Electoral College" for former General George Washington as a candidate to become the country's first president.[19] Implementing a deal worked out even before ratification, the first Congress, which was elected along with Washington, immediately proposed to the states that they would together enact ten Amendments to the Constitution. These became known as the Bill of Rights and mainly protected citizens from federal government abuses of power.

Common Sense

Looking back on this remarkable act of political construction, we can see that the Founders were liberal in the sense that, as participants

---

[18] Some conservatives in America today, like those in The Heritage Foundation within walking distance of the Capitol building, continue to call America a "republic" rather than a "democracy." See www.heritage.org/american-founders/report/america-republic-not-democracy. See also Neil Gorsuch, *A Republic, If You Can Keep It* (New York: Penguin, 2020). Gorsuch was nominated to the Court in 2017 by President Trump (and quickly confirmed by the Senate) after Senate Republicans had refused to hold a hearing on President Obama's 2016 nominee for the same Court seat.

[19] The presidency was greatly innovative, because it gave the president some executive powers formerly wielded by kings even while Americans did not want to install kings who take office by hereditary succession. Therefore, to choose the new executive they fashioned the Electoral College, which is a quasi-democratic institution whereby, originally, "electors" chosen by state legislatures would decide which presidential candidate they would vote for.

in the Enlightenment, they believed that they were able to decide for themselves how to arrange to live together. In modern terminology, they regarded themselves as endowed with "agency," unlike what conservatives such as Edmund Burke would argue concerning the inviolability and/or sanctity of at least some of the most powerful institutions and practices already reigning in existing European states.

In a now-fashionable scholarly view of what happened, we can say that the Founders rejected some traditional narratives, or stories, about how politics should be organized and which regime would be best. Instead, as demonstrated in the *Federalist*, whose newspaper articles were written to convince voters in New York to support ratification, they brilliantly made up a new story fit for a new regime.[20]

Thus in Federalist Paper 14, James Madison proudly asked: "Is it not the glory of the people of America that, whilst they have paid a decent regard to the opinions of former times and other nations, they have not suffered a blind veneration for antiquity, for custom, or for names, to overrule the suggestions of their own good sense, the knowledge of their own situation, and the lessons of their own experience?"[21]

In Federalist Paper 1, Alexander Hamilton agreed: "It has frequently been remarked that it seems to have been reserved to the people of this country, by their conduct and example, to decide the important question, whether societies of men are really capable or not of establishing good government from reflection and choice."[22]

Here, we can sidestep a little. Such quotations show that the *Federalist* took a page from Thomas Paine's very popular *Common Sense* (1776), to the point where his approach underlies their political

---

[20] I discuss the cardinal importance of political narratives, or stories, in David M. Ricci, *Post-Truth American Politics: False Stories and Current Crises* (New York: Cambridge University Press, 2023), esp. pp. 21–31. As for the volume of collected Federalist Papers so admired later, it is a little embarrassing to recall that, when they originally appeared in New York newspapers, they did not persuade New York residents, who voted against ratification before later changing that vote.

[21] *The Federalist: A Commentary on the Constitution of the United States, Being a Collection of Essays Written in Support of the Constitution Agreed upon September 17, 1787, by the Federal Convention* (New York: Modern Library, 1937), p. 85.

[22] Ibid., p. 3.

thought.²³ I will return in Chapter 6, "Information," to the matter of "common sense," because I believe that it is disappearing or has already disappeared in America. We will consider why that is happening, and I will show that its absence should be regarded as hugely problematic for democratic politics and good citizenship.

Sovereignty

At any rate, with such thoughts in mind – that is, while thinking for themselves – the Founders hammered out a constitution which does not even mention the concept of sovereignty and therefore does not fall victim to what we may call "the French temptation" of popular sovereignty. Yes, its Preamble asserts that "We the People of the United States … do ordain and establish this Constitution for the United States." But, once the Constitution was ratified, not the people but their founding document became the highest law in the land and the final arbiter of what "the people" are permitted to do.²⁴

---

[23] In a way, the Founders' new narrative was not so much a specific and detailed story as it was the basic idea that people are able to use their common sense to create new political institutions. That is so obvious a proposition today that we may forget how unusual it was in its time. In those days, European thinkers who opposed the radical Enlightenment might endorse the following sentiment, from Joseph de Maistre, "On the Generative Principle of Political Constitutions (1809)," in *On God and Society*, ed. Elisha Greifer (Chicago: Henry Regnery, 1959), pp. 3–91, esp. p. 3: "One of the greatest errors of a century [the eighteenth] which professed them all was to believe that a political constitution could be created and written *a priori*, whereas reason and experience unite in proving that a constitution is a divine work and that precisely the most fundamental and essentially constitutional of a nation's laws could not possibly be written."

[24] I am using the term "French temptation" to describe the notion that sovereignty is unlimited and should be wielded by a particular person or representatives of the population. This is rather than the notion that the population lives within a set of rules, or laws, such as those flowing from a constitution, written or not. Donald Trump is a recent, and deplorable, example of a modern politician who apparently believes in the French concept of sovereignty, which was expressed by France's Louis XV in 1766 as follows: "It is in my person alone the sovereign power resides … It is from me alone that my courts derive their existence and authority; and the plenitude of this authority, which they exercise only in my name, remains always with me … It is to me alone that the legislative power appertains without any dependence and without any division … The whole public order emanates from me." Louis XV is quoted in Alfred Cobban, *In Search of Humanity: The Role of the Enlightenment in Modern History* (New York: George Brazillier, 1960), p. 209. For the king's entire address to his *parlements* (royal courts), see https://revolution.chnm.org/d/236.

Eventually, of course, there was a horrible quarrel, called the Civil War, about whether the Constitution did or did not permit states to secede from the Union. And slavery was, thank heavens, abolished from America as a result of that quarrel. But Americans, unlike many Europeans, are so unfamiliar today with the concept of sovereignty that they don't even have jokes about it, like the old English notion, not current today, that Parliament can do anything except turn a man into a woman.[25]

Terms

Again, I have highlighted in this chapter terms that can help us frame current challenges to democracy and good citizenship. They are cyclical history, monarchy, aristocracy, democracy, tyranny, oligarchy, anarchy, mob rule, mixed regime, demagogue, republic, republican virtue, the sovereign, sovereignty, the social contract, nation, popular sovereignty, the Terror, Napoleon, the liberal tradition, the Electoral College, narratives, stories, common sense, and the French temptation.

---

[25] In one of his God-complex moments, Donald Trump 2.0 revisited this joke by declaring that the federal government will from now on recognize only two sexes, male and female. For his Executive Order to that effect, see www.whitehouse.gov/presidential-actions/2025/01/defending-women-from-gender-ideology-extremism-and-restoring-biological-truth-to-the-federal-government/.

3 VOCATIONS

Let us sum up. A vision of democracy arose in Greece, evoked some doubts but fueled Athenian greatness, evolved next into republicanism in Rome, limped along during centuries of enthusiasm for one-man rule, but reached into the Enlightenment and, from there, wound up in America's thirteen colonies. The Founders then committed the new country to democracy but enfolded that commitment to rule-by-many within a mixed government that would, hopefully, prevent the constitutional regime from deteriorating into anarchy or mob rule.[1]

Assuming that public life is often stressful and that no regime performs faultlessly, we can say that, with some ups and downs, the American regime has worked well.[2] Consequently, American

---

[1] On anti-democratic restraints that the Founders built into the Constitution, see J. Peter Euben, John R. Wallach, and Josiah Ober (eds.), *Athenian Political Thought and the Reconstruction of American Democracy* (Ithaca, NY: Cornell University Press, 1994), esp. pp. 76–78. See also Robert A. Dahl, *How Democratic Is the American Constitution?* (New Haven: Yale University Press, 2001); Sanford Levinson, *Our Undemocratic Constitution: Where the Constitution Goes Wrong (And How We the People Can Correct It)* (New York: Oxford University Press, 2006); and Erwin Chemerinsky, *No Democracy Lasts Forever: How the Constitution Threatens the United States* (New York: Liveright, 2024).

[2] There are blemishes on America's political record. But, over time, it can be regarded as fulfilling a metaphor promoted by the moderate conservative philosopher Michael Oakeshott, in a lecture on "Political Education," in his *Rationalism in Politics* (New York: Basic Books, 1962), p. 127, where Oakeshott postulates that the ship of state sails on a voyage

constitutionalism is almost 250 years old, which makes it the world's longest running democracy and surely one of the most successful.

Then the Electoral College in November 2016 elected Donald Trump even though many commentators noticed that he was not particularly committed to what the Founders had created.[3] After which, watching him pompously signing his John Hancock with a Sharpie (or Magic Marker) during four years in the White House, dancing in and out of his gingerbread house at Mar-a-Lago, or hacking around on his various golf courses, just made things look worse. Thus:

> Donald Trump ... admired "strong men" and the politics of strong men, hated the free press, was indifferent to the survival of the Western alliance, [and] intensely disliked the EU ... He had no ideological attachments to liberal democracy ... He was populist, instinctively authoritarian, and nationalist. Worst of all, he promulgated the "big lie" that he won the November 2020 presidential election, which he lost by a large margin, thereby undermining the foundations of American democracy.[4]

Of course, Trump was and is only symptomatic. He is on our minds all the time, and especially since he won reelection in 2024. But the truth is that challenges to American democracy, as we shall see, did not start with Trump and will not end with him. Furthermore, he did not create the conditions of his success but only exploited systemic flaws, sentiments, and practices that were already in place.

Modernity

Therefore, we should consider how a political space opened up for someone like Donald Trump in Washington. We should ask what went

---

whose course is not predictable but which must be kept "afloat and on an even keel" by sensible and even traditional seamanship.
[3] For example, Yascha Mounk, *The People vs. Democracy: Why Our Freedom Is in Danger and How To Save It* (Cambridge, MA: Harvard University Press, 2018), p. 2: "For the first time in its history, the oldest and most powerful democracy in the world has elected a president who openly disdains basic constitutional norms – somebody who left his supporters 'in suspense' whether he would accept the outcome of the election, who called for his main political opponent to be jailed, and who has consistently favored the country's authoritarian adversaries over its democrat allies."
[4] Martin Wolf, *The Crisis of Democratic Capitalism* (London: Penguin, 2023), p. 2.

wrong in America's political institutions instead of them inspiring constructive action by democratic citizens. And we should analyze the job of such citizens in America today and ponder whether or not they are doing it as well as they should. That is, not well according to what Athenian citizens had to do in classical Greece, but well within the conditions of modern life.

In other words, "democracy," yes, described at least partly by terms formulated centuries ago. But also "modernity," yes, which consists of conditions that Athenians did not know, which together generate disruptive behavior that American democracy today, as a regime maintaining rule-by-many, must confront and deal with successfully.

But how to get a useful grip on a phenomenon as complicated and far ranging as modernity? As a political scientist, I usually write about my discipline's research findings and propositions, about what my colleagues in that discipline see as present or lacking in our political surroundings. In this book, however, I will explore unease about American democracy by highlighting concepts relevant to that subject but first promoted by Max Weber, the great German sociologist.[5]

Two Lectures

More than a century ago, Weber delivered two brilliant "vocation" lectures.[6] The first was entitled "Science as a Vocation" (1917) and the second was entitled "Politics as a Vocation" (1919). Both are well known in academic circles and are especially familiar to sociologists, historians, and political scientists, who interpret them variously.[7]

Accordingly, I will add my understanding of what Weber said to what other scholars have said about him. In this project, my view is not deeply academic, because I will not follow Weber into

---

[5] From political theory, see Wendy Brown, *Nihilistic Times: Thinking with Max Weber* (Cambridge, MA: Harvard University Press, 2023).
[6] See David Owen and Tracy B. Strong (eds.), *Max Weber: The Vocation Lectures* (Indianapolis: Hackett, 2004), or Paul Reitter and Chad Wellmon, *Charisma and Disenchantment: The Vocation Lectures* (New York: New York Review Books, 2020).
[7] For example, Hans Gerth and C. Wright Mills, *From Max Weber: Essays in Sociology* (New York: Oxford University Press, 1958); Fritz Ringer, *Max Weber: An Intellectual Biography* (Chicago: University of Chicago Press, 2004); and Brown, *Nihilistic Times*.

major intellectual controversies that swirled in his time, touching on Immanuel Kant, Friedrich Hegel, Karl Marx, Friedrich Nietzsche, Sigmund Freud, Ernest Troeltsch, Georg Simmel, and Werner Sombart, and relating to communism, socialism, syndicalism, liberalism, nationalism, and more.[8]

Accordingly, I will not so much write here about Weber's academic career as I will use some of what he observed as a springboard for what I want to suggest about American politics today. To that end, my view of Weber's thinking focuses on what he said about politics in characteristically modern states, as if he can be viewed as a scholar who was especially interested in how Western public life changed during the Enlightenment and became something modern – like America today – which he set out to describe.

Modernity Again

The term "modernity," and its adjective "modern," have attracted considerable academic speculation about when modernity appeared, about why it appeared at that time, about what people expected from it – progress, for example – and about how early examples from European states were eventually joined by multiple examples of modernity, were expressed in various cultures, and appeared relatively recently in non-Western societies such as Iran, India, and China.[9]

I will not elaborate on such scholarly distinctions but will use an ordinary, everyday understanding of modernity, backed up by scholars, which relates to what happened, roughly speaking, first in Europe and later in America. That ordinary view illuminates enough of where we are for my purposes.

---

[8] For a philosophical view, based on intellectual history, and highlighting some of the scholarly disputes conducted in Weber's time, see Brown, *Nihilistic Times*, pp. 60–83. Brown describes Weber as deploring a loss of belief in basic moral values, especially among scientists. She attributes this mainly to the rise of new (Enlightenment) ideas, whereas I add to her analysis by attributing the loss, most recently, to an unmanageable flood of messages in "the information system" (see Chapter 6, "Information").

[9] For example, see Peter Wagner, *Modernity as Experience and Interpretation: A New Sociology of Modernity* (New York: Polity, 2008); Peter Wagner, *Modernity: Understanding the Present* (New York: Polity, 2012); and Peter Wagner, *A Sociology of Modernity: Liberty and Discipline* (New York: Routledge, 2016).

Format

As a matter of format, however, I remind readers that I am not suggesting a "theory" about citizenship. Accordingly, what is new in *Defending Democracy* is not what it reveals for the first time about this or that circumstance or event but that, when they are assembled as they are here in an "essay," such items, described in relevant terms, suggest a sensible way of considering the complex social and political situation in which we find ourselves.[10]

Most scholars specialize within the framework of their disciplines and, very usefully, investigate small and specific matters, like Weber noted when he discussed their work in "Science as a Vocation" (1917). They therefore do not usually offer such a wide perspective. But doing so can be helpful in a confusing time, I think, so that is what I am aiming at.[11]

Keeping this format in mind, let us step up now to Max Weber's ideas about modernity.

Max Weber

While Germany was still waging World War I, a local chapter of the Free Students Alliance in Munich invited Weber to address its members on the subject of "intellectual work as a vocation." These were students

---

[10] Academic readers may want to consider this point in terms of methodology. In a way, *Defending Democracy* has no methodology. My inspiration on this score is the historian William McNeill, who described his "method" as follows: "I get curious about a problem and start reading up on it. What I read causes me to redefine the problem. Redefining the problem causes me to shift the direction of what I'm reading. That in turn further reshapes the problem, which further redirects the reading. I go back and forth like this until it feels right, then I write it up and ship it off to the publisher." McNeill is quoted in John Lewis Gaddis, *The Landscape of History: How Historians Map the Past* (New York: Oxford University Press, 2002), p. 48. Arthur Schlesinger, Jr., offered another version of the same tale. See his "History and National Stupidity," *New York Review of Books* (April 27, 2006): "History is not self-executing. You do not put a coin in the slot and have history come out. For the past is a chaos of events and personalities into which we cannot penetrate. It is beyond retrieval and it is beyond reconstruction. All historians know this in their souls." See www.nybooks.com/articles/2006/04/27/history-and-national-stupidity/.

[11] See William Egginton, *The Splintering of the American Mind* (New York: Bloomsbury, 2018), pp. 65–69, 74–80, who observes that specialization (he writes about "hyper-specialization") in academic fields discourages many scholars from what he calls the "broad, boundary-breaking kind of thinking," and which I [D.R.] am trying to express in this book.

who admired Germany's great universities, such as those in Heidelberg, Leipzig, and Berlin, which were known for their commitments to academic freedom, scientific research, and the pursuit of moral excellence.

Science as a Vocation

In response to this invitation, Weber delivered the lecture entitled "Science as a Vocation" (1917). In it, he spoke about science in the European sense, which includes searches for understanding in intellectual fields across the board, where "science" is a rational pursuit of (a) knowledge in what we now call the natural sciences, like physics and biology, but also a rational pursuit of (b) knowledge in what we call social sciences and the humanities, such as in the English "political science," the French "science politique," or the German "politologie."

As Weber described science, it is an enterprise in which, since the Enlightenment, young researchers have aspired to discover new facts, and to fashion new understandings, about a great many aspects of human life and the natural world. Here are the manifestations of a rational pursuit of "knowledge" rather than mere "opinion."

In this sense, science, based on reasoning and innovation, and entailing theories, laboratories, instrumentation, conferences, and professional journals, is an activity that did not exist in earlier times, which admired clear thinking more than fact collecting because people in those days had few means for effectively collecting facts. Eventually, however, spurred by the exciting discoveries, some intellectual and some technological, of men like Nicolaus Copernicus, Galileo Galilei, Isaac Newton, Francis Bacon, Gottfried Leibniz, René Descartes, and John Locke, science became, since the Enlightenment, a "vocation" of vital importance to the modern society we now live in.

On this score, where for Weber the term "science" referred to how practitioners are committed to seeking the truth in all fields of knowledge, and where those fields entail tangible means of discovery – thus pitting Reason against Theology, experiments against revelation, and laboratories against logic – Weber observed that modern society suffers from "disenchantment."

Disenchantment was Weber's term for how the condition we call modernity rests upon how, over generations, old narratives about

(1) the *shape* of society (say, a doctrine of "the divine right of kings" which justifies monarchy at the top of "a great chain of being") or about (2) the *purposes* of society (say, a story of "original sin" which requires the pursuit of salvation via clergymen who constitute, in effect, an anointed aristocracy), were rejected first by scientists and then by many other people. Furthermore, because we still rely on science, embodied in the work of men and women like Charles Darwin, Louis Pasteur, Marie Curie, Albert Einstein, and Jonas Salk, we continue to reject many old narratives and remain disenchanted.[12]

Politics as a Vocation

A year after Weber lectured on "Science as a Vocation," World War I ended with an armistice between the Entente Powers, or Allies, and the Central Powers, who were mainly Germany, Austria-Hungary, and the Ottoman Empire. Almost simultaneously, Germany's Kaiser Wilhelm II abdicated, a communist revolution broke out in Berlin and was suppressed, the Weimar Republic was established, and Germany entered an era of enormous political turmoil.

Consequently, the Munich chapter of the Free Student Alliance again invited Weber to address them, this time on the subject of politics. Subsequently, Weber delivered his lecture entitled "Politics as a Vocation" in 1919.

In that lecture, Weber started by describing the modern state as a constellation of rulers, institutions, practices, and sentiments. This state, which Weber defined as evolving out of medieval European societies, exercises a "legitimate monopoly" of "power," sometimes referred to as "force," within its own territory.[13] And

---

[12] Weber did not claim that *all* people after the Enlightenment became disenchanted. What he meant was that disenchantment is a hallmark of modernity even though many people who believe in enchantment still live in what we call the modern world. This is true especially of those people who remain religious, who remain committed to propositions for which there is no empirical proof or disproof. Accordingly, it would be accurate to say that Weber saw modernity as entailing *more* disenchantment, but not *complete disenchantment*, than had appeared in previous eras. On the persistence of religiosity in the modern world, even among those who use scientific creations such as antibiotics and smartphones, see Mario Vargas Llosa, "The Opium of the People," in *Notes on the Death of Culture* (New York: Picador, 2016), pp. 153–196.

[13] From Owen and Strong, *The Vocation Lectures*, p. 33.

within states that are democratic, "politicians" are leaders who seek, by running in elections, to obtain a share of the state's power and then exercise it on behalf of their interests and/or those of their constituents.

Most important, politicians as we now know them appeared in Europe along with the rise of modern democracy. This was because, ever since democracy reigned in Athens, no one in later-day monarchical or aristocratic regimes had to address and lead citizens, who originally came from the Greek *demos*, because there were none. That is, post-classical states were not full of modern voters.

History on this point was clear to Weber. Nowadays, members of the *demos* have not acquired the old, enchanted sort of power embodied in Europe's kings and queens (certified by God's endorsement) or in the Christian clergy (empowered by Peter's keys to heaven). But they are widely regarded, in principle, as natural law bearers of "popular sovereignty," for the first time in history.[14]

Consequently, democracy in both principle and practice became increasingly common. And that was especially so after the French nation, in *The Declaration of the Rights of Man and of the Citizen* (1789), took the king's place as France's "sovereign." The result there was that someone – say, of special skill, or inspiration, and/or ambition – would have to speak to newly empowered citizens and enlist their support in favor of formulating and administering particular state policies.

It is in this sense that we can say that "politics" – which entails speaking with citizens to help them rule – became a second new vocation, after "science," in modern societies. The matter is complicated, however, by how politicians, who do the necessary speaking, may staff the state's institutions or promote various policies.

Legitimacy

On this score, Weber described three possible sources of "legitimacy" whereby states may rule their people. These are (1) *tradition*, or the

---

[14] The "first time" because, in Athens and other Greek democracies, the concept of "sovereignty" had not yet been invented.

eternal past, (2) *legality*, or competence based on rational rules, and (3) *charisma*, or the gift of grace.[15]

In other words, depending on which sorts of institution, or which mix of them, exist in any particular state, politicians in that state will either work within acceptable traditions, or they will promote rational–legal practices, or they will enjoy such personal talent (charisma) that they will be able to impose their will, expressed in voter-supported policies or causes, to some or a considerable extent on those traditions or practices. Or they will work within some mix of all of these.

Bureaucracy

Bureaucracy accompanied all three of the ruling factors. Generally speaking, Weber highlighted the increasing rationality of modern societies, in that they assigned bureaucrats to do more and more of the necessary work in many realms. These people he defined as being chosen not because of family ties (say, like among European aristocrats) or political connections (say, like in the American spoils system) but for their competence (perhaps ascertained via civil service examinations) at performing the work that had to be done.

The problem with states increasingly relying on bureaucracies, said Weber, is that bureaucratic entities can wind up pursuing their own interests for gain in any given situation (which amounts to what scholars call "functional rationality") rather than the general and longer term interests of society (which amount to what scholars call "substantive rationality").[16] For this reason, he warned that rationality in human institutions – military, economic, and political – while extraordinarily effective in some respects, can become an "iron cage" around members of a modern society, preventing them from exercising flexibility and creativity.[17]

---

[15] Owen and Strong, *The Vocation Lectures*, p. 34.
[16] F. William Howton, *Functionaries* (Chicago: Quadrangle Books, 1969), esp. pp. 13–44.
[17] It was an idea whose time had come. Thus, almost simultaneously with Weber, Franz Kafka was writing his great dystopian novels about the crushing powers of bureaucracy. See *The Trial*, published posthumously in 1925, and *The Castle*, published posthumously in 1926.

Charisma

But that is where, according to Weber, "charisma" becomes a force that constantly challenges staid bureaucratization as the hallmark of modern society. It is, in fact, unusual politicians, (a) imbued with at least some degree of charisma, and (b) accepted by citizens who will follow them into sometimes uncharted waters, who (c) enable society to avoid being stifled by obstinate organizations that cannot adjust their structure and practices to an ever-changing world. So, in a way, charismatic politicians can become essential players who help modern societies to avoid stagnation.

Absolute Convictions

Unfortunately, charisma can also become dangerous, because exceptional leaders, precisely because they are exceptional, may persuade their followers to move in new but undesirable directions. For this reason, Weber observed, in "Politics as a Vocation," that leaders who uncompromisingly champion what he called "absolute convictions" may convince their followers to endorse imprudent policies.[18] Much better, he thought, for such leaders to try to calculate "the consequences" of those convictions and then moderate their actions accordingly.

Here, Weber famously recommended that politicians will adopt what he called an "ethic of responsibility," whereby leaders should exercise restraint if, in the light of practical expectations, that seems sensible. And if that is his recommendation to politicians, the implication is that such an ethic is relevant to scholarly work as well.

As Weber put it, values and facts are inherently different entities, therefore scholars should not permit their values to bias the outcomes of their research into facts. In which case, Weber was saying, in effect, that, as a matter of ethical obligation, they should help their students and the public to acknowledge facts, such as the potential *consequences* of an office-holder or candidate's commitments, or his "cause" (in German, *sache*).[19]

---

[18] For example, a Christian leader like Martin Luther might call on his followers to "do what is right and leave the outcome to God." Owen and Strong, *The Vocation Lectures*, p. 83.

[19] Ibid., p. 41. This is an enormously complicated point in Weber's "Politics as a Vocation," and I will leave other scholars to try to resolve it. It involves Weber's assumption that

This notion – of politicians promoting visions, or worldviews, or "causes" in Weber's term – was familiar to American Pragmatists, such as William James and John Dewey, who in Weber's time encouraged everyone to take into account the consequences of thought and deed in many realms.[20] It is not a matter we need to discuss here, but we will return to it later, because it is important to consider how the scattershot political thoughts and deeds of Donald Trump might be regarded, or not, as a "cause" today.

Two Vocations

In sum, according to Weber, two new social roles emerged in Western societies which we often regard as modern. There is room for disagreement on what exactly "modernity" consists of (and also on what exactly "the West" is), because modernity is a concept rather than a tangible thing like a giraffe or carrot which can be defined scientifically and conclusively.[21]

However, in Weber's view, and in mine, it is useful and convenient to think of modernity as starting during the Enlightenment (i.e., by rejecting some traditional beliefs) and continuing afterwards to promote Science and Reason (thus perpetuating disenchantment) in Western countries and, at least to some extent, in non-Western countries as well.[22]

---

facts and values are inherently different, wherefore social scientists should deal with the former and not the latter. In which case, if some politicians seem to us morally disastrous [value challenged], all that Weber and his scientific colleagues can do – appropriately – is talk about how the consequences of what those politicians offer to voters would help or damage their society and the people in it.

[20] Weber called for such investigation in the framework of an "ethic of responsibility." I wrote about that ethic in David M. Ricci, *Post-Truth American Politics: False Stories and Current Crises* (New York: Cambridge University Press, 2023), pp. 143–157.

[21] Sociologically speaking, modernity is regarded as including most or all of liberal democracy, private property, the rule of law, limited government, open markets, and individualism. See, in n. 9 p. 39, Peter Wagner's books on this.

[22] On the reign of disenchantment, see Charles Taylor, *A Secular Age* (Cambridge, MA: Harvard University Press, 2007). On its extension to much of the world, see Niall Ferguson, *Civilization: The West and the Rest* (New York: Penguin, 2011), who notes that the "Rest," especially in Asia, are coming to resemble the West in at least six "novel complexes of institutions and associated ideas and behaviors." These include competition, science, property rights, medicine, the consumer society, and the work ethic.

Calling the new roles that emerged "vocations" (in German, *beruf*) in the English translation of Weber's lectures may be confusing, but I will regard Science and Politics as, roughly speaking, necessary additions to the important medieval European roles, or "professions," or "callings," of doctors, lawyers, and priests. I will also grapple with the fact that professions, or vocations, originally embodied specific ethical obligations, such as a doctor's duty, according to the Hippocratic Oath, to serve the patient's health and do him or her no harm.

On the one hand, I am using the term vocation in the sense of a "calling," which is what early Protestants, who were of special interest to Weber, did.[23] For example, the Puritans who came to the Massachusetts Bay Colony believed that God "calls" various people (e.g., judges, blacksmiths, weavers) to different kinds of work, the total of which is a well-rounded and effective Christian community.[24]

On the other hand, I will consider how, in a way, we should regard citizenship not just as one practical calling among others – like cobblers and plumbers – but as a new "profession." That is because if citizens won't do their work with some ethical consideration beyond personal gain, we may suffer not just from ugly shoes and leaky faucets but also from the creeping establishment of tyranny in our society.

Citizenship as a Third Vocation

Now we come to brass tacks, because Weber's teachings on modernity suggest some very large and important implications. Chief among those is what he missed, because Weber didn't explore and didn't analyze a third necessary modern role, beyond those of Science and Politics.

This third role is Citizenship. "Subjects" have inhabited many regimes for centuries. But "citizens" barely existed after Athens and Rome. Whereas, logically and practically in modern post-Enlightenment societies, citizens are present because, to the extent that those societies

---

[23] Weber's greatest work along these lines was *The Protestant Ethic and the Spirit of Capitalism*, ed. Talcott Parsons, intro. R. H. Tawney (orig., 1905; New York: Scribner's Sons, 1958).
[24] The ideal Christian community is described as a balanced collection of "callings" by the great English Puritan divine William Perkins around 1600. See excerpts from his "A Treatise of the Vocations or Callings of Men," in *Puritan Political Ideas 1558–1794*, ed. Edmund S. Morgan (Indianapolis: Bobbs-Merrill, 1965), pp. 35–73.

have decided to be democratic, they not only require but also must cultivate the practice of citizenship.

We can speculate on why Weber wrote about only two rather than three new vocations in his sociology. Maybe it was because the students at Munich University only invited him to give two guest lectures in 1917 and 1919. But maybe it was because, beyond lacking a further invitation, Weber was not entirely enthusiastic about democracy even though he recognized, while living in the fiercely nationalistic Germany of Prince Otto von Bismarck and Kaiser Wilhelm II, that rule-by-the-many was rising, like it or not, in Europe as part of post-Enlightenment civilization.[25]

Or maybe, as a German liberal, Weber liked democracy but thought that democratic thinking, or independence of mind, would be overwhelmed by the power of public (state) and private (capitalist) bureaucracies (via the iron cage). The danger there, for Weber, was that most individual citizens, not being outstandingly talented, might not be able to freely choose rulers or serve well in office because they might be in thrall to conditions and ideas imposed on them by bureaucracies.[26]

On this score, much of Marxian social theory had not yet deteriorated into Leninism or Stalinism and was regarded by forward-looking scholars as intriguing and possibly accurate in the early twentieth century. Therefore, Weber might have sympathized with the Marxian notion that "false consciousness" would prevent most citizens, and especially the less educated and prosperous among them, from reasoning and voting sensibly, on behalf of their real interests.

Special People

Or maybe Weber understood that citizenship is so difficult a business, for so many people, that he had to propose the ineffable notion of

---

[25] De Tocqueville's faint enthusiasm for American democracy was expressed in his warning about the danger of what he called the "tyranny of the majority." Which is to say that a minor French aristocrat, twenty-six years old, arrived in America, traveled here and there, talked with various local citizens, some probably quite uncouth, and then left behind in his writings some disdain for the *hoi poloi*.

[26] On this point, see especially Brown, *Nihilistic Times, passim*.

charisma to deal with it. That is, "special people" – presumably charismatic – will come along to make up for our personal deficiencies, in an age of clashing principles and rudderless citizens, by somehow rejecting extremism fueled by absolute convictions and embracing instead the ethic of responsibility.

As for what exactly charisma is, beyond being a cover word in classical Greek for something mysterious, Weber did not know. But, as if it were like pornography at issue in the United States Supreme Court, he wrote as if he, and we, will "know it when we see it."[27]

Or, finally, maybe Weber did not postulate and describe a vocation of citizenship because he died in 1920 at age fifty-six of the Spanish flu, and therefore his career simply had not got around to exploring fully the work of citizens in modern societies.

Demagogues

Whatever, a second large implication of Weber's take on modernity is that, when he legitimized the vocation of politics, where politicians serve democracy as vital intermediaries, he made way for people who may turn out to be appalling political actors. After all, if politicians are indispensable in modern states because those states are democracies, what happens to the lesson we learned about Alcibiades?

For more than 2,000 years, sober thinkers remembered Alcibiades as a speaker who addressed the Athenian Assembly and prompted it to send the Athenian army and navy to besiege Syracuse, where, according to Thucydides, thousands of Athenian soldiers and sailors died. Consequently, in Western political thought, Alcibiades became the most famous exemplar of the "demagogue" who, at any time, might appear and lead citizens into disaster.

But then, according to Weber, "politicians," whose job is exactly what Thucydides feared – which is to speak to empowered citizens – became necessary characters in modern states. And that, in

---

[27] For the meaning of charisma, I am quoting what Supreme Court Justice Potter Stewart said about pornography in his concurring opinion for the case of *Jacobellis v. Ohio* (1964).

a way, means that an opening became available in America for any wacko like Donald Trump – aka "politician" – to go to the big tent and try out his act.

All Are Citizens

We will come back to the problem of demagogues. For the moment, let us note that there is a fundamental difference in real life between Weber's two vocations and the third.

This is because politicians and scientists choose their vocations, and subsequently work, more or less successfully, within a set of known objectives and practices rather than doing something else with their lives. But we are all citizens, not by choice but because democracy is a political regime which bestows that station upon most of its residents automatically, usually by birthplace or by family.

Yet there is a huge difference of characteristics between those people known as scientists or politicians and those people known as citizens. This is because, unlike scientists and politicians, a country's people as a whole (more or less the ancient *demos*) do not become citizens by agreeing to pursue a set of known ends.[28] Rather, without personal volition, they occupy that station inherently, while engaged with other citizens in a constant dialogue, between them and us, and politicians, advocates, and activists, about what it is that we are all supposed to do in that station.[29]

Consequently, even without exploring what goes on in the public life of many modern societies, we can assume that, for example, between Washington and Honolulu, there is a vocation, or calling, or kind of work, not freely chosen, but practiced since the Enlightenment

---

[28] When immigrants apply for American citizenship, they swear or affirm to accept certain constitutional principles. It is an inspiring occasion which I have witnessed. However, it is not the same as agreeing to a set of instructions about how to espouse and apply those principles. For the exam, see www.uscis.gov/sites/default/files/document/questions-and-answers/100q.pdf.

[29] James A. Morone, *The Devil We Know: Us and Them in America's Raucous Political Culture* (Lawrence: University Press of Kansas, 2014), p. 3: "American political culture is a work in constant progress. There is no one deep creedal value, no obdurate set of fundamental ideas. Instead, Americans engage in a long, loud, and constant clash about the meaning of their nation."

by "citizens," who in an analytical sense must be present and operating in America next to Weber's scientists and politicians because America has chosen to be modern and therefore democratic.

Unfortunately, as we shall see, this third vocation is a maddeningly complicated affair.[30]

The Smallest Public Office

Put that another way. The modern citizen is charged with filling "the smallest public office," which is a part of the power structure in any democratic state.[31] He or she is, in other words, the person who Weber's modern politician talks to and courts, so that it is citizens who, roughly speaking, while prodded and enticed by politicians, legitimately choose the modern officials who make and enforce laws and administer public policies.

But if modern citizens are slated to play a crucial civic role in post-Enlightenment times, we sometimes overlook the fact, which is slightly odd, that, unlike what defines other vocations, we have fashioned neither personal requirements for the job nor instructions on how to do it.[32]

So, what can we say about this special sort of vocation? In plain English, who are these citizens in modern democratic states, what are they made of, and what should they do alongside scientists and politicians?

More to Come

In this chapter, I used Weber to add to our fund of terms, now including modernity, vocation, scientists, politicians, disenchantment, power,

---

[30] For example, analytically separate legal, political, and moral aspects of citizenship are discussed in David Ricci, *Good Citizenship in America* (New York: Cambridge University Press, 2004), *passim*, but esp. pp. 6–8.

[31] Joseph Tussman, *Obligation and the Body Politic* (New York: Oxford University Press, 1968). See also David Shelbourne, *The Principle of Duty: An Essay on the Foundations of the Civic Order* (South Bend, IN: Notre Dame University, 2001).

[32] See Chapter 5, n. 32 for the misunderstanding promoted on this score by Judge Richard Posner.

legitimacy, traditions, charisma, legality, bureaucracy, functional rationality, substantive rationality, absolute convictions, the ethic of responsibility, and false consciousness.

These expand the analytical vocabulary at our disposal for the rest of this essay, while I am now switching to consider my world and era rather than what surrounded Weber.

4 DEMOCRACY

Weber was an intriguing scholar. But questions about modernity are not merely academic today. They are massively concrete and thunderously urgent, front and center, because, in what worried thinkers now call the Age of Populism, and someday may call the Age of Trump, some citizens find themselves desperately vulnerable and battling fearfully to preserve liberal democracy.[1]

---

[1] Nowadays, we usually add "liberal" to "democracy," because with democratic electoral machinery you can wind up with Hitler, but with "liberalism," historically speaking, as "an art of living" or as "a comprehensive way of life," or as "reciprocity, freedom, and fairness," we assume that something like Hitler won't happen to us. For the scope of liberalism in this sense, see Michael Walzer, *The Struggle for a Decent Politics: On Liberal as an Adjective* (New Haven: Yale University Press, 2023), and Alexandre Lefebvre, *Liberalism as a Way of Life* (Princeton: Princeton University Press, 2024). Specifically on behalf of liberal democracy, see John B. Judis, *The Populist Explosion: How the Great Recession Transformed American and European Politics* (New York: Columbia Global Reports, 2015); Wendy Brown, *Undoing the Demos: Neoliberalism's Stealth Revolution* (New York: Zone Books, 2015); Jan-Werner Muller, *What is Populism?* (Philadelphia: University of Pennsylvania Press, 2016); Yascha Mounk, *The People vs. Democracy: Why Our Freedom Is in Danger & How to Save It* (Cambridge, MA: Harvard University Press, 2018); David Runciman, *How Democracy Ends* (New York: Basic Books, 2018); Timothy Snyder, *The Road to Unfreedom: Russia, Europe, America* (New York: Tim Duggan, 2018); Steven Levitsky and Daniel Ziblatt, *How Democracies Die* (New York: Crown Books, 2018); Nadia Urbinati, *Me the People: How Populism Transforms Democracy* (Cambridge, MA: Harvard University Press, 2019); and Yascha Mounk, *The Identity Trap: A Story of Ideas and Power in Our Time* (New York: Penguin, 2023).

Warnings issued by such thinkers include nightmare visions of where modern politics might be going. As William Butler Yeats expressed this point in "The Second Coming" (1920): "Things fall apart; the center cannot hold ... What rough beast, its hour come round at last, Slouches towards Bethlehem to be born?"

Yeats did not know exactly where the modern world was going in his time, and he knew even less about what is coming now. However, since Americans in 2016 elected a troubadour who warbles non-stop to lure them into a political wasteland on behalf of a fantasy entitled "Make America Great Again" (MAGA), anxiety over the fate of democracy has grown immensely.[2] And the behavior of citizens is at the center of that anxiety. How could so many of them have chosen freely to elect such an obvious crank to the most important public office in the land?[3]

The Democratic Commitment

Indeed, how could they? I will start trying to answer that question by looking at what happened when the American experiment adopted, more or less, what we call "democracy." To say that the Founders brilliantly created a "mixed government" with democracy inside of it tells us only part of the story because, as years passed, American pacesetters strengthened the citizenship basis for that government.

No one planned what happened in advance, and not everything went smoothly. Nevertheless, for generation after generation – except during the Civil War and after it in the Jim Crow South – most Americans reaffirmed their country's devotion to the democracy they had adopted. And that meant that, in at least four realms – of party

---

[2] On false stories and Trump's specific MAGA story, see David M. Ricci, *Post-Truth American Politics: False Stories and Current Crises* (New York: Cambridge University Press, 2023). MAGA is like a Rorschach ink blot. It justifies many different interpretations. For example, as I write these lines, Trump's second term in the White House is unfolding, and some aspects of what he is saying and doing remind me of Adolf Hitler's *Mein Kampf* pitch to German voters, not yet called a "populist" pitch, that, if they would support him, he would make Germany great again.

[3] The simplest answers to this question were (1) that many people who voted for Donald Trump didn't know what a president of the United States is supposed to do in Washington, DC, and (2) that the same people regarded Trump's election campaign as a sort of reality show, with little connection to the world beyond show business. I will explore answers like these in later chapters.

activity, of political inclusion, of education, and of journalism – political, social, and economic leaders contributed to fostering citizenship within their constitutional regime.

Therefore, in what follows, I will describe those four realms very briefly. My aim is not to recalibrate the writing of American history but to refer briefly, almost in telegraphy, to some aspects of American public life which evolved usefully but which are now, every one of them, severely challenged by how Americans live together and therefore produce, or do not restrain, parts of the political disorder known as Trumpism.

For lack of a better term to describe the various factors that appeared and affected citizenship, let us say that these four realms provided some of the "wherewithal" that helped people to become citizens and/or practice good citizenship. Elements of wherewithal might include information, tolerance, legal status, jobs, money, property, moral support, inspiration, trust, and more. For convenience's sake, then, I will sometimes refer to "wherewithal" as a category of relevant items rather than enumerating again and again the particular elements at stake.

Functions

Let us also note, for analytical convenience, that active citizenship is a practice which serves, in sociological language, a crucial "function" in America's democratic society. "Functions" are things that must get done – in defense, in culture, in commerce, in demography, in transportation, in agriculture, and more – in any particular society for it to maintain itself from one generation to the next, that is, for a country to be recognizable at one moment as, for example, France, and then, years later, also as France.

On those grounds, in America as a democracy, citizens fulfill the "function" of (1) *choosing* the government, that is, of electing officials who, in a related "function," will (2) *represent* the citizens by expressing their views within governmental institutions.[4] As a matter of function, then, it is crucially important for citizens to be equipped to

---

[4] Sociologists would call those institutions "structures."

do this choosing so effectively that the state will continue and prosper from one generation to another.[5]

1 Parties

It turns out that one realm of wherewithal, which is especially helpful to the citizenship function of choosing, is characterized by political parties. Parties did not appear in the Constitution, and people like Benjamin Franklin and John Adams did not intend for them to arise. The men who met in Philadelphia assumed that America's citizens would vote for candidates mainly on the basis of deference, as if some people who were socially and economically prominent, like former general George Washington – who was a wealthy Virginia planter from one of that Commonwealth's "best" families – would move into politics and ordinary citizens would regard them so highly as to vote in favor of installing them in public offices.

As for how this would happen, the Founders knew that in monarchies, which had been common in Europe historically, small groups of conspirators – usually composed of aristocrats and known as "cabals" – would connive intensively in the king's court, such as the one operating in the glittering, 2,300-room palace at Versailles, to influence his decisions and gain from them.[6]

That sort of intrigue seemed patently undesirable in America, because cabals represented themselves rather than the public, which did not yet have the right to vote within single-ruler regimes. Therefore, President Washington warned, in his Farewell Address, against the "baneful spirit of party" because he thought of parties as cabals.[7]

---

[5] In early American terms, James Madison, among others, expressed the need to make sure American voters would have access to information in order to make proper choices. As he put it in 1822 to W. T. Barry: "A popular Government, without popular information, or the means of acquiring it, is but a Prologue to a Farce or a Tragedy; or, perhaps both. Knowledge will forever govern ignorance: And a people who mean to be their own Governors, must arm themselves with the power which knowledge gives." https://press-pubs.uchicago.edu/founders/documents/v1ch18s35.html.

[6] To English speakers, the word "cabal" sounds vaguely French. In fact, it is an acronym of the names of five men, Thomas Clifford, the Earl of Arlington, the Duke of Buckingham, Ashley Cooper, and the Duke of Lauderdale, appointed to be ministers in 1667 by England's Charles II. See www.britannica.com/topic/cabal.

[7] See Washington's Farewell Address at www.loc.gov/resource/mgw2.024/?sp=229&st=text.

Nevertheless, politicians in America formed parties because, next to Washington, two ambitious networks of leaders and followers took shape. One, which became known as the Democratic Republican Party, formed around Secretary of State Thomas Jefferson and Congressman James Madison, and the other, known as the Federalist Party, arose around Treasury Secretary Alexander Hamilton and Vice President John Adams. Roughly speaking, the first represented Southern interests (mainly agricultural) while the second favored Northern interests (chiefly commercial).

Representation

Historians observe that American parties had to be invented because they were necessary. The Constitution did not establish a king or prince who would be addressed by schemers close to the throne. Instead, America's mixed government had so many parts that, to make public policy and enforce it – for example, to decide, for the entity known as the United States, how to relate to the French Revolution and the European wars it ignited – open co-ordination had to be established between American politicians operating in various parts of the new government.

Hence parties arose which were not elitist cabals but which became representative instruments, helpful to American citizens because, where the Constitution endorsed democracy for many Americans, parties enabled these citizens to express their sentiments and preferences intelligibly.[8]

Factions

Once established, the unforeseen political parties helped to nourish democracy. But until the run-up to the Civil War, parties also served to rein in what Madison, in *The Federalist*, called the danger of "factions." Factions he regarded as citizens' groups committed not to the public interest but very narrowly to their own.[9] Which meant that, if

---

[8] Representation was necessary because, in a modern democracy, unlike in Athens, American citizens are too numerous to come together in an Assembly and therefore practice "direct" democracy.
[9] Federalist No. 10: "By a faction, I understand a number of citizens ... who are united and actuated by some common impulse of passion, or of interest, adverse to the rights of other citizens, or to the permanent and aggregate interests of the community."

any faction would gain control over much of the government, its members might become tyrannical in the sense of using it mainly to promote their own ends.

What parties did, however, without intending to do so, was to enlist factions into what became over generations a mainly two-party system, where the national parties, which were eventually the Jacksonian Democrats against Benjamin Harrison's Whigs and later Abraham Lincoln's Republicans, each contained multiple factions.[10]

That is, the parties enlisted various groups in the population. The result was that national parties not only united their own politicians in order to make policies and administer them but also moderated the course of public life, because party leaders could only enact policies that took into account multiple group interests.[11]

Consequently, political extremism was usually prevented, in line with the understanding, since Aristotle had expressed it, that mixed government was built on the idea of different population sectors having to compromise with other sectors.

This balancing act broke down before the Civil War (1861–1865) when the issue of slavery increasingly polarized the country, thus drawing between parties a line which impeded flexibility and compromise. As a result, the parties, severely divided, could find no compromise on that issue, and therefore went to war.[12]

---

[10] Political scientists say there are usually only two national parties in America because they are competing for an indivisible prize, which is the single-member presidency rather than a multi-member parliament.

[11] See Ricci, *Post-Truth American Politics*, p. 45, n. 93, where I explain how Federalist No. 10 was fully appreciated only after World War II. Until then, the standard view was that earlier Americans divided approximately into Hamiltonians and Jeffersonians, or Federalists and Anti-Federalists. See Richard Hofstadter, *The Progressive Historians: Turner, Beard, Parrington* (New York: Vintage, 1970), esp. pp. 167–284, which comments on Charles A. Beard's *An Economic Interpretation of the Constitution* (1913). The post-World War II understanding – which de-emphasized class conflict – of American politics as based on multiple and ever-shifting groups, was promoted by, among others, political scientist Robert A. Dahl, *A Preface to Democratic Theory* (Chicago: University of Chicago Press, 1956), esp. pp. 4–33. For conservatives, that understanding of factions appears in, among other books, George F. Will, *The Conservative Sensibility* (New York: Hachette Books, 2019), *passim*. Referring to Federalist No. 10 frequently, Will praises James Madison as the greatest Founder.

[12] Some of the sequence of first success and then failure is described in Sean Wilentz, *The Rise of American Democracy: Jefferson to Lincoln* (New York: Norton, 2005), *passim*.

After the war, in exchange for receiving the presidency with help in the Electoral College from Democrats, Republicans in 1877 abandoned Southern Blacks by agreeing to let white Democrats control public life in the South. Those white people, later sometimes called Dixiecrats, imposed racial segregation, known originally as the reign of Jim Crow, now known as apartheid. Then, in the mid 1900s, the two major parties achieved some compromises on social and economic legislation, including civil rights, until, on a national scale, late in the twentieth century, left-wing Democrats and right-wing Republicans divided into a second polarization that now plagues American politics, as we will see.

2 Inclusion

A second realm of "wherewithal" contributions to good citizenship, these more intentional than the unexpected presence of parties, accompanied the parties' rise when politicians began the long process of enfranchising more and more Americans.[13]

Article I in the Constitution authorizes each state to determine voting rights within itself. Consequently, at the country's birth, most of the former colonies maintained property qualifications for their voters. The restriction was left over from when the original states had belonged to the British Empire. But this situation clashed with the national commitment to democracy because where, for example, property and/or tax-paying qualifications obtained in voting, for whatever offices, some citizens were, in effect, like Orwell's pigs in *Animal Farm*, more equal than their peers.

Therefore, as new Western states such as Tennessee, Ohio, and Indiana arose and entered the Union while authorizing universal white manhood suffrage, several older states dropped most of their previous qualifications. Then, from 1820 to 1830, America watched the state governments of Massachusetts, Virginia, and New York conduct full-blown debates on the franchise issue.

In those debates, some speakers promoted pro-democracy arguments, such as the notion that if a man bore arms on behalf

---

[13] Historians cannot always generalize on this issue because the Constitution (in Article 1) allowed the states to maintain different voting requirements and they did.

of the state, he should be entitled to participate as a voter in the state's common affairs. And other speakers promoted pro-property arguments, such as the idea that propertied men have a special stake in the maintenance of law and order, whereas the masses, if empowered, will fall prey to demagogues and precipitate mob rule.[14]

Fortunately for everyone, many Weberian politicians, who were already operating out of parties they had created, wanted to expand the franchise in order to acquire new voters for those parties. Therefore, they did so, regardless of pro-property arguments in Massachusetts, Virginia, and New York.

The franchise further expanded, according to the Constitution at least, when, in consequence of the Civil War, Amendments Thirteen, Fourteen, and Fifteen were enacted, without help from the South, to free Black Americans and install them as full-fledged American citizens. Here was a case where the national community left the states to decide who can vote but then added the provision that they cannot *prevent* a certain category of citizen from enjoying that civil right. Tragically, for many years, neither Congress nor the Supreme Court forced the white South to obey this new constitutional provision.

Later, other qualifications entered constitutional law when the Nineteenth Amendment (1920) determined that no state can deny the vote to women, when the Twenty-Fourth Amendment (1964) forbade states from requiring the payment of poll taxes as a precondition for voting, and when the Twenty-Sixth Amendment (1971), adopted during the Vietnam War, ruled that no state can deny 18-year-old citizens the right to vote (and perhaps oppose obligatory military service).

3 Education

Inclusion was welcome for preventing domestic friction by eventually extending citizenship to most residents in America. But it did not

---

[14] To have a tangible stake in the existing regime that protects us all is why speakers in the Putney Debates in England (1647) referred to property as a form of "real" estate.

address the question of what those citizens were to do about voting and possibly holding office. Such questions did arise, however, in what we can loosely call the realm of education, which operates mainly under state laws and therefore may maintain somewhat different institutions and procedures from one state to another.

Public Schools

To begin with, there were few public schools in colonial America and most of those, say in Massachusetts, existed to install piety in children, which means that they aimed at maintaining faith rather than reinforcing citizenship. Which was not surprising because, until the Revolution, Americans were "subjects" rather than "citizens."

However, this traditional system of instruction became untenable when, having established a democratic United States, the Founders and their successors had to consider two large questions of principle.

The first was how to promote equality. That is, if "all men are created equal," like the Declaration of Independence says, society should not make them unequal because some of them will receive a tax-funded education in a public school and others will not. Second, if, in a democracy, "the people" choose the government and some of them even serve in it, they should not be left so ignorant that, for sure, they will do either or both of those things badly.

Consequently, early nineteenth-century education activists, such as William Ellery Channing and Horace Mann, strongly recommended taxpayer-funded public education for most children, who would grow up to exercise not just piety but also citizenship rights. Consequently, by the time the Civil War broke out, more than 50% of all white children (defined as 11- or 12-year-olds) were enrolled in public schools in the South, and up to 80% of similar children were enrolled in the Northeast.[15] These schools handled basic literacy but, little by little, were supplemented by newly invented high schools and an expanded system of higher education.

---

[15] Johann N. Neem, *Democracy's Schools: The Rise of Public Education in America* (Baltimore: Johns Hopkins University Press, 2017), p. 2.

Two additional things are worth remembering here. One is that public schools taught reading, writing, and arithmetic, but also fostered the culture that gradually took shape around an America dedicated, as we have seen, to its special brand of democracy. In that sense, the books which were used, such as the famous McGuffey Readers introduced in the 1830s, were full of sayings, proverbs, aphorisms, jingles, stories, and other inspiring elements of a distinctively American way of looking at life.[16]

In which case, instillation of that culture – mostly white and mostly Protestant for several generations – became a useful prop for good American citizenship in the sense that it united the original children and introduced new ones – such as immigrant Germans, Irish, Jews, and Italians – to what America was all about.

More Schooling

The second thing to understand here is that American education moved forward, via post-elementary schools and higher education, not only because ideals such as democratic citizenship drove it but also because educators accepted a responsibility for keeping up with the modernity noted by Weber. On that score, while rejecting many longstanding stories underlying, say, France's "old regime" before the Revolution, Enlightenment thinkers promoted Science and Reason, with the result that, as the nineteenth and twentieth centuries wore on, there was more and more to learn and therefore more and more need for schooling.[17]

This reality was recognized, for example, by the Federal Depository Library Program (1813), which still exists today, whereby federal publications – embodying new knowledge – are deposited and made available to citizens in libraries throughout the land. The same commitment to Science and Reason produced the Morrill Land Grant

---

[16] For example, stories included "The Hare and the Tortoise," "The Little Chimney Sweep," and "Waste Not, Want Not." Moral inspiration included "The Battle of Blenheim" (Southey), "The Village Blacksmith" (Longfellow), and "Speech before the Virginia Convention" (Patrick Henry).
[17] Alexis de Tocqueville, *The Old Regime and the French Revolution* (orig., 1856; New York: Dover, 2010).

Acts of 1862 and 1890, which allocated federal lands in each state to support colleges, which later grew into universities, for teaching "agriculture and the mechanic arts ... to the industrial classes in the several pursuits and professions in life."[18]

A similar sentiment spurred the creation of public libraries, among them very large collections like in the Library of Congress (1800) and the Boston Public Library (1848), and a scattering of smaller libraries throughout the land which was helped by the astonishing philanthropy of coal and steel magnate Andrew Carnegie, who built almost 1,800 libraries in American towns and cities.

4 Journalism

Once the Constitution took effect, journalism took a place we can regard as next to formal schooling. Being a purveyor of information, it could help citizens to act effectively in modern society.[19]

Accordingly, Michael Schudson recently defined journalism as "the business or practice of regularly producing and disseminating information about contemporary affairs of public interest and importance ... [which is] normally presented as true and sincere, to a dispersed and usually anonymous audience so as to publicly include that audience in a discourse taken to be publicly important."[20]

The Party Press

Except that American journalism didn't start off as public-minded. Instead, the first parties sponsored newspapers which were less interested in such lofty goals as truth and more committed to editorializing on behalf of their friends and patrons.

---

[18] For example, these include Cornell, MIT, Wisconsin, Ohio State, Texas A&M, Purdue, Auburn, U.C. Berkeley, Michigan State, and Rutgers. The quotation is from the Morrill Act of 1862.

[19] Jurgen Habermas describes newspapers as "preeminent" instruments in what he calls "the public sphere," and in which citizens from civil society discuss political issues and form public opinion. See his *The Structural Transformation of the Public Sphere: An Inquiry into a Category of Bourgeois Society* (Cambridge, MA: MIT, 1991), esp. pp. 181–196.

[20] Michael Schudson, *The Sociology of News*, 3rd ed. (New York: W. W. Norton, 2011), p. 3.

It was thus an Age which, for several decades, fostered "the party press." For example, the *National Gazette*, the *National Intelligencer* and the *Washington Advertiser* praised Democratic-Republicans and "informed" readers with stories about bad people and evil deeds in the other party. Meanwhile, officials and candidates of that other party, the Federalists, were extolled by rival newspapers such as the *New York Evening Post*.

Party newspapers were sold, but not very profitably, mainly to loyalists by subscription. Then they were driven out of circulation when the *New York Sun* appeared in 1833 and was followed by the *New York Herald* in 1835. Printed in large numbers on rotary presses, those newspapers, not politically partisan, and soon joined by imitators, were hawked, one copy at a time, on the streets of their cities. Thus the paperboy was born.

The Yellow Press

Here was "the yellow press," competing fiercely against rivals in town, and characterized by intense sensationalism, if not fabrication, in order to entice profitable customers, who were not committed by subscription, every day.

Eventually, such newspapers, led by owners like Joseph Pulitzer and William Randolph Hearst, ratcheted up sensationalism to the point where, without any confirmed evidence, they declared the Spanish guilty of sinking the USS *Maine* battleship in Havana harbor, and thus contributed to an outburst of hysteria in America that ignited the Spanish–American War in 1898.

Professionalism

Fortunately, at least some part of American journalism changed course again when owners of the *New York Times* proclaimed in 1893 that it would report only on news that was "fit to print." There was a market for this sort of quality, it turned out, which became a standard for professional reliability that enabled such newspapers – like *The Times*, the *Washington Post*, the *Baltimore Sun*, the *Chicago Tribune*, the *Los Angeles Times*, and a host of excellent imitators – (a) to enlist subscribers who didn't need sensationalism to attract them, and (b) to earn enough money from advertising to stabilize the industry financially.[21]

This qualitative high point didn't last long, though, because, like party flexibility, inclusion, and public education, the journalistic prop for good citizenship is severely challenged today by what is known as "click-bait" journalism, to which we will return.[22]

Social Capital

Let's take stock for a moment. What we have seen so far, about four realms relating to citizenship, can be described as fostering growth of the modern democratic resource called "social capital." This is a term which many academic thinkers adopted and refined after Robert Putnam introduced it to them in *Bowling Alone* (2000).[23]

Putnam argued that Americans after World War II were less and less bowling in leagues and therefore more and more bowling as individuals or with just a few friends. He also observed that the same people were increasingly unlikely to join social organizations like the Elks, the Knights of Columbus, and the American Legion.

The point was that, in Putnam's view, doing things together generates healthy democratic sentiments and interactions, whereby people meet other people, sometimes of very different origins and outlooks, and thereby learn how to get along with them comfortably and constructively. In this sense, large networks of people, in effect bowling together rather than alone, fostered "social capital," which sustained social and political prosperity along with the other sort of capital,

---

[21] The "party press," the "yellow press," and the "stable press" are terms used by Ryan Holiday, *Trust Me, I'm Lying: Confessions of a Media Manipulator*, rev. and exp. ed. (New York: Penguin, 2017).

[22] Click-bait journalism consists of many ploys, all designed to attract our attention to various journalistic products – from interviews to articles, from blogs to podcasts, and more. An excellent analysis and critique of these ploys, showing how they sacrifice quality of material for quantity of clicks, leading to "mindless" attention spikes, appears in Franklin Foer, *World Without Mind: The Existential Threat of Big Tech* (New York: Penguin, 2017), *passim*.

[23] Robert Putnam, *Bowling Alone: The Collapse and Revival of American Community* (New York: Simon & Schuster, 2001), pp. 31–180.

familiar to bankers and stock brokers as the "financial capital" that sustained industrial and commercial prosperity.

What I am suggesting, then, is that forward movements in party competition, political inclusion, education, and journalism all strengthened citizens' abilities which generated a good deal of social capital.[24] To recall this now reminds us of what can be accomplished in these four realms because, in recent decades, leading up to Donald Trump's descending the golden escalator, none of them, as we will see, continued to work as well as they used to work.

5 A Democratic Arena

A fifth "wherewithal" realm, which was not exactly tangible but vital nevertheless, was a special arena in which citizenship came to be exercised. This arena arose as an adjunct of science, that is, as part of the search for truth. It took center stage in America's early democratic society but, as we shall see, it has fallen down on the job we still need it to perform today.

In the nineteenth century, philosopher John Stuart Mill had this arena in mind when he promoted the concept of what we now call a "marketplace of ideas." Thus, he insisted, in *On Liberty* (1859), that modern societies should permit freedom of speech in order to search for the truth.[25]

Science will bring us new propositions, said Mill, about the natural world and also about living together in it. Accordingly, it is up to us to treat these propositions open-mindedly, winnowing them to the point where some of them will seem truer than others. But even when we reach that point, we should continue to doubt and discuss, so that if there is an error in what we believe to be true, we will find it. But, if we will see that there is no error, we can go forward with renewed confidence. That is, free speech is a win–win situation.

---

[24] For example, that the acquisition of knowledge and participation in associations are sources of social capital, spurred by political activity and journalism, is explored in Henry Milner, *Civic Literacy: How Informed Citizens Make Democracy Work* (Hanover, NH: University Press of New England, 2002), *passim*, but esp. pp. 13–24.

[25] John Stuart Mill, *On Liberty* (orig., 1859; New York: Oxford University Press, 1980).

The implicit, post-Enlightenment message of Mill's argument for free speech was that, in a modern society, later described by Weber, where Science and Reason are regarded as more reliable than faith and revelation – that is, in a democratic society open to new ideas – people practicing good citizenship will act in that marketplace. While there, they will promote what they believe to be true via parties and elections and education and journalism; other people will do the same; and society as a whole will move forward by, hopefully, a process of civil discussion and peaceful decision-making.[26]

American Adoptions

In the turbulence of politics, Americans have not always been as fair and open-minded as Mill recommended. Still, in 1915, the American Association of University Professors (AAUP), in its Declaration of Principles, adopted a commitment to free speech as a necessary context within which scholars can contribute to social progress by proclaiming and discussing any ideas, no matter how unconventional, which seem to them worth considering especially by teachers and students.[27]

In other words, the AAUP adopted Mill's view as a suitable ethic for modern scientific communities. So there, in a way, with considerable impact on the world of education, they declared their devotion to how Weber's "science as a vocation," in many academic disciplines, should proceed.

Furthermore, just a few years later, Supreme Court justices Oliver Wendell Holmes, Jr, and Louis Brandeis, forecasting progress, famously dissented over the issue of freedom of speech in *Abrams v. United States* (1919). Lower courts had convicted Jacob Abrams and several other agitators of distributing anti-war pamphlets and thereby violating the Sedition Act of 1918.[28]

---

[26] Mill wasn't making predictions about which new ideas might be judged true. By coincidence, though, his *On Liberty* and Charles Darwin's *Origin of the Species* were both published in 1859, and many people are still aiming the one at the other.

[27] See www.aaup.org/NR/rdonlyres/A6520A9D-0A9A-47B3-B550-C006B5B224E7/0/1915 Declaration.pdf.

[28] The Sedition Act was repealed in 1920 on the grounds that it violated the First Amendment.

Consequently, Holmes and Brandeis joined in a dissent which declared that "when men have realized that time has upset many fighting faiths, they may come to believe ... that the best test of truth is the power of thought to get itself accepted in the competition of the market, and that truth is the only ground upon which their wishes safely can be carried out. That at any rate is the theory of our Constitution. It is an experiment, as all life is an experiment."[29]

Thus, two leading judges in the highest court in the land, whose view on this matter was accepted by many of their successors, came down on the side of a forward-looking ethic for what Weber called "politics as a vocation" – that is, for politics as a tolerant and constructive exchange of ideas in a modern, mixed government.[30]

In the following year of 1920, in protest against the pre-McCarthy McCarthyism of this era, the American Civil Liberties Union was founded. Under the leadership of Roger Baldwin, it defended civil rights but, especially, went as high as the Supreme Court to promote the constitutional right of free speech.

The Rise of Doubts

So far, I have been mainly optimistic about post-Enlightenment citizenship. No one believed that American democracy was perfect, but progress took place in the realms I have briefly described and, except for in and around the Civil War disaster, Americans for several generations quarreled over more or less routine issues of the day – some contested very fiercely – and spent little time worrying about whether democracy was collapsing, or whether it was feasible.

However, in the late nineteenth and early twentieth centuries, serious doubts about democracy began to arise, not necessarily everywhere, but certainly among thinkers whose peace of mind on this subject has always been, and will always be, an important source

---

[29] See https://usa.usembassy.de/etexts/democrac/43.htm.
[30] I am highlighting the views of Holmes and Brandeis on free speech, which were eventually accepted, more or less, by the court majority. So that is a "wherewithal" plus for citizenship. But those views were, at the time, straws not in the wind but in a gale of speech suppression enforced during the war by the Wilson Administration. The suppression, a minus for "wherewithal," is discussed in Chapter 5, "Muddling."

of confidence in America. Many of those thinkers regarded America as "exceptional" for its pro-democratic vision and practices, symbolized in the great Statue of Liberty in New York City's harbor that has greeted millions of "huddled masses," including my four grandparents from Romania and Italy, "yearning to breathe free."[31]

The Problem of Individuals

The radical Enlightenment's move to democratic citizenship rested on considerable optimism about the ability of many people – but not all of them and not all of the time – to behave intelligently and appropriately to their circumstances.

On that score, our modern concept of citizens and what they do emerged from large notions of Science and Reason. That is, Science will constantly provide new information to everyone, and Reason will enable citizens to use that information to challenge old, unfounded stories about how to organize society. Thus "disenchantment" will grow and modern communities will commit themselves to secular knowledge more than to theological understandings and objectives.

As time passed, however, Western social scientists, trying to achieve what they regarded as objective accounts of human nature (via Reason), proposed that individuals might be incapable of handling new information (derived from Science) effectively.

Sigmund Freud, for example, said that our minds are not built for thinking rationally. Instead, he claimed that our mental powers are invested in an "id," an "ego," and a "super-ego." By this he meant that the *id* rests on our instincts (which are natural inclinations); that each *ego* rests on an individual's personal organization of those instincts; and that his or her *super-ego* is what we sometimes call a "conscience," which is an outside force, usually derived from shared social standards, which restrains, more or less, each person's ego.

In this amalgam, there are so many combinations of factors that no one can know in advance how most collections of such

---

[31] There was more to Emma Lazarus' great poem "The New Colossus," which she wrote to raise money to finance the base of the Statue of Liberty, and which is now inscribed there. See the discussion in www.theatlantic.com/entertainment/archive/2018/01/the-story-behind-the-poem-on-the-statue-of-liberty/550553/.

complicated people will behave. Political scientists run into this puzzle when they do election studies and are unable to predict how voters, in their totality, will respond to what they are told by experts (who are Weber's scientists) and by candidates (who are Weber's politicians).[32]

Puzzled or not in voting research, however, serious thinkers since Freud are likely to believe, as opposed to currents of optimism about Reason that reigned earlier in the modern age, that we can't count on as many people to be as rational as we would like all citizens to be.

Moreover, many Western economists – for example, Alfred Marshall who, like Freud, already lectured and published professionally in the late nineteenth century – very persuasively promoted "marginal utility" theory. With this theory, they highlighted not an objective grasp of reality (Reason) in our preferences, that is, our buying according to our objective "needs." Instead, they proposed that buying according to subjective "wants" will make people happy, each differently from others, if only in the short run.[33]

Those economists, who powerfully promoted capitalism in America, accepted new commercial notions such as "product differentiation," whereby a Model T Ford and a Chevrolet sedan were similar as instruments for providing basic and reliable transportation but a consumer might decide to buy the Chevrolet rather than the Ford because he or she found happiness (utility) in its color (not black) or shape (eventually, tailfins).

In the long run, this sort of pick-and-choose between objectively similar products might lead, with little or no protest, to free market theories that approved the power of advertisements to sway

---

[32] Variety in voting studies shows up, for example, in Nolan McCarty, Keith T. Poole, and Howard Rosenthal, *Polarized America: The Dance of Ideology and Unequal Riches* (Cambridge, MA: MIT Press, 2008); Andrew Gelman, *Red State, Blue State, Rich State, Poor State: Why Americans Vote the Way They Do* (Princeton: Princeton University Press, 2010); Morris P. Fiorina, Samuel J. Abrams, and Jeremy C. Pope, *Culture War? The Myth of a Polarized America* (New York: Pearson, 2005); Steve Kornacki, *The Red and the Blue: The 1990s and the Birth of Political Tribalism* (New York: Ecco, 2018); and Alan I. Abramowitz, *The Great Alignment: Race, Party Transformation, and the Rise of Donald Trump* (New Haven: Yale University Press, 2019).

[33] Alfred Marshall, *Principles of Economics* (London: Macmillan and Co., 1890). See also William Stanley Jevons, *The Theory of Political Economy* (London: Macmillan and Co., 1871), pp. 1–2, who famously resolved the paradox of objectivity vs. subjectivity when he announced that "value depends entirely upon utility."

modern people's thinking. Which they do, sometimes enticing consumers into buying unnecessary or even dangerous commodities – such as, recently, those like civilian Hummers and Big Macs – because, after all, those objects make their buyers immediately happy.[34]

Group Thinking

Not long after doubts about individual rationality moved into the social sciences, researchers began to notice that groups of such individuals were also less than rational enough. Here Gustave Le Bon's *The Crowd* (1895) pointed to what he called "the mental unity of crowds." That is, when people act together in groups – say in political parties, in legislatures, in committees, in juries, in church congregations, and in other important social entities – they often get swept up in shared enthusiasms, sometimes as wide as ideologies, and sometimes as narrow as specific decisions.[35] The problem there is that those enthusiasms may be comfortable but not true.

Weber saw this when he talked about some politicians promoting attractive "causes" which might lead to bad results, and Freud himself stepped in with his *Group Psychology and the Analysis of the Ego* (1922), where he said that crowds tend, via "the herd instinct," to accept their Leader's vision of what to do. This meant that the Leader's preferences, no matter how destructive, can become a sort of super-ego that will convince people in the crowd that they should accept whatever policies he or she promotes even if those violate traditional restrictions such as moral principles laid down, in their consciences, by religious and philosophical authorities.[36]

---

[34] Some of this story appears in William Leach, *Land of Desire: Merchants, Power, and the Rise of a New American Culture* (New York: Vintage, 1993). See also Susan Strasser, *Satisfaction Guaranteed: The Making of the American Mass Market* (Washington, DC: Smithsonian Institution Press, 1989). Some of the ways in which advertising contributes to the subjective yardstick of economic utility were first analyzed for economists in Edward Hasting Chamberlin, *The Theory of Monopolistic Competition: A Re-Orientation of the Theory of Value* (Cambridge, MA: Harvard University Press, 1933).

[35] Published in English in 1896. See Le Bon, *The Crowd: A Study of the Popular Mind* (New York: Dover, 2002), Book I, Chapter I, on the law of mental unity of crowds.

[36] Sigmund Freud, *Group Psychology and the Analysis of the Ego* (orig., 1922; New York: W. W. Norton, 1975). See Ch. IX on the herd instinct, pp. 81–89. Published in German in 1921.

The Rise of Demagogues

Soon after Freud made this point, the ultimate Leader, Adolf Hitler, offered another insight into what ordinary men and women were or were not capable of doing, in the way of Reason, when he described what he called "the big lie." Hitler accused Jews of blaming General Erich Ludendorff for Germany's World War I defeat. Then he explained that this was no ordinary falsehood but an example of "the big lie."

As Hitler put it in his *Mein Kampf* (1925):

> in the big lie there is always a certain force of credibility; because the broad masses of a nation are always more easily corrupted in the deeper strata of their emotional nature than consciously or voluntarily; and thus, in the primitive simplicity of their minds, they more readily fall victims to the big lie than the small lie, since they themselves often tell small lies in little matters but would be ashamed to resort to large-scale falsehoods.[37]

In other words – for our purposes – Western thinkers, including Americans, began to understand that politicians, who Weber saw as an essential part of modern societies, might work not to enlighten citizens but to manipulate them for undesirable ends. And that, of course, is exactly what happened when famous big liars like Hitler, Mussolini, Stalin, and Franco came onto the political stage, shoved aside traditional or legal rulers, and, in many European countries between World War I and II, installed not liberal democracy but fascist or communist regimes.

Whereupon, pro-democratic thinkers were unable to decisively refute anti-democratic partisans who claimed that most people are incompetent and should be led by authoritarian parties and leaders. The problem was that, against fascists and communists, you could not argue very persuasively that the masses were Reasonable when you had already proved that they were not.[38]

---

[37] Adolf Hitler, *Mein Kampf*, trans. Ralph Manheim (Boston: Houghton Mifflin, 1943), ch. X.
[38] This problem is highlighted in Edward A. Purcell, *The Crisis of Democratic Theory: Scientific Naturalism & the Problem of Value* (Lexington, KY: The University Press of Kentucky, 1973).

The Power of Expertise

That individuals were not always competent, that groups were more likely to disagree than to promote consensus, and that leaders constantly threatened to ignore public opinion in favor of planting in the public their own opinions – these were all factors that led to an important debate in the 1920s between the journalist Walter Lippmann and the philosopher John Dewey on the role of "experts" in modern society.

Lippmann led off with *Public Opinion* (1922) and *The Phantom Public* (1925). In general, he argued that most people are motivated by what he called "stereotypes" and which he thought were preconceptions about the nature of the world and other people in it, like the warlike Hun, the philandering Frenchman, the wily Oriental, the miserly Jew, and so forth. As for politicians, he charged them with promoting such stereotypes while talking to crowds, in which case, collective action, even when it arises from democracy, may be unreasonable, as Le Bon and Freud said.[39]

Lippmann didn't run for public office, but he knew that what he said about politicians deploying stereotypes was true because he had promoted official stereotypes in America while working for the Committee on Public Information (the so-called Creel Committee). This was a federal agency created to design and distribute propaganda intended to arouse in America anti-German sentiments during World War I.[40]

On the other hand, Lippmann didn't assume that, because politicians know how to fashion and promote stereotypes, they are themselves animated by Reason. Much of their time is devoted to getting ahead, whereupon they have to rely on other people to supply them

---

[39] Walter Lippmann, "Stereotypes," in *Public Opinion* (orig., 1922; New York: Free Press, 1965), pp. 53–68.

[40] On the creation and dissemination of official stereotypes during World War I, see Harold D. Lasswell, "Chapter IV: Satanism," in *Propaganda Technique in the World War* (orig., 1938; Mansfield Center, CT: Martino Publishing, 2013), pp. 77–101. In England, George Orwell promoted government propaganda during World War II, and he was so horrified by it that he wrote *1984*, which was published in 1949, to describe a future regime that, basically, brainwashes its citizens. Literary critics were not impressed by *1984*, but it continues to be sold today as an extraordinary warning against official mind control.

with information and theories (hopefully reasonable) about most public matters. And these other people cannot be ordinary citizens at large, because such citizens are in thrall to stereotypes.

In which case "experts," who presumably are knowledgeable, at least in their own fields, must be trained and deployed as advisors to political officials and administrators. At that point, however, the democratic public still exists but becomes, in effect, a "phantom" rather than a legitimate source of popular mandates.[41]

Against such a pessimistic view of civic capacities, Dewey offered, in *The Public and Its Problems* (1927), a stout defense of democracy.[42] What good will it do if politicians will receive public policy advice mainly from experts, he said, if only citizens at large know how they feel and what they need from government day to day? Here is a shoe-that-pinches argument going back all the way to Aristotle.

Furthermore, politicians must receive some input from the public because, if only experts shape policy, the American political regime will become an "oligarchy" run for their benefit – that is, run for the few rather than for the many.[43] There, updated for modern society, is the bad form of aristocracy, according to the Greek matrix.

But most importantly, Dewey, as a Pragmatist philosopher, insisted on maintaining democracy not because modern citizens are rational enough to certainly make wise decisions but because they are sensible enough to maintain an arena that can deal with "uncertainty." Like in scientific communities, said Dewey, citizens can make social and economic discoveries which are tentatively true. Government can then devise tentative, rather than permanent, public policies in accordance with those understandings, and we can afterwards test those policies to see which ones are worth retaining, still theoretically tentative, and which ones deserve to be abandoned.[44]

---

[41] Walter Lippmann, *The Phantom Public* (New York: Macmillan, 1925).
[42] John Dewey, *The Public and Its Problems: An Essay in Political Inquiry* (orig., 1927; Athens, OH: Ohio University Press, 2016).
[43] Ibid., pp. 221–225.
[44] A standard description of the scientific method in these years appeared in Morris R. Cohen, "Method, Scientific," in *Encyclopedia of the Social Sciences* (New York: Macmillan, 1933), Vol. X, p. 89: "The progressive character of science shows that its essence is to be sought not in the content of its specific conclusions but rather in the method whereby its findings are made and constantly corrected."

In other words, by comparing modern politics to work performed in the Enlightenment realm of Reason by scientific communities, Dewey proposed that public opinion should be commended as a useful input into the marketplace of ideas. Here, he claimed that the *best* ideas, like in scientific work, which would not necessarily be *perfectly true*, will win in the end.[45]

Dewey was not tilting at windmills. As a realist, he welcomed the input of experts because, like Lippmann, and Weber, he understood that the modern world and how we might live in it were becoming more complicated and difficult for amateurs to understand. But for Dewey, citizens are *also* welcome in that marketplace because, together, they possess an unmatchable range of specific understandings that should be taken into account in overall decision-making.[46]

The Turning Point

Hence, there occurred notable episodes in the work of parties, in the unfolding of political inclusion, in the evolution of public education, and in the development of journalism. Together, these bedrock events and institutions, fostering capacities for democratic citizenship, all appeared in America. And later we will see how what is left of them today still affects citizenship.

Meanwhile, the country became increasingly aware of incompetent individuals, rudderless groups, dangerous demagogues, and essential but unrepresentative experts. Therefore, by World War II, more and more of democracy's contestable points were coming into view – modernity's dirty political laundry, so to speak – and were being discussed soberly by serious American thinkers.[47]

---

[45] The debate between Dewey and Lippmann and the move by Dewey and later Karl Popper to a science-based model of modern democracy are described in David M. Ricci, *The Tragedy of Political Science: Politics, Scholarship, and Democracy* (New Haven: Yale University Press, 1984), pp. 99–132.

[46] It was as if Dewey were proposing "the public" as a collective substitute for Weber's "charismatic" leaders who can occasionally break out of modern bureaucracy's iron cage.

[47] Among scholarly disciplines, political science was particularly stressed by increasing doubts and skepticism concerning democracy before World War II. Members of the discipline formally committed themselves collectively to teaching good citizenship but had difficulty agreeing on how they could do that satisfactorily. See the analysis of this problem in Ricci, *The Tragedy of Political Science*, pp. 66–96.

Which means that we should move on and consider what came into view after World War II, during which President Franklin Roosevelt had called upon Americans to build and staff an "arsenal of democracy," and during which, on behalf of what Protestant minister Reinhold Niebuhr had called "the children of light," Democrats and Republicans alike fought a terrible war to defeat the "children of darkness."[48]

At that point, as we will see, new trends prepared the ground for Donald Trump to come down the escalator.

---

[48] On the arsenal of democracy, see https://millercenter.org/the-presidency/presidential-speeches/december-29-1940-fireside-chat-16-arsenal-democracy. For Reinhold Niebuhr, see his *The Children of Light and the Children of Darkness: A Vindication of Democracy and a Critique of its Traditional Defense* (orig., 1944; Chicago: University of Chicago Press, 2011).

5 MUDDLING

If we are going to consider "trends" that paved the way for Donald Trump – who is, basically, illiterate in public affairs – to take center stage in America, we are challenged to consider the landscape of American life as it developed in recent generations. And that, in a way, is impossible because the target embraces too large a number of possibly relevant people, events, and ideas. We can, however, consider only some of them and hope that the analysis will leave us with a useful collection of impressions. Or, in a way, we are going to look at a forest instead of its trees.

The Cold War

So let us start, in this chapter, by considering how serious thinkers regarded democracy after World War II. They came out of the 1930s with a sense that democracy was still admirable compared with more authoritarian alternatives, such as those that arose in Europe. But when confronted by new claims, domestic and foreign, about how, in reality, democratic citizens are not as competent as they might need to be, American thinkers did not agree to any conclusively persuasive explanations of why government by the many was inherently admirable.

Nevertheless, the country's elected leaders and their followers mobilized 16 million men and women to fight a worldwide war against fascism and, together with America's allies, triumphed.[1] So the democrats must have been doing something right, but thinking about their achievements was muddled.[2]

Then came thinking in response to the Cold War. The idea there was to recognize the size and nature of the forces that had been defeated, and to resolve to confront similar forces, or "contain" them, in communist states like the Union of Soviet Socialist Republics (USSR) and The People's Republic of China (PRC).

To that end, Hannah Arendt, who was a Jewish refugee from Nazi Germany, wrote *The Origins of Totalitarianism* (1951), which showed especially how ordinary people had not understood quickly enough what horrors a pathological German demagogue could generate and therefore had not opposed him adequately. The outcome, in classical terms, was rule by a "tyrant" in Berlin, although Hitler wrapped himself in a racist ideology which claimed that the "dictator" was actually ruling commendably on behalf of "the many."[3]

Arendt's analysis was ponderous and, given her personal experiences, heavily focused on the Jewish question. But Carl Friedrich and Zbigniew Brzezinski followed it up with *Totalitarianism, Dictatorship, and Autocracy* (1956) in order to describe, especially to college students, six "features" of totalitarian regimes, which were "an ideology, a single party typically led by one man, a terroristic police force, a communications monopoly, a weapons monopoly, and a centrally directed economy."[4]

Their work, intentionally or not, complemented *The God that Failed* (1950), wherein six prominent intellectuals, including Arthur

---

[1] We have mostly forgotten how massive the efforts to that end were. American armed forces, with worldwide obligations, now possess close to 5,000 battle tanks. Half of those are held in reserve, which means that they are not immediately available for combat. In World War II, the United States produced 88,000 battle tanks. See https://nationalinterest.org/blog/buzz/us-military-has-astounding-4650-m1-abrams-tanks-212509.
[2] See Edward A. Purcell, *The Crisis of Democratic Theory: Scientific Naturalism & the Problem of Value* (Lexington, KY: University Press of Kentucky, 1973), pp. 115-196. See also, for general background, John Tipple (ed.), *Crisis of the American Dream: A History of American Social Thought, 1920-1940* (New York: Pegasus, 1968).
[3] Hannah Arendt, *The Origins of Totalitarianism* (orig., 1951; New York: Meridian, 1958).
[4] Carl Friedrich and Zbigniew Brzezinski, *Totalitarianism, Dictatorship, and Autocracy* (orig., 1956; New York: Praeger, 1961), p. 9.

Koestler and Richard Wright, told harrowing tales of how, as men of the Left, and therefore as anti-fascists in the 1930s, they personally came to understand how Marxian ideas, promoted by the Soviet Union, were used to foster the maintenance of police states and concentration camps.[5]

The End of Ideology

In the sequence, one upshot of America's contest with international communism during the Cold War was a scholarly move in the direction of arguing that the main problem was Communist "ideology." In this view, ideological thinking was based on systematically misunderstanding the nature of politics and society. That is, it was based on believing in catechisms of misleading principles, like the Marxian notion of dialectics and the linked Marxian doctrines of a capitalist ruling class, economic exploitation, false consciousness, and class wars.

The argument against ideology suggested that American democrats should avoid the dangers of such misleading thinking by seeking pragmatic solutions to social problems. In this "end of ideology" view, the main political objective was not to espouse some all-embracing vision of rearranging the political regimes of this world but to focus on the nitty-gritty of, for example, obtaining a five-cent per hour wage increase (in the mid 1950s) here and there.[6] Progress and prosperity could thus be achieved gradually – in a process of one "piecemeal social reform" after another – without risking the sort of civil wars encouraged by Marxian notions like "the workers" throwing off their "chains."[7]

---

[5] Andre Gide, Richard Wright, Ignazio Silone, Stephen Spender, Arthur Koestler, and Louis Fischer, *The God That Failed* (orig., 1950; New York: Bantam, 1959).

[6] Seymour Martin Lipset, *Political Man: The Social Bases of Politics* (orig., 1960; New York: Anchor Books, 1963), p. 442.

[7] The notion of "piecemeal social reform" came from the philosopher Karl Popper. I have described his ideas and their importance to the end of ideology movement in David M. Ricci, *The Tragedy of Political Science: Politics, Scholarship, and Democracy* (New Haven: Yale University Press, 1984), pp. 114–132. On the Marxian notions cited here, see the last lines from Karl Marx and Friedrich Engels, *The Communist Manifesto* (1848): "The Communists ... openly declare that their ends can be attained only by the forcible overthrow of all existing social conditions. Let the ruling classes tremble at a communist revolution. The proletarians have nothing to lose but their chains ... Workingmen of all countries, unite!"

Daniel Boorstin chipped in to the new mood with *The Genius of American Politics* (1953), in which he claimed that there was not really much to worry about, because most Americans were not tempted by domestic or foreign ideologies. As Boorstin put it, politics in America did not promote any overall plan but expressed "givenness," by which he which meant that existing physical and geographic conditions in the New World permitted, when necessary, useful practical experimentation – for example, the economic and social programs of the New Deal.[8]

The point was that, culturally speaking, most Americans assumed that their founding moment had produced political institutions which did not need substantial repair or replacement. Consequently, said Boorstin, Americans did very little philosophizing about this attachment to past principles, but lived a public life of somewhat mindless continuity, which worked well for them. In which case, he assumed they would ignore the ideological threat posed by communists.

It was a time of relative quietism. Nevertheless, these threads of Cold War thinking did not mean that such thinkers thought democracy was always working wonderfully in America. More to the point, they thought that life in Russia and China was worse.[9] As for America, for example, Seymour Martin Lipset analyzed what he regarded as relentless and dehumanizing work in modern American factories, where major corporations like Ford and General Motors organized output based on Frederick Winslow Taylor's managerial advice about treating workers like machines and then exploiting every opportunity to speed up production lines mercilessly.[10] Thus, in effect, Lipset

---

[8] See the discussion of "givenness" in Daniel J. Boorstin, *The Genius of American Politics* (Chicago: University of Chicago Press, 1953), pp. 8–35.

[9] Thus one journalist at the time suggested defeating Soviet Communism by using the Strategic Air Command to bombard Russians with Sears Roebuck catalogs.

[10] Seymour Martin Lipset, "Work and Its Discontents: The Cult of Efficiency in America," in Daniel Bell, rev. ed., *The End of Ideology: On the Exhaustion of Political Ideas in the Fifties* (orig., 1960; New York: Free Press, 1965), pp. 226–272. Frederick Winslow Taylor's advice appeared in his *Principles of Scientific Management* (New York: Harper & Brothers, 1911), where he referred to ideal pig iron workers as "intelligent gorillas." If Lipset and Bell were writing today, they would probably accuse large corporations like Amazon and Walmart with continuing to pursue this sort of merciless efficiency. See www.propublica.org/article/inside-documents-show-how-amazon-chose-speed-over-safety-in-building-its-delivery-network.

offered scholarly sympathy for Charlie Chaplin's frantic efforts as an assembly line worker in his film entitled *Modern Times* (1936).

The Tragedy Syndrome

Parallel with the Cold War, another wave of responses to American democracy after World War II promoted less quietism while it embodied the modern, post-Enlightenment quest for Reason. Thus, professors in many academic disciplines – such as history, sociology, philosophy, political science, economics, and psychology– were social scientists whose new vocational activity, which was not always benign, had earlier caught the attention of Max Weber.[11]

I have described this syndrome in an earlier book, but I will summarize here what I said there.[12] As universities expanded in the twentieth century, and as more experts were needed to understand life in increasingly complicated societies, more "social studies" professors were checking out old stories and institutions as nineteenth-century scientists before them had done to even older stories and institutions.

In this process, later-day professors pursued the important, post-Enlightenment, and scientific aim of creating new "knowledge" rather than purveying mere "opinion." It was like Plato's wise men coming out of *The Republic*'s cave, into the sunshine, if we want to think of them in classical terms.

Unfortunately, however, there were serious downsides to this activity, which engaged many thousands of practitioners. The first downside was that a great many old beliefs could be disproved, sometimes easily, because many of them were based on convictions formed before modern tools for acquiring solid knowledge were available. For example, the notion of "self-evident truths" in the Declaration of

---

[11] That Science is not always benign, after the atomic bomb was invented and dropped in 1945, is the main theme in Friedrich Durrenmatt, *The Physicists* (orig., 1961; New York: Grove Press, 2010). This drama features three inmates in an insane asylum: Johann Mobius, Albert Einstein, and Isaac Newton. Mobius is a real scientist pretending to be insane to hide himself and the fact that he has discovered how to make new weapons that would enable political control of the world, and Einstein and Newton are pretenders who are spying on Mobius to find out what he has discovered in order to convey that knowledge to their respective governments.

[12] Ricci, *The Tragedy of Political Science*, esp. pp. 209–248.

Independence. Why were these self-evident, and to whom were they obvious?

The catch was this: What if some tales or convictions, even if wrong, might be helpful for serving as shared sentiments – like the *Declaration*'s self-evident truths – that help people live together peacefully and prosperously even if in error?[13] And if that were the case, how could potentially dangerous social scientists find, among themselves, guidelines for placing some useful but inaccurate subjects out of bounds, so to speak?

The second downside to this steady pursuit of Reason was that, even when some curious professors might sense, uneasily, that they might be undermining comity and stability, or law and order, their career success depended on demonstrating this or that, more or less, no matter what. So how could they stop?

That is, most professors get promoted in universities according to the rule of publish or perish. In economic terms, that is their "business model." Therefore, they are impelled to conduct research and publish the results, if possible, regardless of what they are investigating. Moreover, the louder and more dazzling their propositions, the more promotions they can earn. But again, who will tell these practitioners, of the "soft" sciences, when to stop? Who will tell them that, about certain subjects, their personal gain might be outweighed by a social loss?

In other words, who will hold them to Weber's "ethics of responsibility," which calls for testing ideas to ascertain their possible consequences? For example, if professors are going to undermine an old story, are they not somehow obliged to formulate a new story that will serve just as well to hold society together?[14]

---

[13] This point was raised by Edmund Burke against Dr. Richard Price (a Protestant minister), and the common-sense philosophy of Thomas Paine, when Burke extolled the efficacy of our "prejudices" as opposed to using "reason" to shape and administer a government. For Burke on prejudices, see his *Reflections on the Revolution in France* (1790), Part I, Book 6, Section 2. There, Burke writes the famous lines: "[W]e are generally men of untaught feelings ... [Instead] of casting away all our old prejudices, we cherish them ... because they are prejudices; and the longer they have lasted and the more generally they have prevailed, the more we cherish them. We are afraid to put men to live and trade each on his own private stock of reason, because we suspect that this stock in each man is small ... Prejudice renders a man's virtue his habit ... Through prejudice, his duty becomes a part of his nature."

[14] David M. Ricci, *Post-Truth American Politics: False Stories and Current Crises* (New York: Cambridge University Press, 2023), pp. 170–182.

Put that another way. It is "functionally rational" – that is, personally *profitable* – for professors to do their work well as prescribed, that is, to use modern research techniques to show, for instance, via publication, that an old story about elected leaders being steadily responsive to voter preferences is unrealistic. But where is the "substantive rationality" – that is, the social *welfare* – in that publication?[15]

Whatever, as more and more scholars pursued the vocation of science by publishing, there appeared interesting studies of democratic behavior during, roughly speaking, the Cold War years. I am listing a few of those studies here.[16] I won't discuss what they said because, when taken together, they offered only a learned hodgepodge of understandings

---

[15] I describe such a prize-winning political science book in ibid., pp. 200–205. Recognizing this problem is a theme in moderate conservatism today. For example, see Alasdair MacIntyre, *After Virtue* (Notre Dame, IN: Notre Dame University Press, 1981); Stephen L. Carter, *The Culture of Disbelief: How American Law and Politics Trivialize Religious Devotion* (New York: Anchor Books, 1994); Rodney Stark, *The Victory of Reason: How Christianity Led to Freedom, Capitalism, and Western Success* (New York: Random House, 2005); Paul W. Kahan, *Putting Liberalism in its Place* (Princeton: Princeton University Press, 2005); Patrick J. Deneen, *Why Liberalism Failed* (New Haven: Yale University Press, 2018); and Steven D. Smith, *The Disenchantment of Secular Discourse* (Cambridge, MA: Harvard University Press, 2019).

[16] The following books are listed only as a sample of works that I found interesting. I do not mean to suggest that they were more important than others which I did not cite here because space is limited. Bernard R. Berelson, Paul F. Lazarfeld, and William N. McPhee, *Voting: A Study of Opinion Formation in a Presidential Campaign* (Chicago: University of Chicago Press, 1954); Angus Campbell, Phillip E. Converse, Warren E. Miller, and Donald E. Stokes, *The American Voter* (Chicago: University of Chicago Press, 1960); Henry B. Mayo, *An Introduction to Democratic Theory* (New York: Oxford University Press, 1960); E. E. Schattschneider, *The Semi-Sovereign People: A Realist's View of Democracy in America* (New York: Holt, Rinehart, and Winston, 1960); Thomas Landon Thorson, *The Logic of Democracy* (New York: Holt, Rinehart, and Winston, 1962); James MacGregor Burns, *The Deadlock of Democracy: Four-Party Politics in America* (Englewood Cliffs, NJ: Prentice-Hall, 1963); Gabriel A. Almond and Sidney Verba, *The Civic Culture: Political Attitudes and Democracy in Five Nations* (Princeton: Princeton University Press, 1963); V. O. Key, *The Responsible Electorate: Rationality in Presidential Voting, 1936–1960* (Cambridge, MA: Harvard University Press, 1966); Peter Bachrach, *The Theory of Democratic Elitism: A Critique* (Boston: Little, Brown and Company, 1967); Penn Kimball, *The Disconnected* (New York: Columbia University Press, 1972); Michael J. Crozier and Samuel P. Huntington, *The Crisis of Democracy: Report on the Governability of Democracies to the Trilateral Commission* (New York: New York University Press, 1975); Norman H. Nie, Sidney Verba, and John R. Petrocik, *The Changing American Voter* (Cambridge, MA: Harvard University Press, 1976); Robert A. Dahl, *Dilemmas of Pluralist Democracy: Autonomy vs. Control* (New Haven: Yale University Press, 1982); Benjamin Barber, *Strong Democracy: Participatory Politics for a New Age* (Berkeley: University of California Press, 1984); Francis Fox Piven and Richard A. Cloward, *Why Americans Don't Vote* (New York: Pantheon, 1988).

and generated no research consensus about the nature of citizenship and its practices. Only their overall thrust was clear, and it showed that democracy is more complicated and fallible than we used to think, if only because we hadn't thought about it frequently or systematically.

Which is not surprising. And it does not trouble me, because while scholarly talk about democracy in this interim era left students and public audiences somewhat up in the air, that was not problematic for what I am exploring because, anyway, things were about to get much worse.

1 Parties

What happened was that conditions for good citizenship deteriorated in every realm I discussed in previous chapters. Chief among them was the realm of party politics which, as we saw, was an arena where Weber's politicians spoke to citizens and helped them to express their sentiments and preferences. In this sense, party politics had to be invented in America and then became a necessary condition for democracy in that country as it grew during its early generations.

Except for when the two national parties polarized over the issue of slavery and then fought the Civil War, healthy party politics (not necessarily gracious or elegant) had consisted, in effect, of collecting factions and competing (peacefully) for power against other collections of factions.[17] It was paradoxical, then, that at the same time that Americans were condemning communists during the Cold War by arguing that their ideological thinking was an authoritarian sin, America's Republican Party went from being a flexible collection of factions to being an ideological entity as opposed to the Democratic Party which continued, not very smoothly, to embrace various interest groups.[18]

---

[17] American parties as competing collections of factions – attracted by gravitational forces to either a sun or a moon – was the guiding thesis in Samuel Lubbell, *The Future of American Politics* (New York: Harper & Row, 1952). This book won the American Political Science Association's Woodrow Wilson Foundation Award in 1952 for the best book that year in government, politics, or international affairs.

[18] The descent of the Republican Party into ideological inflexibility is described in Geoffrey Kabaservice, *Rule and Ruin: The Downfall of Moderation and the Destruction of the Republican Party, from Eisenhower to the Tea Party* (New York: Oxford University Press, 2012).

Jacob Hacker and Paul Pierson described this outcome as undermining democracy by moving away from the political center in American life, which they assumed includes a mixture of groups, some more Left and some more Right, among whom compromises can be hammered out so that Americans can go forward together, more or less.[19] Thus, Hacker and Pierson joined other scholars in arguing that Republicans, with their ideological springboard, became culpable for systematically distorting the realm of party politics whereas Democrats, who are not always or necessarily admirable, are, if at all, guilty only of routine power plays and maneuvers.[20]

Moving Right

Milestones on the way to transforming Republicans into an ideological powerhouse are by this time well known.[21] We can describe them in terms of "conservatives," like Senators Barry Goldwater (R-AZ) and Strom Thurmond (R-SC), wresting leadership of the party away from "moderates," like Governor Nelson Rockefeller (R-NY) and Governor William Scranton (R-PA). On this score, Thurmond, who was an out-and-out racist from South Carolina, moved from the

---

[19] Jacob S. Hacker and Paul Pierson, *Off Center: The Republican Revolution & the Erosion of American Democracy* (New Haven: Yale University Press, 2005). See also Alan I. Abramowitz, *The Disappearing Center: Engaged Citizens, Polarization, and American Democracy* (New Haven: Yale University Press, 2019). On earlier liberal praise for pragmatism and flexibility of the center, see Arthur Schlesinger, Jr., *The Vital Center: The Politics of Freedom* (Boston: Houghton Mifflin, 1949). After Trump's election in 2024, one can argue that Trump won because, this time, he, rather than the Democrats, was at the center of American thinking. That argument would assume that, because Trump boosted racism and misogyny (against his Black and female opponent), similar sentiments probably motivated the people who voted for Trump. But that proposition would assume that most people who voted for him agreed with his policy talk, whereas I believe that many such people may have admired him less for his policy proposals and more because of his entertainment value, which is sometimes described by pundits as his "authenticity." In which case, the center of voter *sentiment* hasn't shifted but voter *behavior* has.

[20] Along this line, of ideology vs. vague generalities, see D. J. Dionne, Jr., Norman J. Ornstein, and Thomas E. Mann, *One Nation after Trump: A Guide for the Perplexed, the Disillusioned, the Desperate, and the Not-Yet Deported* (New York: St. Martin's Press, 2017), which calls, p. 3, on Democrats to pull themselves together around a "vision – a hopeful and unifying alternative to his [Trump's] dark and divisive assessment of our country's prospects."

[21] I am intentionally not using terms like "sect," "cult," or "tribe" because they might project scholarly implications I do not wish to suggest here.

Democratic Party into the Republican Party in 1964, just in time to back Goldwater.²²

Goldwater received the Republican presidential nomination in that year after voting against the Civil Rights Act of 1964 on the grounds that it would violate "property rights" (to choose one's customers) in public accommodations and therefore justify a "federal police state of mammoth proportions."²³ At the same time, moderate Republican Senators like Everett Dirksen (R-IL) and Jacob Javits (R-NY) voted to overcome a Southern filibuster in the Senate and then joined forces with non-Southern Democrats to enact the most important civil rights legislation since the Nineteenth Amendment (1920), which guaranteed American women the right to vote.

Following his lurch to the right, Goldwater announced to the 1964 Republican convention that his guiding principle was that "extremism in the defense of liberty is no vice" – that is, it is entirely moral to leave the white South at liberty to perpetuate Jim Crow segregation.²⁴ Consequently, he lost the popular vote in November 1964 to Lyndon Johnson by 27 million to 43 million votes but, as a harbinger of further Republican popularity in the white South and Southwest, Goldwater won the electoral votes of Arizona and five Deep South states.

---

²² He was also a hypocrite. After Thurmond died at age 100, his bi-racial daughter Essie May Butler, born out of wedlock, revealed his paternity in her autobiography *Dear Senator: A Memoir by the Daughter of Strom Thurmond* (New York: Regan Books, 2005).

²³ See his speech at www.nytimes.com/1964/06/19/archives/text-of-goldwater-speech-on-rights.html.

²⁴ In our concern with citizenship, we should note that, around the time that Goldwater was proclaiming his support for states' rights, the former Republican governor of California, Earl Warren, was writing the court's decision in *Brown v. Board of Education* (1954). In that case, speaking for a 9–0 majority of justices appointed by Democratic and Republican presidents, Warren observed that: "Today, education is perhaps the most important function of state and local governments. Compulsory school attendance laws and the great expenditures for education both demonstrate our recognition of the importance of education to our democratic society. It is required in the performance of our most basic public responsibilities, even service in the armed forces. *It is the very foundation of good citizenship.* Today it is a principal instrument in awakening the child to cultural values, in preparing him for later professional training, and in helping him to adjust normally to his environment. In these days, it is doubtful that any child may reasonably be expected to succeed in life if he is denied the opportunity of an education. Such an opportunity, where the state has undertaken to provide it, is a right which must be made available to all on equal terms" (emphasis added).

New Alliances

Growing Republican electoral success in the old Confederacy was predicted by thinkers who saw that Republicans could gain power in state and federal elections by pursuing what they called "the Southern Strategy," which meant pursuing votes in the white South and the fast-growing Southwest.[25] Efforts in that direction were usually conducted by what we now call "dog whistles" rather than clear statements of racial prejudice. An example appeared when Ronald Reagan opened his 1980 presidential campaign in Mississippi by announcing, like Goldwater had earlier, to a mostly white county fair crowd, that he believed in states' rights and would restore them if he were elected.[26]

The genial Reagan, with his entertaining fables about "welfare queens" – the hint was that most of them were Black – was a more attractive candidate than the sometimes-abrasive Goldwater.[27] In addition, and very importantly, he introduced into Republican rhetoric the reassuring notion of "supply-side economics."

This notion, which was simple enough to be sketched on a cloth napkin by its author Arthur Laffer, was never endorsed by most leading economists.[28] Still, it promised that if federal taxes would be reduced, money consequently left in private hands would be invested productively, employment would expand, workers' incomes would rise, and painless tax revenues from increased economic growth would balance the budget so that the country would achieve perpetual prosperity.

By endorsing this notion, Reagan was, in effect, turning the Republican Party into a champion of what is now called

---

[25] Kevin Phillips, *The Emerging Republican Majority* (orig., 1969; Princeton: Princeton University Press, 2014).

[26] See Reagan's speech at www.zinnedproject.org/news/tdih/reagan-speech-at-neshoba/.

[27] See "'Welfare Queen' Becomes Issue in Reagan Campaign," *New York Times* (February 15, 1976), p. 51: "'There is a woman in Chicago,' the Republican candidate [Reagan] said recently to an audience in Gilford, N.H. during his free-swinging attack on welfare abuses. 'She has 80 names, 30 addresses, 12 Social Security cards and is collecting veterans benefits on four non-existing deceased husbands ... she's got Medicaid, getting food stamps, and she is collecting welfare under each of her names. Her tax-free cash income alone is over $150,000.'" Journalists discovered no such woman in Chicago.

[28] Despite Dr. Laffer's small reputation among leading economists, President Trump awarded him in 2019 the Medal of Freedom, which is the nation's highest civilian honor, for inventing "supply-side economics." See https://trumpwhitehouse.archives.gov/briefings-statements/remarks-president-trump-presentation-medal-freedom-dr-arthur-laffer/.

"neoliberalism," where public officials should "unleash" capitalism and private entrepreneurs will do the rest. We will return to this marriage of Republicanism and neoliberalism, which is actually a *ménage à trois* because there are many Democrats who also admire neoliberalism.

At any rate, supply-side economics was a promise which reached out to less affluent white voters and even some union members. These were often Governor George Wallace (D-AL) enthusiasts in the 1960s and 1970s, sometimes living in the Midwest, who opposed school busing in urban areas, who regarded Vietnam War protesters as unpatriotic, who scorned hippies as coddled youngsters, who felt that religious and family values were mocked by Americans who promoted the "Counterculture," who suffered from the neoliberal export of American factory jobs to, say, China, Vietnam, Indonesia, and Mexico, and who might abandon their long-time alliance with New Deal Democrats and turn into the kind of hard-hat workers whom Fox News would eventually cultivate.[29]

Severe Polarization

After President Reagan retired in 1989, Republican attention increasingly focused on Speaker of the House Newt Gingrich (R-GA), who promoted his "Contract with America" as a platform around which conservative Republicans on the Hill could rally.[30] The Contract proposed tax cuts on capital gains, a line-item veto, funding for an anti-ballistic-missile defense system, cancellation of many federal business regulations, raising estate tax exemptions, funding fewer Social Security pensions, and enabling more private retirement accounts.

Gingrich succeeded in polarizing the two parties in Congress with such ideas, to the point where Republicans, unlike in earlier years, began to vote almost unanimously against any Democratic proposals

---

[29] On Fox News and its relation to hard-hats, see Reece Peck, *Fox Populism: Branding Conservatism as Working Class* (New York: Cambridge University Press, 2019).
[30] Newt Gingrich, *Contract with America: The Bold Plan by Rep. Newt Gingrich, Rep. Dick Armey, and the House Republicans to Change the Nation* (New York: Times Books, 1994).

no matter how intrinsically worthy.³¹ But he failed to remove from office the president. The House of Representatives voted to impeach Bill Clinton, but the Senate voted not to convict him for un-presidential behavior with Monica Lewinsky, which wasn't seemly but also wasn't a crime.³²

Dissimilar Parties

Eventually, Trump arrived to take command of a Republican Party which conservatives like Goldwater, Reagan, and Gingrich had redesigned.³³

---

³¹ This anti-Democratic solidarity did not relate to whether a particular policy proposal was worthy or not but to the fact that it was proposed by Democrats. For example, on March 21, 2010, the Affordable Care Act, sometimes known as Obamacare, passed the House of Representatives by a vote of 219–212 with not a single Republican voting to approve it. This after Republicans and Democrats together, in both houses of Congress, voted to enact Medicare in 1965. Moreover, in 2021, the John Lewis Voting Rights Act was approved by the House of Representatives without a single Republican vote in favor, after which the bill was kept off the Senate agenda by the threat of a Republican filibuster. Only one Republican senator voted for cloture. This happened years after senators of both parties overrode a Southern filibuster threat and voted in favor of enacting the Voting Rights Act of 1965.

³² The 7th Circuit Court Judge Richard A. Posner, widely admired as a conservative intellectual, explained that "intelligent evaluation" of the Lewinsky "mess" requires us to recognize both private and public morality, where society "imposes" the latter as a code on every "profession and vocation, including that of a political leader." This is simply not true, because there is no such "imposition." Professions like medicine and law have codes of conduct written and certified by their practitioners, whereas, even though Weber conceived of politics as a vocation, it has no such standards, defined by the public or politicians themselves. As to whether Posner believed that Clinton should have been impeached or convicted, he offers a welter of "on the one hand this" and "on the other hand that" arguments, but declares that Clinton's "conduct in the Lewinsky matter has been sufficiently shocking to raise questions about his capacity to conduct public business responsibly." That is, Posner is "shocked" and "raises questions," therefore Clinton should be convicted. See Richard A. Posner, *An Affair of State: The Investigation, Impeachment, and Trial of President Clinton* (Cambridge, MA: Harvard University Press, 1999), esp. "Chapter 4: Morality, Private and Public," pp. 133–169, and 173. See also, on the Right, William J. Bennett, *The Death of Outrage: Bill Clinton and the Assault on American Ideals* (New York: Free Press, 1998). Bennett argued that because Clinton had no respect for laws, he committed adultery and then lied about it. In which case, all Americans should be outraged, should understand that Clinton violated his constitutional obligation to enforce the "rule of law," and therefore should tell their representatives in Washington to impeach him and remove him from office. After Bennett wrote, Clinton was impeached by the House but not convicted by the Senate.

³³ On the ideas that came to inform most Republicans, see David Ricci, *Why Conservatives Tell Stories and Liberals Don't: Rhetoric, Faith, and Vision on the American Right* (Boulder, CO: Paradigm Publishers, 2011).

But first, Mitch McConnell (R-KY), the Majority Leader of the Senate, broke every custom and tradition of Congressional behavior and courtesy, in the name of ideological solidarity, by enlisting his Republican senatorial colleagues to ignore their constitutional obligation to conduct a hearing for someone whom Barack Obama, a Democratic president, had nominated for a seat on the Supreme Court.[34]

This ploy demonstrated that America now had two very different parties, one commonly known as conservative and the other usually seen as liberal. But we should note that the conservatives were considerably united on ideological grounds, whereas the liberals had no clear doctrine but were a collection of interest groups or, in earlier language, "factions." Factional strength relative to other factions in the Democratic Party varied over time, whereby the party's policy proposals expressed not a creed but a list of preferences, sometimes clashing, arising from groups like, recently, pro-Palestinians and pro-Israelis in Michigan.[35]

2 Inclusion

What I referred to earlier as a realm of "inclusion" has become, regrettably, an arena for "exclusion." During the nineteenth and early twentieth centuries, inclusion slowly but commendably extended democratic participation in America's "mixed" government. At the same time, the white South managed to resist Reconstruction after the Civil War and disenfranchise most of its Black citizens via segregation and violence, thus setting an example of how activity in this realm could go backwards.

Eventually, in response to what was, after all, a national disgrace of Jim Crow segregation, moderate majorities of Republicans

---

[34] The Constitution, Article 2, Section 2, says that the Senate will or will not confirm (proffer "advice and consent" on) appointments. But it does not say *when* that will happen, so McConnell and his colleagues waited until Trump was elected and inaugurated, whereupon Neil Gorsuch was nominated by Trump and confirmed by the Senate.

[35] On this fundamental difference between the parties, and on some of its consequences, see Matt Grossmann and David A. Hopkins, *Asymmetric Politics: Ideological Republicans and Group Interest Democrats* (New York: Oxford University Press, 2016). On Democratic lists of preferences, see David Ricci, *Politics without Stories: The Liberal Predicament* (New York: Cambridge University Press, 2016), pp. 132–154.

and Democrats together in the House and Senate enacted the Voting Rights Act of 1965. That Act imposed federal supervision on voting and other election procedures throughout the country. It thus eliminated many discriminatory Southern practices, such as literacy tests, "proof" of moral character, and "voter dilution" via election district border changes. As a result, Black voting rates across the former Confederate states climbed substantially.

Subsequently, however, the increasingly ideological Republican Party, attracting white racists, and especially strong in the South, turned to deliberate efforts to exclude rather than include a great many citizens.[36] The main targets for exclusion were various "minorities" – especially Blacks, Latinos, and Asians – who would probably vote Democratic if they were not excluded.[37]

Techniques

Conveniently for us, Carol Anderson collected data on these efforts and grouped the different schemes into voter ID laws, voter roll purges, and ploys that rigged electoral rules.[38] Of course, because there are fifty states and each has its own laws, we can note here only a few cases that shed light on what happened.

In states like Mississippi, Texas, Wisconsin, Ohio, and North Carolina, citizens must present government-issued photo-IDs, such as a passport or a driver's license, at polling stations in order to vote. In those states, Republican officials have argued that the requirement of a government photo-ID is designed to prevent fraudulent voting by people who are, for whatever reason, not qualified to vote.

Plaintiffs against the same laws argue that poor people – likely to be minority members and vote Democratic – are least likely to possess

---

[36] This point is denied by conservatives like Dinesh D'Souza, who argued that Republicans were "color blind" rather than "racist." See Dinesh D'Souza, *The End of Racism: Principles for a Multiracial Society* (New York: Free Press, 1995), *passim*, but esp. pp. 163–170.
[37] What happened was especially ironic because the Republican Party, led into war by Abraham Lincoln, eventually used that war to spearhead, via Amendments Thirteen to Fifteen, the great inclusion of Black Americans into citizenship with full voting rights.
[38] Carol Anderson, *One Person: No Vote: How Voter Suppression Is Destroying Our Democracy* (New York: Bloomsbury, 2019).

such ID documents and least able to afford the cost of obtaining them, such as, for example, from a difficult-to-access state office which issues photo-IDs especially for voting purposes.

Such a law for Indiana was upheld 2–1 by the 7th Circuit Court of Appeals in 2007 and then upheld again, 6–3, by the Supreme Court in *Crawford v. Marion County Election Board* in 2008. No instances of voter fraud were presented in defense of the law.[39] But the appellate judges concluded, with Reagan-appointee Richard Posner in Chicago leading the way, that there was an overriding state interest in preventing *future* instances of fraud and therefore the law did not constitute some sort of updated poll tax forbidden by the Twenty-Fourth Amendment.

Soon afterwards, in *Shelby County v. Holder* (2013), by voting 5–4, the Republican-packed Supreme Court gutted the supervisory provisions of the Civil Rights Act of 1965. The Court said that such national supervision violates "basic principles of federalism" – that is, states' rights – and, anyway, because that supervision was devised forty years ago, it "has no logical relationship to the present day."[40]

In other words, supervision would no longer be needed to repair conditions in once openly racist states which, according to the Supreme Court, and over the years, had become racially tolerant. It was like giving a green light to red states, mainly in the South and Midwest, to keep potential Democrats, often Black Americans, away from voting booths with voter ID laws or other ploys.

Purging voters from registration lists is technically allowed by the National Voter Registration Act of 1993, because it authorizes state officials to periodically update voters' rolls. The problem there, which was weaponized by Republican state officials, emerged from Republican election administrators deciding how to define "ineligible" state residents.

---

[39] There was no obligation to present such evidence because these were not courts of first instance. It is also true, however, that no evidence of fraud was presented in the federal District Court, where the case started and which *is* a first instance court.

[40] For *Shelby County*, see www.supremecourt.gov/opinions/20pdf/19-1257_g204.pdf. For additional Supreme Court gutting of 1965 Civil Rights Act protections, in *Brnovich v. Democratic National Committee* (2020), see www.supremecourt.gov/opinions/20pdf/19-1257_g204.pdf.

When those administrators used "non-voting" as a criterion, as if a person registered but voting only infrequently should be removed because he or she obviously is flighty, unserious, capricious, erratic, socially disconnected, and so forth, millions of people, many of them young, poor, and belonging to minorities, were struck from voter rolls in Republican-controlled states, often without warning.

Therefore, they might show up on Election Day and, by surprise, be denied the right to vote. This happened, for instance, in Florida in time for the 2000 federal election. There, 173,000 voters were purged before Election Day by Secretary of State Katherine Harris, who happened to be the co-chair of George Bush II's presidential campaign in Florida that year. Then, on Election Day, Governor George Bush (R-TX), who happened to be the brother of Governor Jeb Bush (R-FL), won Florida's twenty-five electoral votes by receiving 537 more votes than Al Gore (D-TN) out of almost 6 million votes cast.[41]

Rigging the Rules

Let's skip Anderson's third category of exclusion – which is a matter of rigging election rules, gerrymandering outrageous electoral districts, opening very few polling stations in densely populated urban areas, doing the same for drop boxes, and more – because its acts are both brazen and depressing. They came to a pinnacle of partisan nastiness when, in 2000, officials in Florida's Republican state government (a) refused to recount the uniquely designed "butterfly" ballots processed by defective voting machines in that state on the grounds that doing so would infringe George W. Bush's constitutional rights, and when (b) this obvious stonewalling was upheld a few weeks later by the national Supreme Court's Republican justices in a 5–4 unsigned (*per curiam*) opinion.[42]

---

[41] See www.britannica.com/event/Bush-v-Gore.

[42] The "butterfly" ballots in Palm Spring County were a post-election source of contention because Pat Buchanan received there more than 2,000 votes from people who would normally vote for Democrats, including Jewish residents whose community disliked Buchanan because they considered him to be anti-Semitic or close to it. On the butterfly ballot issue, see www.gsb.stanford.edu/faculty-research/publications/butterfly-did-it-aberrant-vote-buchanan-palm-beach-county-florida.

The opinion was written anonymously, but it was endorsed by William Rehnquist, Clarence Thomas, Anthony Kennedy, Samuel Alito, and Sandra Day O'Connor, lest we forget.[43] They ruled that continuing the recount would amount to "unequal treatment" and therefore violate George W. Bush's constitutional rights under the Fourteenth Amendment. Justices O'Connor and Kennedy added, in a concurring opinion, that the decision would not apply to future cases. This they phrased in legalese: "Our consideration is limited to the present circumstances, for the problem of equal protection in election processes generally presents many complexities."[44] In other words, at least these two justices were aware that there was no principle underlying the decision they had just signed.

Neoliberalism

As we saw, Ronald Reagan introduced, to the increasingly ideological Republican Party, the language of supply-side economics, which says, leave more taxable profits in private hands so that entrepreneurs will grow the economy and thereby provide prosperity for everyone, including precarious workers. Here was the neoliberal notion that justified the party's enacting federal tax cuts which increased the national debt and therefore required ever larger interest payments that left fewer tax receipts to be applied to social welfare projects – such as schools, libraries, police, public transportation, environmental clean-up, and parks – which benefit ordinary people.

In that sense, supply-side economics is an exclusionary device which serves the interests of wealthier people, such as federal bond holders, before those of rank-and-file citizens, who own little of the national debt and its Treasury bonds.[45] Without listing here additional

---

[43] *Bush Et Al. v. Gore Et Al.* (2000), see the decision at https://tile.loc.gov/storage-services/service/ll/usrep/usrep531/usrep531098/usrep531098.pdf.

[44] This stipulation is noted by Jeffrey Toobin, *Too Close to Call: The Thirty-Six-Day Battle to Decide the 2000 Election* (New York: Random House, 2002), p. 265. Most people are not lawyers and do not read opinions issued by Supreme Court justices. This one, though, is worth the effort. In effect, O'Connor and Kennedy said that the decision they just signed forbids robbing a bank on Main Street in Zenith but does not apply to any other banks.

[45] As I wrote this book, Elon Musk was designated by incoming president Donald Trump to head a new "Department of Governmental Efficiency," where he will be charged with

rounds of Republican tax cutting through the careers of George Bush I, Newt Gingrich, George Bush II, and Donald Trump, we can take two Supreme Court decisions – first of all *Citizens United v. FEC* (2010) and second *McCutcheon et al. v. FEC* (2014) – both decided by 5–4 votes, as emblematic of this Republican commitment to modern exclusion based on wealth.[46]

From roughly 1790 to 1830, as we saw, American states that had property requirements for voting dropped them in a move toward increased democracy. Now the Republican Party, having packed the Court, was reinstalling the early disparity between people of more and less property. This time the gap was between those whose interests are served or not served by candidates who seek campaign contributions.

It is that simple. You are not excluded physically from the electorate, but your presence, accompanied by modest means, becomes in many cases immaterial to politicians who believe that they must raise a great deal of money to win elections.[47]

---

shrinking federal governmental expenditures. This comes when, as a result of tax cuts enacted under several Republican presidents, the federal budget deficit is approaching $2 trillion annually. In that situation, yearly interest on the national debt is now close to $1 trillion (which is more than the entire yearly defense budget), and much of this interest money goes to a minority of Americans who can afford to buy government bonds and Treasury notes. In other words, such people pay lower taxes than in the past (because of the cuts) and also receive more interest payments than previously (because of the debt), leaving federal agencies smaller than they might be otherwise. For now, it is not clear in which programs or agencies federal expenditures will decline. It is possible, though, and maybe even likely, that Musk and his associates will try mainly to reduce social and economic services that help ordinary more than wealthy people. Elon Musk, for example, doesn't need Social Security or Medicare or veterans' benefits. And, of course, even if services are reduced, the interest payments (to economic winners) will remain to be paid. Information on the deficit and interest payments is available at www.cnbc.com/2024/09/12/interest-payments-on-the-national-debt-top-1-trillion-as-deficit-swells.html.

[46] A previous Supreme Court decision was *Buckley v. Valeo* (1976) which, in the name of free speech, permitted multimillionaire William Buckley and future candidates to spend on their campaigns unlimited amounts of their own money. That decision later permitted billionaire Michael Bloomberg to spend $102 million, or $174 per vote, on his campaign for a third term as New York City's mayor in 2009. See www.nytimes.com/2009/11/28/nyregion/28spending.html. In the 2020 Democratic presidential primary elections, Bloomberg spent over $900 million of his own money and got nowhere. On this, see www.nytimes.com/2020/03/20/us/politics/bloomberg-campaign-900-million.html.

[47] The loss of democracy, when money is empowered, is a main theme in Lawrence Lessig, *Republic Lost: How Money Corrupts Congress – and a Way to Stop It* (New York: Twelve, 2012).

The move to, in effect, enfranchise money occurred when the court held that corporations have the same right as individuals to make "independent campaign expenditures." What this amounted to was that the First Amendment protects the right of free speech, wherefore all "persons," living or legally defined, including corporations, have a right to spend money to express their opinions to the public, to office holders, and to candidates.

But the court in these two decisions, supported only by Republican judges, also opened the way for so-called super Political Action Committees (super PACs) to solicit virtually unlimited contributions from individuals and groups who were entitled by the Court to make "independent expenditures."[48] The fig leaf of propriety there was that those expenditures could not be "coordinated" with candidates. As if such co-ordination – a word or two here or there, or not even words but winks and nods – could be discovered and would be prosecuted.

The Culture War

Modern Republicans created another exclusionary practice when they began to contest elections on the basis of what they called "culture" rather than economics. This ploy worked through two considerations.

First, if candidates promote neoliberalism openly, they are not likely to win elections. The problem there is that capitalism maintains economic competition which produces winners and losers, where some (a few) people are more able than others (the many) to succeed in whatever work they choose or can manage to find. Over time, this process creates significant income gaps between the few and the many.[49] And

---

[48] This line of legal thinking permitted Elon Musk, who is reputedly worth $260 billion, and who announced his support for candidate Donald Trump in 2024, to award $1 million per day to voters (obviously Republicans) who after October 19, in that election year, signed affidavits of their support for "free speech" and "the right to bear arms." This project was promoted by America PAC, which Musk founded. Musk is entitled by Supreme Court of the United States (SCOTUS) decisions to contribute as much money as he wants to that PAC. On the estimated size of Musk's wealth, see www.forbes.com/profile/elon-musk/.

[49] On modern capitalism and income gaps, see Thomas Piketty, *Capital in the Twenty-First Century* (Cambridge, MA: Harvard University Press, 2017).

some of the less successful may then feel that their lives are "precarious" and may then "resent" their lowly status.[50]

Rightists claim that these gaps will eventually narrow because, if "unleashed," entrepreneurs will create new industries, new products, and new jobs in new workplaces. Leftists reject this sort of thinking, say that it amounts to "trickle-down" economics, and argue that income gaps should be ameliorated by progressive taxation, public works projects, and government regulation. In other words, they advocate a new New Deal.[51]

Second, the Right–Left division on such matters has a long history and has inspired many electoral confrontations.[52] But for almost half a century now, Republicans have developed a way to mainly avoid these confrontations, which are risky for them because the poor, often less talented and usually less endowed with the right sort of parents, invariably outnumber the rich.

Therefore, since the late twentieth century, Republicans have highlighted issues of what they call culture. These issues change from time to time and place to place as popular moods evolve. So Republican complaints have varied. But they have related, for example, to school prayers, to Judeo-Christian values, to unconventional gender couples, to "activist" judges, to environmental "extremism," to gun rights, to abortion "on demand," to pornography, to school choice, to "radical" feminism, to children suing parents, and to the rights of "the unborn."[53]

---

[50] Guy Standing, *The Precariat: The New Dangerous Class* (New York: Bloomsbury, 2014). Some scholars argue that on average, economic growth is up and therefore the nation is wealthier than it used to be. But almost all of the growth has increased the income of elites while income for the lower 50% of American earners has more or less remained constant for the last forty years. For empirical evidence on this extensive inequality, see William Davies, *Nervous States: Democracy and the Decline of Reason* (New York: Norton, 2019), pp. 75–83.

[51] See Michael Grunwald, *The New New Deal: The Hidden Story of Change in the Obama Era* (New York: Simon & Schuster, 2012).

[52] See Amity Shlaes, *The Forgotten Man: A New History of the Great Depression* (New York: Harper Perennial, 2008), and Kim Phillips-Fein, *Invisible Hand: The Businessmen's Crusade against the New Deal* (New York: Norton, 2009).

[53] It is not always clear why the Republican side of the culture war brings together religious and economic conservatives, because religious conservatives tend to favor stable virtuous practices whereas economic conservatives (sometimes called neoliberals) tend to pursue social disruption in search of profit rather than morality. In fact, however, common

Pat Buchanan, who ran unsuccessfully against George Bush I within the Republican Party in 1992 for its presidential nomination, summed up the new approach to his supporters at that party's nominating convention. We are, he said, in the midst of "a cultural war, as critical to the kind of nation we shall be as was the Cold War itself, for this war is for the soul of America."[54] The shift was clear. The party's aim should be less to achieve economic equality and more to safeguard Republican virtue.[55]

A decade later, by which time the culture war thesis had come to characterize much or most of Republican campaigning, Thomas Frank analyzed how it affected his home state of Kansas. Several generations earlier, wrote Frank, in *What's the Matter with Kansas?* (2004), populist and progressive citizens in that state had voted for local politicians who promised to stand up, in Kansas or in Washington, against economic forces like the great railroads and New York banks, the E. H. Harrimans and J. P. Morgans of American life.[56] Now, they were distracted by Republican talk about cultural issues, and therefore they voted mainly for Republican candidates.

Once elected, though, according to Frank, those politicians did little or nothing to rein in neoliberal practices, which encourage privatization, union busting, and deregulation, via free trade, global outsourcing, downsizing, and financial shenanigans such as the frauds committed by Enron and WorldCom. Meanwhile, in Kansas itself,

---

political ground is found when many people in both sectors are brought together by their conviction that government regulation – of, say, religious schools, abortions, guns, and corporations or digital surveillance – is a danger to what they hold dear. So, they unite against people who endorse regulation. I explained this in David M. Ricci, "Chapter Four: Enemies," in *Why Conservatives Tell Stories & Liberals Don't: Rhetoric, Faith, and Vision on the American Right* (Boulder, CO: Paradigm Publishers, 2011), pp. 81–104.

[54] See his speech at https://voicesofdemocracy.umd.edu/buchanan-culture-war-speech-speech-text/.

[55] Readings from the Right in the culture war were supplied by, among others, William J. Bennett (ed.), *The Book of Virtues: A Treasury of Great Moral Stories* (New York: Torchbooks, 1993), and William J. Bennett (ed.), *The Spirit of America: Words of Advice from the Founders in Stories, Letters, Poems, and Speeches* (New York: Torchbooks, 1997). President Reagan appointed Bennett to be chair of the National Endowment for the Humanities and later Secretary of Education. On his own, as a warrior in the culture war, Bennett published *The Death of Outrage* (1998).

[56] Thomas Frank, *What's the Matter with Kansas? How Conservatives Won the Heart of America* (New York: Metropolitan Books, 2004).

main streets were devastated by the activity of Walmarts and other big-box stores located on cheap land outside of town, and the middle class was hollowed out because, said Frank, no elected officials represented its "fundamental," rather than "cultural," needs.[57]

By shifting attention to cultural issues, a move which Frank regarded as a great "derangement" in American life, Republicans plugged into social rather than economic sentiments, some already existing and some evoked by constant fear-mongering, expressed in condemnation of presumably dangerous Democratic "liberals."[58] The result of persuading a large number of citizens to vote on the basis of cultural considerations was that scholars and activists began to talk about "tribes" of voters, or voters inspired by "identity politics."

3 Education

Education for democracy arose in America's formative years very successfully. Elementary schools, junior high schools, high schools, colleges and universities were established and flourished; libraries large and small were founded and widely available; newspapers kept citizens up to date; postal service spread throughout the country and subsidized the circulation of popular, including "muckraking," magazines; scientific knowledge increased, was written up in professional journals and books, and was passed on to students and the public.

We might conclude, then, that institutions in this realm performed so well, although plagued by occasional controversies, of course, that we need say no more about them here. It is also true, however, that significant strains showed up in education during recent decades, and some of those are worth noting as contributing to our populist era.

---

[57] Ibid., p. 1. Frank is a journalist. For an academic version of much the same thesis, see Jacob S. Hacker and Paul Pierson, *Let Them Eat Tweets: How the Right Rules in an Age of Extreme Inequality* (New York: Liveright, 2020). See also Walter Benn Michaels, *The Trouble with Diversity: How We Learned to Love Identity and Ignore Inequality* (New York: Holt, 2007), which argues that turning identity into a political issue detracts attention from consequences of class and wealth.

[58] Frank opened his argument by pointing out (p. 1) that America's poorest county, in rural Nebraska, gave George Bush II more than 80% of its votes in the 2000 election.

Privatization

First of all, close to 8,000 public schools have been privatized.[59] Americans in favor of moving in that direction have argued that public schools are so inefficient that their students learn little and then go on to lives of poverty. That is, the advocates of privatization in effect say that large income gaps in America, seen in slum neighborhoods across the country, which often house minority group members, are not the result of neoliberal economic hardships but of failing instruction in public schools. In which case, ambitious parents should be able to choose a "charter" school for their children, and those should be paid for by public money, say in the form of government-issued vouchers, because, after all, they are neither elitist nor sectarian.[60]

The number of such schools varies from state to state, depending on the convictions of those who run local and state education boards. But the contest itself is clearly drawn.[61] This was not exactly all Republicans against all Democrats but, generally speaking, the more against the less accomplished, for whatever reason.

The argument is offered elegantly. Public schools may have served old-line American children well in the days of McGuffey Readers, and may have successfully introduced immigrant children

---

[59] See https://nces.ed.gov/fastfacts/display.asp?id=30.
[60] Private schools, such as those run by the Catholic Church, have always been funded by private money. This amounts to double taxation, in the sense that parochial school parents, on behalf of their Catholic faith, tax themselves to pay for their child's school but also pay government taxes to support public schools which the child does not attend. Public school enthusiasts argue that even Catholics should pay for public schools because those schools provide an integrating public service – a "public good," in the language of economists – which all citizens, even Catholics, enjoy when it brings a sense of common ends to the entire community. The advocates of privatization reject that claim by insisting that the schools they support deserve government funding because they serve a public purpose by alleviating community-wide poverty in the long run. Governor Ron DeSantis (R-FL) makes the entire issue go away by saying that "if the taxpayer is paying for education [via vouchers or other support], it's public education." DeSantis is quoted in Cara Fitzpatrick, *The Death of Public School: How Conservatives Won the War over Education in America* (New York: Basic Books, 2023), p. 2.
[61] Taking sides on this issue, President Trump in 2017 appointed Betsy DeVos to be his Secretary of Education. At the time, DeVos had graduated from a private high school, was married to the billionaire CEO of Amway, was seriously religious, was a strong privatization advocate, and had contributed time and money to that cause. In other words, she was plainly on one side of the culture war.

to their new lives in America. But the institution of public education, perhaps because of incompetent teachers who cannot be fired because of union protections, no longer works satisfactorily, say privatizers, because so many of its pupils are failing in and out of school.[62]

Therefore public schools must be supplemented or replaced in many jurisdictions and especially in aging, densely populated urban areas where they sometimes suffer from absenteeism, delinquency, violence, and disrespect.

These propositions are supported by hundreds of millions of dollars in grants from, among other sources, many large philanthropies including, for example, the Bill and Melinda Gates Foundation and the Walton Family Foundation.

Opponents of privatization argue that, when private pupils are tested, they do not always, or even often, perform better than pupils in public schools. That is, some charter schools are impressive and some are not. And anyway, measuring by testing ignores a most important characteristic of public schools, which is the fact that, on behalf of democratic equality, they accept all children in the neighborhood, even those who sometimes misbehave because they are troubled by problems at home. Whereas charter schools can pick and choose who to accept because they do not have public responsibility for the entire population.[63]

This last contention highlights an implicit political issue which we touched on earlier. By letting some parents place their children in what amounts to a private school, surrounded by similar children, those parents are, to some extent, participating in class and identity warfare in the country. That is, to make private schools available for free is to enable some groups more easily to wall off their children from other groups of children in the same society. And doing that, according

---

[62] Sometimes conservatives accuse public schools of "dumbing down" children because the schools are in thrall to educational philosophies of liberals like John Dewey, which, in the charge, produce low scores on the SAT and many cases of ADHD. For example, such charges appear in Samuel Blumenfield and Alex Newman, *Crimes of the Educators: How Utopians Are Using Government Schools to Destroy America's Children* (Nashville: Post Hill Press, 2021), esp. pp. 18–21, and 127–134.

[63] The point of principle here is that public schools should not be regarded as "commodities" but as a "public good" which, when it exists, benefits everyone in the community.

to public school advocates, is a serious breach of democratic commitments to tolerance and equality.[64]

Rising Costs

Raising the costs of higher education is another move backward. Here, we can assume that America's several thousand four-year colleges and two-year junior colleges, once established, have provided and continue to provide the education that a democratic society needs.[65] That is not the problem. The problem is that tuition costs and on-campus living expenses have risen sharply for several decades, in which case a great many young people must take out loans in order to study and graduate. Information on this problem is difficult to interpret, because tuition rates and other expenses may be clearly stated yet students subject to them may be paying different bills depending on scholarships and other forms of student aid.[66]

Nevertheless, the Council on Foreign Relations, which is presumably a reliable source, noted that, as of September 2023, over *43 million Americans owed $1.6 trillion in student loans*, mostly borrowed from the federal government.[67]

Various analysts disagree on why higher education costs went up so sharply. For example, some blame professors' larger salaries,

---

[64] Steven Brill, *Class Warfare: Inside the Fight to Fix America's Schools* (New York: Simon & Schuster, 2011), and Dianne Ravitch, *Slaying Goliath: The Passionate Resistance to Privatization and the Fight to Save America's Public Schools* (New York: Vintage, 2020), esp. pp. 268–283.

[65] www.usnews.com/education/best-colleges/articles/how-many-universities-are-in-the-us-and-why-that-number-is-changing.

[66] When I studied as an undergraduate at Johns Hopkins University (1958–1962), four years of tuition added up to about $2,000, which was a sum roughly equal to the price of a small Chevrolet sedan. My middle-class parents, one of whom was a federal lawyer and the other a "housewife," who were not particularly affluent, and the parents of most of my classmates, so far as I know, simply paid for that. At the rate set in 2024, four years of undergraduate tuition at Johns Hopkins will add up to $258,920. I don't know what percentage of students, if any, will pay for all of that out of family resources.

[67] For the council's analysis, see www.cfr.org/backgrounder/us-student-loan-debt-trends-economic-impact. Among other factoids, the council observes that student debt now exceeds debt from all American auto loans and credit cards. For information on how the loans work and how interest payments can pile up, see https://studentaid.gov/understand-aid/types/loans/interest-rates, where the Department of Education explains, perhaps unintentionally, how unbearable the situation has become.

some blame an increase in the number of administrative jobs, some blame decreased state funding, and some blame competitive executive salaries.[68]

For our purposes, the details are unimportant. What is clear and undemocratic is that rising costs constitute a situation in which some people can afford an education which facilitates good citizenship and others are excluded by the cost factor.

Partisans of present conditions claim that successful and mostly well-educated Americans have established a "meritocracy," where the more prosperous rule the country and deserve high standing because of their individual achievements.[69] This is an educational variant of the neoliberal argument that people at the top get there through hard work and creative accomplishments.

Opponents of meritocracy say that, among other reasons, many people who achieve much do so because of luck, or because they were born into well-to-do families – for example, the Kennedys, the Bushes, and the Trumps – or because they benefit from circumstances created by previous leaders in various fields. From this point of view, the bottom line is that many other Americans, without advantages, are not even in the running to participate in the so-called meritocracy regime and are therefore deprived of an equal place in their own society.[70]

4 Journalism

In effect, journalism served Americans for generations as an adjunct of education. After all, journalists searched out information, which

---

[68] Jacob S. Hacker, *The Great Risk Shift: The New Economic Insecurity and the Decline of the American Dream*, rev. ed. (New York: Oxford University Press, 2006), pp. 73–76, argues that permitting public college funding to fall is an example of the way that politicians, mainly Republicans, have made success in modern life less affordable for citizens who are least able to pay to acquire modern skills.

[69] In this sense, "meritocracy" may be regarded as a new form of "aristocracy."

[70] In favor of meritocracy, see Adrian Wooldridge, *The Aristocracy and Talent: How Meritocracy Made the Modern World* (New York: Penguin, 2021). Against meritocracy, see Stephen J. McNamee and Robert K. Miller, Jr., 3rd ed., *The Meritocracy Myth* (Lanham: Rowman and Littlefield, 2014); and Daniel Markovits, *The Meritocracy Trap: How America's Foundational Myth Feeds Inequality, Dismantles the Middle Class, and Devours the Elite* (New York: Penguin, 2019); and Michael J. Sandel, *The Tyranny of Merit: Can We Find the Common Good?* (New York: Picador, 2020).

became the basis for "news," and thereby passed it on – that is, taught it – to citizens. However, that function began to disappear, though not entirely, when CNN started broadcasting news in 1980, offering exciting moving pictures, and sensational interviews of VIPs, proclaimed by celebrity announcers and hosts, around the clock and every day.

Which meant that, for many important events, newspaper articles were turned into obsolete announcements, which were scarcely marketable by the time they could reach customers. Therefore, advertising fees, gained from promoting various commodities and store sales, which had long sustained newspapers, were increasingly directed to television stations.

Later in this book, I will say more about what happened to modern journalism, which moved increasingly away from serious print articles, and how that affects the public wherewithal for good citizenship today. But for now, one development is particularly worth noting.

Gatekeeping

Little by little, even the most competent of journalists lost their "gatekeeping" function. This function we can define as their acquiring and maintaining, by appearance and character, a sort of authority whereby Americans counted on them to sift and winnow presumed information and present citizens with the truth.

Journalists like Walter Lippmann, Edward R. Murrow, Walter Cronkite, and David Brinkley, enjoyed and exercised this sort of authority. It is not that they continually discovered and revealed new facts. It is that when they said that something was a fact, wherever they got it from, their assertion was accepted as true by many citizens across the board.[71]

It is in that sense that journalism was long an adjunct of education, because just as people assumed that competent teachers told their pupils the truth, the same people also assumed that good journalists did the same.

---

[71] Thus, the case of Walter Cronkite, who reported from Vietnam for CBS in 1968 that the war there could not be won but would have to be negotiated to a resolution. See www.washingtonpost.com/national/did-the-news-media-led-by-walter-cronkite-lose-the-war-in-vietnam/2018/05/25/a5b3e098-495e-11e8-827e-190efaf1f1ee_story.html.

But time went by, and the marketplace for ideas (a) expanded greatly, into radio, television, the internet, and social media, (b) received a flood of stuff from entities such as "think tanks," "research institutes," and "trade associations" intent on promoting what was just as much opinion as knowledge, and (c) publicized every sort of well-financed point of view including conspiracy theories and the equivalent of assurances that 2+2=5, or 6.

The problem there was that even top-notch journalists were no longer as credible as they once were, because what they said or wrote got drowned out in the flood of – let's not mince words – "sludge."[72] Some part of it was probably true, but which part? Who could say for sure? Although many television hosts and anchors, like Sean Hannity, Tucker Carlson, Rachel Maddow, and Stephen Colbert, seemed to have no doubts.

The most respected newspaper in the country inadvertently revealed how unreliable it had become, in some respects, when its editors threw in the towel on truth. For more than a century, the *New York Times* told readers on its front page that its journalists wrote up "All the news that's fit to print." The paper still says that.

But for years now, in the Age of Trump, the same editors have back-pedaled to add, also on its front page, that "*The New York Times* publishes opinion from a wide range of perspectives in the hopes of promoting constructive debate about consequential questions."[73]

In other words, the *NYT* will publish exciting opinion articles about current affairs and important public issues. But when it does that, it now leaves its readers to decide if what each author says is true or not. Therefore, the paper's editors no longer serve as gatekeepers. They no longer provide that service. They are merely promoting

---

[72] I am borrowing the term "sludge" from a book that describes how modern public relations firms receive large fees for making bad commodities and corporations look either good or not as bad as they really are. Some of the items upgraded for public regard have included cigarettes, insecticides, growth hormones for meat animals, genetically altered fruits, infant formula, nuclear power stations, plastic foam containers, and herbicides. There is also the special case of praising treated sewage waste (sludge) as a safe crop fertilizer even when it is not safe. On that case, see John Stauber and Sheldon Rampton, *Toxic Sludge is Good for You: Lies, Damn Lies and the Public Relations Industry* (Monroe, ME: Common Courage Press, 1995), pp. 99–122.

[73] The same fudging appears on television, such as when, instead of promising that it will tell "the truth," CNN says that it will tell "the whole story" and "go behind the headlines."

a "constructive debate." Thus they are no longer, in effect, teachers by vocation, but people running a business that consists of circulating messages.[74]

In short, mass media entities today, digital and otherwise, must first attract attention and only secondarily tell the truth about important matters.[75] It doesn't really help much that inconsequential events may be covered credibly. Therefore, if you want to know what Michelle Obama wore when she addressed the 2024 Democratic National Convention, you can learn all about that in a *New York Times* article entitled "A Speaker suited up for battle: Michelle Obama chose a Monse outfit that was understated, but edgy."[76] And if you are interested in the patriotic significance of Melania Trump's Inauguration hat (a "boater-style toque") by Eric Javits and her dress by Adam Lippes, the *New York Times* also addressed that issue.[77] Such articles may be entirely true, for whatever that is worth.

Worse Than It Looks

In this chapter, I observed that, sometimes by intent and sometimes innocently, conditions for democracy deteriorated considerably in the realms of party politics, inclusion, education, and journalism. Those realms were already somewhat familiar to us, therefore what went wrong in them is not especially hard to notice.

Unfortunately, however, democracy is faltering not only in familiar arenas. In fact, the situation is "even worse than it looks," say veteran Washington think tankers Thomas Mann and Norman Orenstein.[78] That is because new realms of "wherewithal" for

---

[74] Which leads James T. Hamilton, *All the News That's Fit to Sell: How the Market Transforms Information into News* (Princeton: Princeton University Press, 2004), p. 7, to say: "News is a commodity, not a mirror image of reality."

[75] Tim Wu, *The Attention Merchants: The Epic Scramble to Get Inside Our Heads* (New York: Vintage Books, 2016).

[76] That is from a Vanessa Friedman article that appeared in the *NYT International Edition*, August 24–25, 2024. The New York version of this article appeared at www.nytimes.com/2024/08/21/style/michelle-obama-dnc-fashion.html.

[77] See www.nytimes.com/2025/01/20/style/melania-trump-hat-inauguration-outfit.html.

[78] See Thomas Mann and Norman Orenstein, *It's Even Worse Than It Looks: How the American Constitutional System Collided with the New Politics of Extremism* (New York: Basic Books, 2012).

democracy – based on evolving technology and confounding especially our efforts to understand reality – have powerfully influenced the thinking and behavior of citizens since the late twentieth century. Consequently, good citizenship is harder than ever to practice.

Consequently, it is to those new realms of wherewithal that I will turn now.

6 INFORMATION

New pieces of wherewithal for good citizenship eventually showed up in a collection of modern communication practices and modern messaging devices, which I call "the information system."

These things, together, function as a "system" because, like nature's ecology, everything in the system tends to be related to everything else. Thus, for example, marketing is linked to evasive vocabulary, smartphones to multi-tasking, advertising to public relations, television to constant entertainment, bad news to click-bait journalism, silo thinking to short attention spans, marketing to post-truth falsehoods, and expertise to propaganda.

Many thinkers and scholars have investigated, and then commented on, parts of the information system. My aim, therefore, is not to add to what they have discovered about it but to note some aspects of what they know in order to show how relevant the system is to the matter of good citizenship.

Meanwhile, one thing should be clear from the start. All parts of the system are elements of "wherewithal" for good citizenship, in the sense that the information and disinformation we receive, and how we receive it, and how we decide what it is worth, determine how we will behave toward every individual whom we meet and also toward the community's public institutions and procedures, such as government agencies and elections. And therein lies their importance for this essay.

In other words, as social psychologists know, information from our surroundings, and not just instincts we may be born with, becomes the stuff we are made of, as private people and as citizens. Therefore, if the information system does not work well, people will have difficulty knowing who they are and how to function in their community. And that is where we are today, because information is not circulating optimally, many people believe very little of what they see or hear, and their trust in the bearers of so-called information is at an all-time low.

Language

So let us start with the sort of talk that dominates the information system in our time. An early turning point, generating very modern messages, was the growth of advertising in the late nineteenth century. One part of the Enlightenment consisted of an Industrial Revolution, whereby open-minded Science and Technology advanced by leaps and bounds while using, for example, coal, steam, timber, steel, sugar, potatoes, petroleum, and cotton to enormously increase the production of useful things from textile mills to railroads, and from food to clothing to housewares, and more.

The welcome result was that, as the Industrial Revolution progressed, fewer Europeans than before suffered from poverty, to the point where, by 1776, Adam Smith could write about how, via support for what became known as capitalism – the division of labor, the protection of private property, enforcement of contracts, and so on – governments could facilitate economic growth and thereby increase what Smith called "the wealth of nations."[1]

Selling

Innovation and investment continued so that, early in the twentieth century, Henry Ford proclaimed that he would "build a motor car for the great multitude."[2] And he did exactly that when he produced the Model T with his extraordinarily efficient assembly lines in

---

[1] Adam Smith, *The Wealth of Nations* (1776).
[2] Henry Ford and Samuel Crowther, *My Life and Work* (Garden City, NY: Garden City Publishing Co., 1922), p. 73.

factories like River Rouge and Highland Park in and around Detroit and Dearborn, Michigan.[3]

This outburst of industrial efficiency, during which America modernized along with Western Europe, was a boon to democracy, because it provided the economic wherewithal for more citizens than ever to participate in civic life. There was a serious hitch, though, because so many commodities – tables, chairs, jeans, pots, and more – could be produced that it was not clear how they could all be sold, even in large and convenient department stores such as Macy's (1858) in New York City and Marshall Field (1865) in Chicago.

What businesspeople feared was that more and more Americans might buy mainly enough to satisfy their needs, after which they might buy less than that or nothing at all. Which meant that some factories, and the stores that marketed their goods, might be left with unsold output and in danger of bankruptcy.

The solution was to entice consumers into desiring more than just what they might "need," and therefore modern advertising was designed to go beyond needs to stimulate "wants."[4] That is, just like political parties emerged to help make mixed government work in America, modern advertising arose to help sustain economic prosperity by selling what were, in a way, surplus commodities.[5]

Parties and Advertising

However, with regard to democracy, there was a sharp difference between parties and advertising. Parties, on the whole, were good for democracy, providing healthy circumstances for the practice of citizenship, whereas advertising, as it grew, injected into American talk

---

[3] David Ricci, *Good Citizenship in America* (New York: Cambridge University Press, 2004), p. 139. In 1910, before Ford installed the assembly line, a Model T chassis took 12 hours and 28 minutes to produce. In 1914, on the assembly line at Highland Park, the same chassis required only 1 hour and 33 minutes.

[4] I mean here "modern" advertising, because earlier advertisements, which were not widespread, consisted of a few factual sentences, such as "a new brick house, to be let or sold, near Lewes, with a barn, stable, pond, and 20 acres of cleared land."

[5] The link between the Industrial Revolution that spawned capitalism, and the capitalism that spawned a surplus of commodities, used to be a favorite theme of economic historians. See Peter d'A. Jones, *The Consumer Society: A History of American Capitalism* (Baltimore: Penguin Books, 1965).

a large measure of duplicity, dissembling, exaggeration, and manipulation. Thereafter, powerful messages entailing such distortions, and causing enormous damage to everyday integrity – that is, to the simple pursuit of truth – continued and even grew to the point where, today, they are frightfully influential in the information system.

Public Relations

For example, one problematic extension of advertising appeared early in the twentieth century with the growth of public relations. Here was a new kind of work which, in effect, constituted advertising on behalf of businessmen (in those days) and their institutions rather than just their products.

It was entirely logical that public relations would arise because, if means of persuasion would become available, tycoons might want to use them for protection. And they did lean in that direction because some of them believed, like Le Bon wrote in *The Crowd* (1895), that "crowds" (the many) might rise up against corporate leaders (the few). And what was democracy, at least potentially, if not a sort of crowd?

Ivy Lee, a former New York newsman and pioneer in the field of public relations in early twentieth-century America, put the matter caustically: "The people now rule. We have substituted for the divine right of kings, the divine right of the multitude."[6] And the truth was that, spurred on by muckraking progressives like Frank Norris, *The Octopus* (1901), Ida Tarbell, *The History of the Standard Oil Company* (1904), and Upton Sinclair, *The Jungle* (1907), many ordinary Americans came to regard great corporations like US Steel and Armour (meatpacking) as greedy and brutal.

The solution worked out by Lee and his colleagues was to make their corporate clients look better. In Lee's case, which became notorious, this was most famously displayed in his work on behalf of the Rockefellers, following what became known as the Ludlow Massacre. In that bloody event, twenty-one striking miners, wives, and children were killed on April 20, 1914 by National Guardsmen and private

---

[6] Quoted in Start Ewen, *PR! A Social History of Spin* (New York: Basic Books, 1996), p. 75. Ewen, pp. 64–67, *et passim*, also notes the link to Le Bon.

guards on behalf of the Colorado Iron and Fuel Company, which the Rockefeller family in New York controlled.[7]

Probably more plainly than most public relations practitioners – sometimes now called "strategists" – would explain today, Lee testified in Congress and described his work for the Rockefellers as an honest presentation of facts. It became clear, though, from what he said, that his job was to present the *client's* facts rather than *all* the facts. In which case, as he testified, his job was to present "the truth as the [mine] operators saw it."[8]

The extent to which Lee, and his colleagues in other cases, succeeded in telling their sort of truth is not possible to calculate. But even if we cannot know how often what they did worked for their clients, we can be sure that at least two general downsides characterized this new professional enterprise that grew out of advertising.

First, the practice of public relations was not truthful in an Enlightenment sort of way, according to the pursuit of Reason. Instead, it was a calculated selection of information slanted on behalf of an advertising aim which, a cynic might say, was not above making a silk purse out of a sow's ear or sometimes, even more crudely, like putting lipstick on a pig.

Second, public relations was work done on behalf of people who could afford it. Which meant that this sort of advertising was fashioned for the financially successful rather than for rank-and-file Americans. On that score, public relations was somewhat undemocratic, because it was a resource available to citizens who were already more equal than others and wanted things to remain that way.

---

[7] See Scott Martelle, *Blood Passion: The Ludlow Massacre and Class War in the American West* (New Brunswick: Rutgers University Press, 2008).

[8] Quoted in Ewen, *PR!*, pp. 79–80. Lee put the matter plainly. I invite readers to compare his language with a self-description of Sowen Strategy Consulting, which is a 21st century business entity that a century ago would have been described as a public relations firm. This firm's website states that "We are pragmatic idealists. We are confidently challenging the hegemony of traditional consulting to design, deliver, and measure solutions that drive cultural change, operational efficiency, and tangible impact." Moreover, Sowen Strategy Consulting describes itself as "a data strategy consultancy. We are the growth partner for those who do well *and* do good. We design data-driven strategies that accelerate your mission so you can: (1) Optimize operations. (2) Demonstrate impact. (3) Unlock capital." Furthermore, "Humility, expertise, and a relentless focus on impactful results comes together through a diverse team of global leaders that bridge empathy and thoughtfulness with a no BS approach."

Propaganda

In the wake of public relations work, disseminating messages on behalf of what came to be called "propaganda" became a severe problem for democratic citizenship. This became increasingly obvious because, as public relations thrived on praising business corporations, propaganda was used by the national government to promote America's participation against Germany and Austria in World War I.

America entered the war in 1917, after President Woodrow Wilson was elected in 1916 to a second term based on the campaign slogan "He Kept Us Out of War." That eventually embarrassing claim had to be marginalized by getting the public to believe that not Wilson but the Germans – the barbaric Huns – were to blame for the president going to war.

However, there were a great many immigrants in America – Irish who didn't like the British, Germans who didn't hate Germany, and Jews and Italians who were struggling to make a living in big city ghettoes – whom leading American politicians and businessmen regarded as unreliable. The fear there was that those people might not be enthusiastic about sacrificing themselves in a far-away war helping people they loathed, or against people they respected, and which seemed, especially to socialists like Emma Goldman and Eugene Debs, to be a terrible conflict that was lopsidedly profitable for American banks and arms manufacturers, or the owners of assembly lines and sweatshops.[9]

Therefore, after America entered the war on April 6, President Wilson on April 17 issued an Executive Order which created the Committee on Public Information (CPI), which was known also as the

---

[9] The staggering human costs of World War I are almost impossible to grasp today. On July 1, 1916, the first day of the Western Front battle of the Somme (the Allies against the Central Powers), which lasted (intermittently) for 141 days, British forces alone suffered over 57,000 casualties, of which 19,240 were killed. See www.iwm.org.uk/history/what-was-the-battle-of-the-somme. Historical knowledge and accurate presentation are not Donald Trump's strong points. Therefore, on May 15, 2025, speaking in Qatar, he declared that the Hamas incursion into southern Israel on October 7, 2023, was "one of the worst days in the history of the world, not only in this region." See that at www.presidency.ucsb.edu/documents/remarks-troops-al-udeid-air-base-doha-qatar. Reports vary about what happened on October 7–8, 2023. Apparently, about 800 Israeli and foreign civilians were killed along with 400 or so security forces.

Creel Committee after its director, George Creel, who was a progressive journalist.

The committee, which was designed along lines suggested by advisors like Walter Lippmann, was an enormous entity, employing up to 150,000 people, publishing pamphlets and a newspaper, suggesting talking points to private newspapers all over the country (including hundreds of foreign language newspapers read by immigrants), paying for thousands of highway billboards stimulating patriotism, hiring tens of thousands of what we would today call "opinion influencers" who, in their communities, would extol the troops and disparage the enemy, financing pro-war movies in Hollywood, and more.

That was the direct side of Washington's propaganda. The indirect side aimed at suppressing dissenting voices. To that end, Congress enacted the Espionage Act of 1917 and the Sedition Act of 1918, which together criminalized most criticism of the government's war policy.

The Supreme Court famously joined this assault on the First Amendment (which protects freedom of speech) in *Schenk v. United States* (1919), when Justice Oliver Wendell Holmes ruled that socialist Charles Schenk had violated the Espionage Act by urging young American men to peacefully oppose the draft. As Holmes said, freedom of speech means you can say anything that does not constitute "a clear and present danger" to other people. Except that, in wartime, to speak against what the government is doing is to promote such a danger.[10]

Most important for us, because it was an enormous move away from maintaining healthy conditions for good citizenship, the committee was not particularly interested in making a rational case in favor of the war. That is, it didn't help the public to actually think sensibly about what was going on in the trenches and shipping lanes.

Creel called his committee "the House of Truth," and doing so reflected his earlier career as a progressive muckraker who had cited facts to arouse public opinion against injustices perpetrated by various "robber barons." But the committee wasn't really interested in truth. Instead, while advertising lore increasingly showed the way, the committee talked very little about facts but preferred to approach citizens on psychological grounds, by stimulating emotions such as fear and

---

[10] See https://supreme.justia.com/cases/federal/us/249/47/.

hostility, and by showing Americans exciting pictures rather than reciting dull statistics.

After the war, in his debate with John Dewey over the nature of democracy, Lippmann, who had worked for the CPI, observed that most people think in terms of "stereotypes." He knew that very well because the committee conducted much of its work by borrowing or creating such illusions.[11]

Then Edward Bernays, who also had worked for the CPI, pointed out in his *Propaganda* (1928) that propaganda amounts to "the engineering of consent."[12] And the Committee was not finicky about observing Enlightenment standards of truth and Reason while it did that. In its view, the end justified the means.

Habits of the Heart

We have noted advertising for commodities, conducting public relations for business corporations, and disseminating propaganda for governments. All three of these were activities designed to persuade, which became inescapable information sources in modern America, and remain so today. Indeed, they are so commonplace that we don't usually notice how effectively they muddle our thinking.

But a best-selling textbook eventually appeared which offered a wide-ranging analysis of American talk that showed how problematic the language of persuasion had become. That book was Robert Bellah and his colleagues' *Habits of the Heart* (1985), which described everyday talk about life in America as revealing traces of three different language traditions, which were biblical, republican, and individualistic.[13]

---

[11] Some of what the committee did, via stereotypes it fashioned, is described in Harold D. Lasswell, *Propaganda Technique in the World War* (orig., 1938; Mansfield Centre, CT: Martino Publishing, 2013), esp. "Satanism," pp. 77–101.

[12] Bernays argued, much like Lippmann, that the public is so irrational and incompetent that it must be led by various experts who, via their use of propaganda techniques, will engineer the public's consent to sensible government action. See Edward Bernays, *Propaganda* (orig., 1928; New York: Ig Publishing, 2005), see esp. "Organizing Chaos," pp. 37–45.

[13] Robert Bellah, Richard Madsen, William M. Sullivan, Ann Swidler, and Steven M. Tipton, *Habits of the Heart: Individualism and Commitment in American Life* (orig., 1985; New York: Harper & Row, 1986).

That is, citizens may not all be familiar with the country's great public statements of its principles, like John Winthrop's sermon entitled "A Modell of Christian Charity" (1630), Jefferson's *Declaration of Independence* (1776), the Founders' *Constitution of the United States* (1787), Abraham Lincoln's "Gettysburg Address" (1864), Franklin Roosevelt's "Four Freedoms Speech" (1941), and Martin Luther King's "Letter from Birmingham Jail" (1963).[14] But Americans of all ranks, now and in the past, have traditionally recognized three kinds of admirable aspirations, which inspire them to promote principles of biblical wisdom, republican virtue, and respect for individualism.[15]

The main dilemma in this tri-partite culture, said Bellah and his colleagues, is that, in their commendable insistence on freedom for all individuals – which did not inform De Tocqueville's "Old Regime" before the radical Enlightenment moved to democracy – Americans pursued not one but two kinds of "individualism."

Individualism

One form was "utilitarian" individualism, typically expressed by Benjamin Franklin when, in his eighteenth-century *Autobiography*, he described how he was born poor but through hard work achieved a comfortable station in life.[16] The problem, for *Habits*, was that a *successful* life in that sense did not always equal a *good* life. Consequently, during the nineteenth century, there appeared an "expressive individualism," as praised in Walt Whitman's *Leaves of Grass*, which focused less on economic achievements and more on creating happy

---

[14] Some of these and other sources are conveniently collected by Robert Bellah, Richard Madsen, William M. Sullivan, Ann Swidler, and Steven M. Tipton in *Individualism and Commitment in American Life: Readings on the Themes of Habits of the Heart* (New York: Harper & Row, 1987).

[15] This analytical point stems from the fact that in *Habits*, Bellah et al. used a vocabulary derived from Alexis de Tocqueville, *Democracy in America*. The Frenchman extended Edmund Burke's insight, in *Reflections on the Revolution in France* (1790), Part 1, Book 6, that our "prejudices" can turn into virtuous "habits" which help to sustain our society over time.

[16] Bellah et al., *Habits* also notes the influence of Franklin's practical aphorisms in *Poor Richard's Almanac*, such as: "God helps those who help themselves." And: "Lost time is never found again."

and healthy individuals. Or, as Whitman said, "I loaf and invite my soul."[17]

But the problem there, said Bellah and his colleagues, is that people who they interviewed for *Habits*, and who wanted to be good people as Whitman recommended, were often not sure of how to do that. Getting ahead was their constant goal, whereas biblical and republican values, while still present, were often overshadowed by the imperatives of success. And that observation makes room for what we have been describing, because one reason why modern Americans may get lost on the way to a good life is that a fourth language, not highlighted in *Habits* but present there between the lines, has upended everyday thinking.[18]

The Fourth Language

The fourth language is a language of persuasion. It is a matter of form rather than substance. It is a matter of how to talk about anything and everything. It became a necessary adjunct of surplus productivity during the Industrial Revolution. It was fashioned, as we saw, in advertising and then extended into public relations and propaganda.

Habits did not discuss the fourth language. Perhaps that was because talking that way is not a matter of ingredient or content but of rhetoric and style. That is, the language of persuasion is not a vehicle embodying longstanding convictions such as republicanism but a practical use of words to inflate consideration for anything, from the trivial to the apocalyptic, from avoiding dandruff to justifying what happened to Hiroshima and Nagasaki. And, as we will see, via the inexorable advance of "information technology," it has infected every sort of modern communications – from newspapers to radios, television, computers, and smartphones.[19]

---

[17] Quoted in ibid., p. 34.
[18] *Habits* does not make the same argument that I am making here. But it discusses what it calls "Transforming American Culture," by which, basically, it means degrading America's tri-partite commitment to traditional values. See ibid., pp. 275–307.
[19] Closer to our own times, practices like advertising, public relations, and propaganda are summed up in the term "spin." Accordingly, Brooks Jackson and Kathleen Hall Jamison, *unSpun: Finding Facts in a World of Disinformation* (New York: Random House, 2007), p. vii, points out that spin "is a polite word for disinformation." Humorously

Most annoyingly, the language of persuasion violates the radical Enlightenment's spirit, which is a commitment to what Thomas Paine called "common sense," and which embodies a moral obligation to find reasonable grounds for living together. The fourth language does this by elevating successful selling – of commodities or corporations or politicians – to the status of a legitimate and respectable activity.[20] Whereas, when compared with the great Enlightenment ideal of Reason, the work of selling (which we sometimes spruce up today by calling it "marketing") often ignores the truth and promotes dissembling.[21]

Monopolistic Competition

So marketing has a very large downside. But many American thinkers have treated it uncritically. That was especially true of mainstream economists, who understood that to constantly change fashions over time, in the shape of cars, furniture, clothing, kitchen utensils, and other commodities, was profitable but distinctly wasteful when serviceable items were thrown out to make way for newer and more fashionable ones.

Such economists therefore invented the theory of "monopolistic competition," which recognized that very large corporations were not competing on the basis of price and affordability but via marketing the results of so-called "product differentiation." Where such differentiation reigned, backed up by advertisements, buying a red Chevrolet

---

but unflinchingly, disinformation is described in *unSpun* as appearing in "tricks" such as "misnomers," "weasel words," "eye candy," "the average bear," "the literally true falsehood," and "the implied falsehood." Promoting disinformation – commercially, socially, and politically – means lying or, like Ivy Lee, not telling *all* of the truth. We will return to such aspects of public talk in Chapter Six, "Information."

[20] Practitioners often rename their activity to make it seem more innocuous than blatant "advertising." Thus today, "reputation management" is fashionable, and image-building professionals insert it into media stories that flatter their clients and disparage their competitors or enemies.

[21] This point is stated briefly by Jules Henry, "Advertising as a Philosophical System," in *Culture Against Man* (New York: Vintage, 1963), pp. 45–99 and esp. p. 50: "Truth is what sells. Truth is what you want people to believe. Truth is that which is not legally false." Additional classic studies on this point include Ivan L. Preston, *The Great American Blow-Up: Puffery in Advertising and Selling* (Madison: University of Wisconsin Press, 1975); and Cynthia Crossen, *Tainted Truth: The Manipulation of Fact in America* (New York: Touchstone, 1996).

sedan might make some customers happier than buying a black Ford sedan even while both provided the same adequate transportation.[22]

The key to this theory was to ignore production costs, which were objective, and highlight happiness, which economists renamed "utility."[23] Happiness was subjective, but it was also, in many cases, a scientifically engineered response to exciting advertising images of the commodity being sold and whoever purchased it.[24]

Now take a step back. To recommend the pleasures of utility was to endorse the practice of ceaselessly aspiring to obtain *more* rather than *enough*, whereby large corporations worked on small consumers emotionally and thereby violated the precepts of what economists

---

[22] Edward Hastings Chamberlain, *The Theory of Monopolistic Competition* (Cambridge, MA: Harvard University Press, 1933). On early Chevrolets versus early Fords, see Ricci, *Good Citizenship in America*, pp. 145–146.

[23] By focusing on "utility" rather than production costs, mainstream economists often manage to give advice while ignoring the likely effects of what they recommend. (On mainstream economists, see David Ricci, *A Political Science Manifesto for the Age of Populism* (New York: Cambridge University Press, 2020), pp. 29–44.) For example, common sense says that there are too many people living in the world today, using up too many natural resources and therefore causing enormous and maybe irreversible ecological damage. Using up resources and destroying the environment in order to get to them, are production costs. In which case, you don't have to be an Einstein at math to welcome steps to reduce the human footprint on Earth's environment. Indeed, we should all welcome any reduction (especially if it is peaceful and/or voluntary) in the number of people, say, when this or that country starts having fewer children than in the past. Instead, mainstream economists say the sky will fall if we don't somehow bring more people (or babies) into countries where that is happening, so that young workers will be available to support retirees. Or, they say, we could make industry more efficient so it can continue to produce the current output with the same number of workers but more automation or AI. What the same economists don't say is that, via sensible political action (that is, common sense), we could change the tax structure in Japan, Italy, or the United States so that taxes would enlist more public money to support old people and therefore help us avoid importing immigrants and continuing to use up the same disastrous quantities of resources that we use today. For an example of regretting population decline, see Daron Acemoglu, "America is Sleepwalking into an Economic Storm," *New York Times* (October 17, 2024). In 2024, Acemoglu, Simon Johnson, and James A. Robinson shared the so-called Nobel Prize in Economics. See that in www.nytimes.com/2024/10/17/opinion/economy-us-aging-workforce-ai.html. The shortfall of babies may appear in anxious popular writing as "the demographic winter." The Trump 2.0 Administration, which does not promote redistribution, is considering boosting American population by paying bonuses to women who give birth. See www.nytimes.com/2025/04/21/us/politics/trump-birthrate-proposals.html.

[24] As for who purchased the commodity, and how he or she might do so from fear or anxiety, see Neil Postman, *Amusing Ourselves to Death: Public Discourse in the Age of Show Business* (New York: Penguin, 1985), p. 128, which points out that "What the advertiser needs to know is not what is right about the product but what is wrong about the buyer." For example, the buyer's fear of "halitosis."

called "consumer sovereignty." Here was another example of ignoring the anti-democratic impact of persuasive language which was, more or less, available to the highest bidder and therefore a resource owned, unequally, by Orwell's pigs.

Nevertheless, because this downside was noticed even by some economists, they provided a justification for it in what Joseph Schumpeter called "another theory of democracy."[25] And which some later scholars called "an economic theory of democracy."[26]

In Schumpeter's view, democracy does not depend on its actors being more or less equal in size and resources, as Westerners have thought since the Greeks. It is, instead, mainly a matter of competition between large actors, backed up by political parties, who seek election and therefore the authority to rule.

In other words, if society's elites compete for your vote, you may be economically slight next to them, but those well-off and powerful people must serve you in order to get your vote. Therefore, in this view, the consumer is reassuringly sovereign, and is in command even when confronting capitalist giants like General Motors, Standard Oil, the Pennsylvania Railroad, and International Harvester.[27]

Schumpeter's theory captivated many economists and political scientists.[28] But it continued to ignore what the fourth language really did in modern societies, which was to help people at the top

---

[25] Joseph Schumpeter, *Capitalism, Socialism, and Democracy*, 3rd ed. (orig., 1942; New York: Torchbooks, 1950), pp. 269–283, esp. p. 269: "the democratic method is that institutional arrangement for arriving at political decisions in which individuals acquire the power to decide by means of a competitive struggle for the people's vote."

[26] See n. 28.

[27] The notion of consumer sovereignty assumes that consumers have a set of desires which drive them to buy from, and thus control, producers who serve those desires. In reality, however, desires do not always arise on their own within us but are sometimes, or often, planted there by force of persuasion, via an advertising process that can be called "preference formation." So that is where large actors can manipulate, more or less successfully, smaller actors. Robert W. McChesney, *Rich Media, Poor Media: Communication Politics in Dubious Times* (orig., 2000; New York: New Press, 2015), *passim*, explains the many ways in which the commercial media system promotes not what all audiences want but what dominant media entities want to sell them in order to maximize profits by, for example, offering a great many cheap and exciting productions infused with sex and violence.

[28] See Anthony Downs, *An Economic Theory of Democracy* (New York: Harper & Row, 1957) and James M. Buchanan and Gordon Tullock, *The Calculus of Consent: Logical Foundations of Constitutional Democracy* (Ann Arbor: University of Michigan Press, 1962).

to shape the thinking of people at the bottom. The manipulation didn't always work, just like advertisements don't always work. But even partial success is presumably more profitable than leaving results to chance.

In which case, Weber's modern politicians, who became the actual candidates, were backed up by an expensive apparatus of persuasion which made them, rather than voters, the real sovereign in America.[29] It was a point made famously, in an economic context, by John Kenneth Galbraith when he observed that, after buying the latest and most fashionable commodities, consumers were still left not within a world which *they* shaped but which *business entities* created for them in order to profit from it endlessly.[30]

The Culture War

An analogous situation obtains in the culture war that rages in America today. Yes, there are real cultural differences between many groups in the country, for example between those who are for or against prayers in public schools, and those who endorse or condemn abortion, and those who appreciate or despise immigration. And members of those groups feel that those differences deserve to be expressed somehow in public life.

But, as we saw, the Republican Party is amplifying cultural differences to fever pitch, to the point where, in many states, such

---

[29] The Open Secrets research group predicts that total spending, including PAC sponsored "outside spending," on the 2024 "federal election cycle" will reach $15.9 billion. See www.opensecrets.org/news/2024/10/total-2024-election-spending-projected-to-exceed-previous-record/.

[30] John Kenneth Galbraith, *The Affluent Society* (orig., 1963; New York: Mentor, 1967), pp. 198–211, described this situation as lacking in "social balance," where the provision of private goods flourished and the supply of public goods languished. As he put it: "The children, though without schools, subject in the playgrounds to the affectionate interest of adults with odd tastes, and disposed to increasingly imaginative forms of delinquency, were admirably equipped with television sets ... The family which takes its mauve and cerise, air-conditioned, power-steered, and power-braked automobile out for a tour passes through cities that are badly paved, made hideous by litter, blighted buildings, billboards, and posts for wires that should long since have been put underground ... They picnic on exquisitely packed food from a portable icebox by a polluted stream and go on to spend the night at a public park which is a menace to public health and morals. Just before dozing off on an air mattress, beneath a nylon tent, amid the stench of decaying refuse, they may reflect vaguely on the curious unevenness of their blessings" (pp. 199–200).

differences outweigh all others. And the politicians who are doing that, like the distinctively corrupt Donald Trump, may care nothing about the virtues they are praising but excel at promoting an electoral war which they believe in little but profit from greatly.

Which means, to an extent which is difficult if not impossible to measure, that here, too, some people from on high are, for personal gain, muddling the thinking of people below them. In the circumstances, as Thomas Frank said about Kansas, some important parts of social and economic life are not being attended to adequately.

The bottom line here is that powerful means of persuasion are used for diverting attention away from what threatens those above; that is, the parties who most encourage us to neglect this imbalance are, in fact, staffed by people who, more than others, deploy elements of the fourth language present in American discourse. That language operates relentlessly in the "information system," especially via the technology of communications to which we now turn.

Technology

Marshall McLuhan set the stage for any serious discussion of modern human communications with his short and powerful aphorism: "The medium is the message."[31] He used the term "medium" here to refer to technologies – like the alphabet, movable type, the steam engine, and the telegraph – which extend human power over our natural or social environment and thus permit us to reorganize how we live together.

McLuhan's insight was that, regardless of how we intend to use new technologies, they will use us beyond what we can imagine we invented them for to begin with. For example, the telegraph could transmit messages faster than steamships or railroads. Wonderful. Really. But one result, unforeseen, was that generals like Ulysses S. Grant and Robert E. Lee could use the telegraph to prepare their armies for battles and conduct a war more massive and ferocious than anyone was expecting.

---

[31] Marshall McLuhan, *Understanding Media: The Extensions of Man* (orig., 1964; London: Abacus, 1973), p. 15.

Or, the men who invented automobiles, such as Henry Ford, thought of them as replacing horses. But it turned out that using cars did much more than that. For example, they completely reshaped cities and towns, ruined much of the natural landscape, speeded up climate change by burning gasoline, and made most chaperones obsolete by providing young and unmarried people with, in effect, movable bedrooms.

Television

McLuhan wrote *Understanding Media* in 1964, while televisions were becoming cheaper and spreading into almost every American household. Their behavior then became the paradigm for later technologies, and especially for some which McLuhan did not live to see, including personal computers, the internet, smartphones, and social media.

Which means that the modern information system, promoting to us messages that are true or false, that are frightening or comforting, that are benign or destructive, looks like it does now because of how television and its imitators transmit information. In a way, then, writing in 1964, McLuhan was saying that, in our relations with other people, we are all living in a world that television made.

Neil Postman highlighted that analytical point in 1985 while offering a far-reaching guide to what television has done to modern society. "Amusing ourselves to death" is the name of television's game, said Postman, along the lines of McLuhan's notion that the medium is the message.[32] That is, in Postman's term, every medium has an "agenda" which will take it further than what we might intend for it to do.

In the case of televisions, said Postman, if we want them to improve our cultural life by broadcasting Shakespearean dramas, they will do some of that. But mostly, and implacably, in the pursuit of profit, they will force us to program the screen with various kinds of (1) entertainment, rather than (2) edification. Thus, if the programs on one television station are not entertaining, viewers looking for an

---

[32] Neil Postman, *Amusing Ourselves to Death: Public Discourse in the Age of Show Business* (New York: Penguin, 1985).

interesting experience will switch to another channel and the first station will go bankrupt.[33]

So what? People who are looking for edification can still turn to newspapers, magazines, and books for serious culture, and then ignore what commercial television offers, right? That is, enthusiastically literate people can simply choose to stay in the Age of Print, which since the Enlightenment has expressed, via careful and effective writing, the achievements of Science and Reason, fiction and non-fiction, right?[34]

Entertainment

Wrong or, at least, highly unlikely, because of the following characteristics, among others, of the information system.[35]

The first characteristic is when Postman says we are amusing ourselves to death, he does not mean that television is full of Bridget Jones movies or *The Simpsons* sitcoms. He means that television promotes entertainment in a "peek-a-boo" manner. He means that television is where "now this event, now that, pops into view for a moment, then vanishes. It is a world without much coherence or sense."[36]

It is a world where small-screen journalists report for one minute on an earthquake and in the next minute tell viewers about the First Lady's dinnerware. Or where the anchor shows us heart-rending casualties of Hurricane Matilda and then, with the ubiquitous

---

[33] Ibid., p. 86–87.
[34] We should put Postman into historical perspective on this point. When he wrote up his notion of each medium having an "agenda," the more conventional view of media scholars was that if journalists and citizens would try harder, it might be possible to produce and sell more quality journalism for newspapers and television because citizens would demand and buy more of it. See, for example, Robert M. Entman, *Democracy without Citizens: Media and the Decay of American Politics* (New York: Oxford University Press, 1989), *passim*, but esp. pp. 129–140. In opposition, Postman claimed, for reasons I describe in the earlier text, that television simply won't give us much Shakespeare. In effect, Entman said: try harder. Whereas Postman said: that mostly won't work.
[35] For a non-scholarly but factual view of what television actually offers us, backed up by many examples from commercial and political life, see Chris Hedges, *Empire of Illusion: The End of Literacy and the Triumph of Spectacle* (New York: Nation Books, 2009). Hedges quotes Postman about entertainment on p. 65, to the effect that America is ruled by a culture in which "all public discourse increasingly takes the form of entertainment." Hedges' book resembles Postman's *Amusing Ourselves to Death* by following movement from an age of words (print) to an age of images (pictures).
[36] Ibid., p. 77.

announcement of "now... this," switches to showing us pictures of the Northern Lights taken in Chicago and Philadelphia. Postman regarded this sort of discontinuity as a form of "vaudeville" on screen.

But that is not all. Postman's insights are especially true for capitalist societies, where neoliberalism reigns.[37] Therefore we should add to his dirge a realistic understanding to the effect that television in such societies, including America, is not going to change for as long as entertainment is demanded of it by the environment, or social ecology, of what Tim Wu called "the attention society."[38]

Second, in that society, "the business model" for television is that sellers must get the attention of buyers, who will not buy unless they know what is on sale. So sellers are willing to pay to advertise their wares wherever there is an audience of the right sort of buyers, and such buyers are available in television audiences. Therefore, in effect, because sellers will pay to place advertisements in front of potential buyers, television stations will make every effort to collect those audiences with entertaining programming in order to have them on hand to sell them to advertisers.

And, of course, the business of selling "audiences," which is what television "users" are, to advertisers is also exactly what digital giants like Google and Facebook do, whereby instantly peddling enormous amounts of data about their users has turned such corporations into entities vastly more wealthy and powerful than "legacy" corporations like General Motors, US Steel, and Dow Chemical, which merely make things.

Third, in this endless loop, said Postman, we must always remember that television is tele*vision*. That is, it is about *seeing* things. Indeed, it insists on seeing things, and that insistence produces two results.

The first result is that pictures are not words but images which communicate something to us directly, as in the saying that "a picture is worth a thousand words." The saying is misleading, though, because

---

[37] Postman notes that, in some areas of the world, powerful governments may use a single broadcaster in order to promote the political regime, in which case the medium doesn't have to amuse in order to attract an audience and advertisers who can go nowhere else.
[38] Tim Wu, *The Attention Merchants: The Epic Scramble to Get Inside Our Heads* (New York: Vintage Books, 2016).

words, which belong to the Age of Print, express propositions based on facts – therefore an entity labeled "lion" is not the same as an entity labeled "horse" – whereas images are not factual in that way but can be interpreted differently depending on who sees them.[39]

Therefore one consequence of the constant presence of pictures on screen is that viewers are being taken here and there, depending on their own emotions, rather than to any particular goal or conclusion set by the pictures. That is, to return to Plato, television leaves us inside the shadowy cave of "opinions" rather than taking us outside, to the sunlit land of "knowledge."

The second result is that because television communicates with us especially via pictures rather than print, television programs are not interested in promoting much serious talk – thus their indifference to "talking heads" – because talk is too likely to sound like something stodgy written in the Age of Print as opposed to exciting images of sports, war, famine, storms, funerals, weddings, the perfect soufflé, and more.[40] And here is a reason for the shortage of (adequately literate) gatekeepers.

The fourth characteristic is that from commercial television's basic operation, additional imperatives follow. There is, for example, the need to measure the audience, because advertisers will pay more if it is large.[41] So Nielson boxes were installed, starting in 1950, and

---

[39] Thus, the philosophical discussions of how, and why, in the Bible's Ten Commandments, we are enjoined not to make graven images, not to set them up because, if we do, then by looking at them we will misunderstand God's role in the natural world and our lives. Television ignores that point, even going so far as to occasionally interrupt the news with fifteen or twenty seconds of images without written or spoken comment, as if just the pictures convey a significant message even though they don't. Viewers don't really know, for example, what happened, and why, to the "falling soldier" whom Robert Capa famously photographed in the Spanish Civil War. See Capa's famous photo at www.metmuseum.org/art/collection/search/283315.

[40] Postman did not foresee the rise of interviews conducted by network stars like Christiane Amanpour or Sean Hannity. On the other hand, such interviews usually don't call upon us to actually do anything about what the interviewee – such as the Ukrainian prime minister, or Rafael Nadal – said, so often their talking also constitutes a form of what Postman would call entertainment, or what Susan Jacoby referred to as "ersatz conversations." See Susan Jacoby, *The Age of American Unreason* (New York: Vintage, 2008), p. 271.

[41] I say "large" but that is not precisely so. Advertisers want not large audiences of just anyone but large audiences of people who can afford to buy. Therefore, they want television shows that will attract such people rather than the poor, the elderly, and the already over-spent.

ratings were invented, to see how many people were watching and who they were.

After that, on the internet, which includes podcasts, blogs, and webinars, ratings could be established even more reliably, by counting computer "mouse" clicks. Therefore, "click-bait journalism" was born, where the work of many journalists is valued today not for its intrinsic excellence but by its entertainment qualities, that is, by its ability to attract more or fewer clicks as evidence of viewing. Accordingly, we are bombarded with headlines like: "Want to Network in Silicon Valley? Bring a bathing suit" ("The Drudge Report"); or, "You Won't Believe the Transformation after This Extreme Makeover!" (*Slate Magazine*).[42]

Fifth, furthermore, televisions, via their entertainment agendas, encourage "silo thinking," or "echo chambers," or "gated communities," or "filter bubbles," whereby audiences get segregated so that people of similar minds are likely to see mostly, or only, messages that agree with their outlook. That happens when "news feeds," driven by algorithms, are created by companies like Facebook, X, and Instagram.

The philosophy there is aimed at filtering information to maintain segregated but tranquil audiences, relatively calm and mostly satisfied, audiences whose members will not be exposed to jarring opinions about the world, audiences who will be emotionally ready to react favorably to advertisements.[43]

Sixth, there is the "bad news" factor. In one sense, tranquility is important. But entertainment is also a matter of getting people's attention, in which case the most entertaining subjects for reporting are those that convey bad news rather than good. One can rejoice at the rescue of a beached dolphin, but one is transfixed by a raging forest fire in California. One can admire a beautiful vineyard in Toscana, but

---

[42] Note also, for example, the *Slate* article entitled "Study Finds Eating Cheese May Reduce Your Risk for This Potentially Serious Health Condition" at www.huffpost.com/entry/cheese-health-condition-reduce-risk-study_l_67780b0ae4b059a6ef87e22e. After "may" and "potentially" remove any predictive value from the title, the article's first sentence introduces the pure entertainment factor with: "This could be 'grate' news for cheese lovers." The article does not say who paid for the "study."

[43] On this point, see Eli Pariser, *The Filter Bubble: How the New Personalized Web is Changing What We Read and How We Think* (New York: Penguin, 2011). See also James G. Webster, *The Marketplace of Attention: How Audiences Take Shape in the Digital Age* (Cambridge, MA: MIT Press, 2014)

one cannot disengage from heart-wrenching scenes of war damage in Kiev or Gaza.

That audiences themselves, under a constant barrage of bad news, may become fearful and reluctant to engage in public activities, is not something that seems to bother most broadcasters. And since it is legal (and profitable) to emphasize the negative, they continue to do so. To the point where, today, newscasts are major sources of foreboding, catalogs of wars after tsunamis, forest fires after violent elections, epidemics after trashing great universities, and school shootings after rising fascists.[44]

Seventh, we should also note the "news cycle." As Postman said, the news is like show business and, because that is so, stations and networks cannot hold the attention of audiences if they broadcast the same show for too long. Even *Cats*, *Phantom of the Opera*, *My Fair Lady*, and *Mamma Mia* eventually closed on Broadway, and *Hamilton* will, too.

One consequence of fading interest, though, is that newscasts tend to stick with one set of events for a few days and then switch to highlighting another set after that.[45] There are some events that get reported for longer stretches of time, for example, the 2024 American presidential election. But most events get caught up in the short-term news cycle, being constantly replaced by the next exciting "story" even when, as matters of real importance, like climate change and environmental destruction, they deserve, in some moral sense, to dominate broadcasts continually and remain there until citizens will demand that their politicians take steps, via government restraining action, to stop the irreparable damage those events are causing.

But that doesn't happen, because the "message" of the "medium" is a "business model" that demands "entertainment" in "the attention society." And there are no longer enough "gatekeepers," as we

---

[44] Psychologists John Tierney and Roy F. Baumeister, *The Power of Bad: How the Negativity Effect Rules Us and How We Can Rule It* (New York: Penguin, 2019), *passim*, explain how our brains "are wired to focus on the bad," whereupon the media's emphasis on bad events gets our attention, which they want to obtain, but which also makes us feel helpless and fearful.

[45] The point here is that "news" is not, objectively speaking, a collection of especially important events in the world but what stations and networks decide, for business reasons, to report on. And if those reporters are in the entertainment business, they will work according to a news cycle.

have seen, who might keep our attention focused – or our noses to the grindstone – on essentials rather than trivial, such as phasing out plastic shopping bags rather watching skateboarding at the Olympic Games.[46]

Eighth, an overarching factor in the information system is what Hollywood producers call "casting." Scholars may say that Abraham Lincoln was not handsome enough to get elected president today but, of course, in 1860, almost no voters actually saw him. Similarly, everyone knows that today you should cast Michael Douglas rather than Woody Allen in the movie role of American president. As for the role of newscaster, Postman pointed out that you would not, as a matter of casting, put on the screen women of advanced age, people who are "overweight or whose noses are too long or whose eyes are too close together. You will try, in other words, to assemble a cast of talking hair-dos."[47]

Ninth, a final factor in what we see, and eventually think we know, is ownership of media entities. In this essay, I am referring to "gatekeepers" as people who, in one way or another – like Walter

---

[46] Many scholars and journalists have wondered why we no longer have as many gatekeepers as we used to. Without getting deeply into the debate they have conducted, it is worth observing here that another way of raising that subject is to note the "decline of trust in experts." For example, see Tom Nichols, *The Death of Expertise: The Campaign against Established Knowledge and Why It Matters* (New York: Oxford University Press, 2017). Here, the ideas of pro-capitalist economists figure importantly, because their model of a "free" marketplace (advocated by, for example, Ludwig von Mises, Friedrich Hayek, Milton Friedman, Robert Lucas, Eugene Fama, Georg Mankiw) assumes that markets will allocate resources optimally, in which case we can derogate the advice of anyone – credentialed or not – who tries to promote information about how markets may actually make some terrible decisions. On the decline of trust in such pro-market economists (experts) and the result, see William Davies, *Nervous States: Democracy and the Decline of Reason* (New York: Norton, 2019), pp. 153–175. Furthermore, scandalous evidence has surfaced about some capitalist entities – such as oil and tobacco companies – which fund scientists (experts) who conduct research and discover that the same companies and their products (cigarettes that cause cancer and fossil fuels that drive global warming) are good for consumers. See Erik M. Conway, *Merchants of Doubt: How a Handful of Scientists Obscured the Truth on Issues from Tobacco Smoke to Climate Change* (London: Bloomsbury, 2011). See also Crossen, *Tainted Truth*, pp. 130–131, on how rising public concern, around 1990, about environmental damage caused by disposable diapers (using non-biodegradable plastic), was reduced, and regulation proposals abandoned, after widely publicized studies showed that disposables caused no more damage than reusable cloth diapers. Critics pointed out that the most effective study was sponsored by Procter & Gamble, the country's largest maker of disposable diapers, including Pampers and Luvs. The disposable diapers soon acquired the name "single-use" diapers, which removes the environment from the picture entirely.

[47] Postman, *Amusing Ourselves to Death*, p. 100. It was a brilliant anticipation of Donald Trump.

Lippmann, John Dewey, Edward R. Murrow, or Oprah Winfrey – possess such personal and cultural authority that audiences will pay special attention to what such thought leaders tell them is important and true, in print or in pictures.

Recently, however, some people of enormous wealth have bypassed the difficult and uncertain process of acquiring personal credibility and simply purchased the power to decide what we will see and hear. For example, to that end, Jeff Bezos, of Amazon, bought the *Washington Post*; Elon Musk of Tesla bought Twitter; Mark Zuckerberg financed, within Facebook and Instagram, algorithms that make selections, or news feeds, of who and what users will see and read; and Meriam Adelson, who is an Israeli-American, and who wields her family's casino earnings of tens of billions of dollars in Las Vegas, Macao, and Singapore, created a free, daily newspaper distributed all over Israel, called *Israel Today*, to promote Prime Minister Benjamin Netanyahu.[48] All four of these media owners showed up as invited guests at Donald Trump's second inauguration in the Capitol Rotunda.

The Marketplace for Ideas

As the poetess said, let me count the ways. In earlier chapters, we saw that there is a crisis of democracy which is actually a crisis of citizenship; we saw that Weber identified the modern figures of Scientist and Politician but said nothing about the equally modern, and essential, figure of Citizen; we saw that the Founders committed the nation to democracy without knowing how citizens would or should behave; and we saw that, for several generations, except during the Civil War and mainly in its Southern aftermath, America's parties managed to foster citizenship fairly well.

---

[48] In February of 2025, Bezos instructed his editors at the *Washington Post* to begin accepting for publication only op-ed article submissions which endorse the principles of "personal liberties and free markets." In other words, guest writers at the *Post*, which is an institution presumably committed to defending free speech, will be published only if they promote the economic philosophy of Milton Friedman and neo-liberalism. On this administrative decision by a billionaire who earlier attended the Trump 2.0 inauguration ceremony, see www.nytimes.com/2025/02/26/business/media/washington-post-bezos-shipley.html.

Eventually, however, we also saw that, in the twentieth century, Science and Reason challenged the very concept of a legitimate sovereign *demos* which Enlightenment thinkers had planted in America; and that, in recent decades, an ideological Republican Party, plus new "medium" technologies such as televisions and smartphones, created a space in America for the appearance of Donald Trump, who is a demagogue of remarkable if not admirable talent, and who is a reality showman of extraordinary flair – a square peg in a square hole – in the attention society.

Moving on from that sequence, we assumed that the supply of information in a modern society constitutes a crucial element of "wherewithal" for fostering in citizens the capacities needed for them to practice citizenship *well* in democracy's smallest public office. Based on that assumption, we took stock, very briefly, of important aspects of the information system so that we would eventually be able to consider whether or not that system is doing what we need it to do to nurture good citizenship and maintain democracy.

That is the question we must address now, and we are especially ready to consider it via many terms which usefully describe things we need to understand as aspects of a "marketplace for ideas," where information is available to us as citizens but not, as we shall see, anywhere near optimally.

Those terms all connect us to understandings directed at the worlds of psychology, consumerism, and communications. They include – and there really are lots of them – needs, wants, advertising, public relations, propaganda, the engineering of consent, the republican, biblical, and individualist languages of public discourse, utilitarian and expressive individualism, the language of persuasion, monopolistic competition, product differentiation, consumer sovereignty, the economic theory of democracy, mediums, messages, agendas, entertainment, the attention society, the peek-a-boo world, the "now … this" formula, television news as vaudeville, the media's business model, pictures, images, talking heads, click-bait journalism, silo thinking, echo chambers, filter bubbles, news feeds, bad news, and the news cycle.

7 DYSFUNCTION

I have talked so far about creating citizens and providing them with conditions and resources to act as *good* citizens if only we knew what behaving that way requires. In effect, therefore, I have discussed a sort of Stage One in "the vocation of citizenship," which pertains to achieving the "wherewithal" needed to become active citizens. This as opposed to Stage Two, which is about how to act as citizens with the available wherewithal, especially in the four realms of party activity, inclusion, education, and journalism.

So let us now put Stage One behind us, analytically speaking, to return to a fifth realm which we considered briefly in Chapter 3, which is the "arena" praised by John Stuart Mill, the AAUP, Oliver Wendell Holmes, Jr, Louis Brandeis, John Dewey, and many other thinkers, in which citizens can make their preferences and choices known. In other words, let us return to the democratic "marketplace for ideas."

The main Stage Two point to explore here is this: even if you are curious, alert, and knowledgeable, and if you want to practice the vocation of citizenship, you will aim, in most cases, at connecting with other people in order to do the job well.

For example, Rosa Parks on her segregated bus made the right move – actually refusing to move – personally. But that act, of good citizenship on her part, had its desired effect only when other citizens, including Martin Luther King, Jr., joined her protest and instituted the bus boycott in Montgomery, Alabama, which led federal courts to ban segregated public buses as unconstitutional.[1] Which means that good citizenship is something we do best with other people, so that our shared sentiments will move society in desirable directions.

According to the Constitution, and in America's mixed government, it would seem that the signature place to do well with others is at a certified polling booth. But in fact, no matter whether we are in "red" or "blue" states, we have to arrive at that booth thinking clearly and coherently if the mandate we will deliver, together, is going to make sense.[2]

So we should note now that, in the matter of thinking, citizens in America who were invited to vote in 2024 a third time for Donald Trump – who was a convicted felon, a public policy nitwit, and an oaf – had to deal with what we should recognize as "a great dysfunction." That dysfunction becomes obvious if and when we ask how ordinary people, who are surrounded by weird conditions in the marketplace for ideas, can think straight today.[3]

Fracturing Attention

To address that question, we don't need to collect complicated, voluminous, or arcane research findings. And we don't need to conduct specific investigations about something defined as a great dysfunction. It is enough that we will look around at what is going on, see what many people are saying about it, and draw sensible conclusions.

---

[1] The federal district court ruling in Alabama was *Browder v. Gayle* (1956). The Supreme Court affirmed the Browder decision later in the same year. See https://civics.supremecourthistory.org/article/browder-v-gayle.

[2] We should recall James Madison in Federalist Paper #14, wherein he declared: "Is it not the glory of the people of America that, whilst they have paid a decent regard to the opinions of former times and other nations, they have not suffered a blind veneration for antiquity, for custom, or for names, to overrule the suggestions of their own good sense, the knowledge of their own situation, and the lessons of their own experience?"

[3] What follows in the text above is in line with what Sissela Bok said in *Lying: Moral Choice in Public and Private Life* (New York: Pantheon Books, 1978), p. 85: "to be given false information about important choices in their lives is to be rendered powerless." And she wrote that before lying in public became so widespread that we now try to understand how and why citizens and politicians permit it to characterize many communications in the Age of Post-Truth.

For example, we have already seen that the "attention society" compels individuals and firms to try, powerfully and relentlessly, to get our attention. There is nothing mysterious about that. It is not a secret. And it is not illegal.

But that there is a campaign to make us notice such sirens (and we might remember how dangerously the original Sirens tempted Ulysses on his way home in *The Odyssey*) does not mean that all of us will be approached with the same pitch because, in fact, we are not all the same people and will not respond similarly to the same pitches.

For example, in a program featuring Disney cartoons, capitalists will not advertise Lipitor or cosmetic surgery. Moreover, a professional wrestling match is not likely to promote Estée Lauder's "advanced night repair." And newscasts are not sponsored by crib makers, because CNN and Fox News usually attract older viewers who are no longer raising small children.

Rather, advertisers direct their programming to this or that part of the general public, to these or those people who are likely to buy this or that commodity. It is not that capitalists, who are citizens like the rest of us, think it is good for society if they will fracture our attention and thereby contribute to shattering our community. But it is good for business, which is what they are of a mind to do. On that score they know, and so do we, that what is good for General Motors, or Facebook, is not necessarily good for America or any other country.[4]

Confirmation

We can use the term "confirmation" to refer to an excuse occasionally offered by the attention seekers, because sometimes they say that they are not responsible for fracturing sentiments in the marketplace but are merely, in all innocence, confirming what they know we want to hear. In which case, we, and not they, are doing the fracturing.[5] That is,

---

[4] Yuval Noah Harari, in his *Nexus: A Brief History of Information Networks from the Stone Age to AI* (London: Fern, 2024), pp. 195–202, explains how, in 2016–2017, Facebook inadvertently "helped fan the flames of anti-Rohingya violence in Myanmar (Burma)."

[5] This is the excuse offered by Mark Zuckerberg, for example, when he declares that Facebook merely helps people to get in touch with other people. In other words, he is doing no more than helping them to pass messages back and forth. Therefore, his

their algorithms, driving news feeds, are not creating filter bubbles but only providing the comfort we seek to obtain by being surrounded by our own, and familiar, opinions.[6] Kurt Anderson, unpersuaded by such notions, caustically suggests that selections made by internet algorithms amount to a "stark version of Gresham's law, the bad driving out – or at least overrunning – the good."[7]

At any rate, the confirmation thesis is, in fact, an elegant version of the notion of "consumer sovereignty," which we met in Chapter 5 and which is no truer now than it was when I described it there. The notion of consumer sovereignty assumes that consumers, including all citizens, have desires for various commodities and that producers seek to serve the totality of those desires by making the sought-after commodities available.[8]

---

consumers are in charge, not Facebook. In the real world, though, his company, like the Rockefellers, came to be so disliked that, helped by public relations people, he changed its name to Meta, which means nothing at all and does not remind us that it is still Facebook and he is still Mark Zuckerberg. Standard Oil used the same strategy and became Exxon.

[6] We should compare the news-feed world with the world of schooling. In the former, an algorithm sends you a message about something you already know; in the latter, the teacher conveys to you something you don't know. The first is entertainment; the second is education.

[7] Kurt Anderson, *Fantasyland: How America Went Haywire: A 500-Year History* (New York: Random House, 2017), p. 418. Anderson's book explains how many aspects of American life – including clothing, politics, gambling, restaurants, religion, and more – even before television, morphed into forms of entertainment. So, he wasn't surprised (pp. 252–264) that Ronald Reagan, an entertainer (who sometimes confused reality with what he saw in movies), was elected president twice in the 1980s and that Bill Clinton appeared in 1992 on the Arsenio Hall late-night show wearing Ray-Ban Wayfarers and playing "Heartbreak Hotel" on his saxophone. On Reagan's occasional references to movie scenes as if they described real-world events, see Michael Rogin, *Ronald Reagan the Movie: And Other Episodes in Political Demonology* (Berkeley: University of California Press, 1988).

[8] The notion that consumers are in charge of what they get from producers, rather than having their thoughts and preferences manipulated by advertising (from producers), is demolished in Erik Larson, *The Naked Consumer: How Our Private Lives Become Public Commodities* (New York: Penguin, 1994), *passim*, but esp. 15: "As consumers, we see Oz. We don't see the little man behind the curtain." About quality production, Larson continued: "Suppose God's product development team had first tried out His creations on a panel of average Americans – would the lobster and artichoke have made the convenience cut?" See also Benjamin R. Barber, *Consumed: How Markets Corrupt Children, Infantilize Adults, and Swallow Citizens Whole* (New York: Norton, 2007), where advertisers may talk about "empowering" children and adults but are really manipulating them emotionally. It is a system wherein people make individual choices but have little or no understanding of how those choices add up to public consequences that can only be repaired by political decisions which are anathema to pro-capitalist thinkers. For example, Barber (p. 35) notes that a civilian Hummer owner feels good about his chariot but "squanders fossil fuel resources, pollutes the environment, and makes the United States more dependent than ever on foreign oil resources – contributing quite inadvertently to

In the real world, however, guided by advertising experts, producers can work to plant desires in consumers and, if the planting takes hold, the producers, continuing to use the language of persuasion, can very powerfully cultivate those desires so that they will stimulate either commercial buying, in stores and online, or political buying, such as choosing to "buy" this or that candidate with our vote on Election Day.

It is a practice which, as we have seen, generates "polarization," and there are examples of persistent face-offs constantly at hand in the marketplace for ideas. We see, for example, that some Americans believe, like Franklin Roosevelt did, that government can play a positive role in society,[9] and we see that other Americans, like Ronald Reagan, believe that government is not the solution but the problem itself.[10]

Furthermore, we see that some Americans, most likely Democrats, believe that "the system" is broken for not delivering enough services, whereas others, who are mostly Republicans, believe that "individuals" should accept more "responsibility" for their own poverty or other failures.[11] Or we see that some Americans, likely to be

---

the justification for Middle East military interventions he otherwise vehemently opposes." And that means (pp. 291–339) that Americans who are expected to be both normal consumers and good citizens suffer from a kind of schizophrenia between the two roles, which have different objectives.

[9] See his "Four Freedoms" speech at www.archives.gov/milestone-documents/president-franklin-roosevelts-annual-message-to-congress which discusses government's moral obligation to promote freedom of speech, freedom of worship, freedom from want, and freedom from fear.

[10] Ronald Reagan, "First Inaugural Address" (January 20, 1981): "In the present crisis, government is not the solution to our problem; government is the problem ... If we look for the answer as to why, for so many years, we achieved so much, prospered as no other people on Earth, it was because here, in this land, we unleashed the energy and individual genius of man to a greater extent than has ever been done before ... It is no coincidence that our present troubles parallel and are proportionate to the intervention and intrusion in our lives that result from unnecessary and excessive growth of government." For support of this thesis, see Jonathan R. T. Hughes, *The Governmental Habit Redux: Economic Controls from Colonial Times to the Present* (Princeton: Princeton University Press, 1991) and James Bovard, *The Rise of the State and the Demise of the Citizen* (New York: St. Martin's, 1999).

[11] A leading example of blaming "the system" is Richard Delgado and Jean Stefancic, *Critical Race Theory: An Introduction* (New York: New York University Press, 2017), *passim*, but esp. p. 8: "racism is ordinary not aberrational – 'normal science' – the usual way society does business." On the right, praise for individualism framed as opposition to tribalism and identity politics by groups, is a central theme in Victor David Hanson, *The Dying Citizen: How Progressive Elites, Tribalism, and Globalization Are Destroying the Idea of America* (New York: Basic Books, 2021).

Trumpists, believe that men should guide the country, whereas other Americans, more likely Democrats, are ready to help women to break glass ceilings on this score.

Such bifurcations sometimes work at cross purposes, for example when right-wing activists like Phyllis Schlafly, who are comfortable with traditional female roles, reject feminism,[12] and when Black Republican men, like Clarence Thomas, who entered Yale University Law School within the framework of an affirmative action admissions policy, preach the gospel of personal success.[13] So there is room for considerable muddling here, but that is precisely the point.

Muddling

We can speak of "muddling" as (a) what the liberal, democratic, Enlightenment marketplace of ideas generates now, instead of (b) the clarifications that John Stuart Mill hoped it would produce. Not being religious, Mill believed that, in a philosophical sense, we can never achieve absolute truth. He argued, though, that a process of constant and moderate examination of many social principles and propositions can move us in the direction of truth, and that that is the right thing to do.[14]

---

[12] Phyllis Schlafly, *Who Killed the American Family?* (Chicago: WND Books, 2014).

[13] Clarence Thomas, *My Grandfather's Son: A Memoir* (New York: Harper Perennial, 2008).

[14] Here is how Mill envisioned what we later called the marketplace for ideas. John Stuart Mill, *On Liberty* (orig., 1859; New York: Liberal Arts Press, 1956), pp. 64–67: "the free expression of all opinions should be permitted on condition that the manner should be temperate, and do not pass the bounds of fair discussion … The gravest [of offenses] … is to argue sophistically, to suppress facts or arguments, to misstate the elements of the case, or misrepresent the opposite opinion … The worst offense … which can be committed by a polemic is to stigmatize those who hold the contrary opinion as bad and immoral men." Mill would have been horrified by any of Ann Coulter's or Mark Levin's books. For recent research into how far the current marketplace for ideas is from Mill's original prescription for it, see Jeffrey M. Berry and Sarah Sobieraj, *The Outrage Industry: Public Opinion Media and the New Incivility* (New York: Oxford University Press, 2014). Outrage includes mockery, name calling, belittling, obscene language, character assassination, slippery-slope argumentation, and more. The problem is that it works, they say, for politicians personally and for media entities financially. Thus: "At the individual level, outrage discourse may undercut our tolerance of other views and promote misunderstandings about public issues. At the institutional level, outrage is working to stigmatize compromise and bipartisanship, and undercutting the political prospects of more moderate

But what is happening nowadays in Mill's marketplace? America maintains that marketplace with modern technology including radios, televisions, computers, the internet, the cloud, algorithms, and our smartphones. But what is actually going on in this arena that surrounds everyone?

On the one hand, there is the "culture war." In that war, people talk less about what to do and more about who, say, in the Washington "swamp," is doing anything. And that is a constant invitation to preaching scorn and hostility, a practice at which Donald Trump excels.[15]

In the circumstances, comity goes out the window, even though Mill insisted that the marketplace would only work if participants in it respected each other. Where is that respect now, when Senator Mitch McConnell (R-KY), the Senate majority leader, proudly announced in 2016 that he would not permit the president of the United States, a Democrat, to appoint a new Supreme Court justice to replace Justice Antonin Scalia, a Republican?

And who is to stop the marketplace from being flooded by every sort of nonsense, by false accusations, by conspiracy theories, and by a stunning quantity of what I call intellectual "sludge"? The Supreme Court has ruled, for example, in *Citizens United v. FEC* (2010) and *McCutcheon v. FEC* (2014), that wealthy Americans, no matter what, or how outlandish, their sentiments and preferences might be, can use as much money as they want to promote in politics whatever they like.

---

voices" (p. 221). From the Right, blaming outrage on the Left, see Mary Katharine Ham and Guy Benson, *End of Discussion: How the Left's Outrage Industry Shuts Down Debate, Manipulates Voters, and Makes America Less Free (and Fun)* (New York: Crown Forum, 2017).

[15] Many other conservatives in the culture war match Trump on this score. For example, before Trump and his associates began to complain about the Washington "swamp," Marvin Olasky told his readers a farmer's daughter story. See Marvin Olasky, *Compassionate Conservatism: What It Is, What It Does, and How It Can Transform America* (New York: Free Press, 2000), p. 190: "'Momma,' the young lady called out [from the yard, where she was milking the family cow], 'there's a man here to see you.' The mother looked out the kitchen window and replied, 'Haven't I always told you not to talk to strangers? You come in this house right now.' The girl protested. 'But Momma, this man says he is a United States senator.' The wise mother replied, 'In that case, bring the cow in with you.'"

The result, not surprisingly, is that people of every sort throw into the marketplace, especially in the form of social media snippets, every sort of nonsense which Mill hoped we would disprove but which today, even when disproved, will be sponsored again by some enthusiast and made to appear repeatedly.

Means of Attention

I will in a moment return to the information system and its drawbacks. But first, to frame how we might understand that system in our society, we should note how George Orwell and Aldous Huxley, two of England's great dystopian novelists, from different but complementary angles of analysis, approached the subject of thinking, or not, as it might take place in societies controlled by modern political regimes.

George Orwell

In *1984*, George Orwell, who thoroughly understood the promotion and suppression of ideas, described Winston Smith as declaring that to be free in Oceana is to be entitled to say, out loud and without fear of retribution, that "two and two make four."[16] Winston (and George) never imagined, though, that this rational, scientific equation, which is a matter of obvious, unmistakable, and total truth, might be drowned out nowadays by people who simply insist that, in effect, two and two make five.[17] Or that a UN report on human-made climate change is "fake news."[18]

---

[16] George Orwell, *1984* (orig., 1949; London: Penguin, 2008), p. 84.
[17] I admit that I am using this example figuratively and that I have not seen anyone actually claim that two and two make five. But I have seen passionate people who make what I consider to be similarly preposterous claims.
[18] For example, Senator James Inhofe (R-OK), *The Greatest Hoax: How the Global Warming Conspiracy Threatens Your Future* (New York: WND, 2012), *passim*, rejects the conclusions of 2,500 scientists who, in reports from the Intergovernmental Panel on Climate Change (IPCC), insist that global warming, caused by human activity, generates climate change, disastrous floods, raging forest fires, species extinctions and other catastrophes. He also believes (pp. 70–71) that, no matter what the vast majority of scientists say, climate change will not seriously disrupt seasonal weather because God promised that "As long as the earth remains, there will be springtime and harvest, cold and heat, winter and summer, day and night" (Genesis 8:22). In support of climate-change denialism, see Marc

And how are we to avoid this dysfunction when everyone hires his or her own "expert"? Who should we listen to when there is a "think tank" or "institute" shouting out every sensible or bizarre idea?[19]

Moreover, where are the authoritative thinkers who will help us to understand what in the marketplace really deserves our attention if everything there glitters? We know that not all that glitters is gold. But who will tell us what in the marketplace is dross, and why should we believe him or her when Sean Hannity and Jimmy Kimmel are competing for our attention? The business model here aims not to illuminate the world but to keep us in front of commercials.

Aldous Huxley

With his *1984* story, published in 1949, Orwell helped us to understand some aspects of where we are today by commenting on brutal methods – such as war mongering, police violence, constant surveillance, newspeak, and doublespeak – for manipulating the thinking of citizens. But we should also keep in mind Aldous Huxley's *Brave New World*, published in 1931, because Huxley told the story of a future state which designed children to be born out of laboratory bottles, and then shaped them, with chemicals and behavioral training, into distinct castes of people – from Alphas to Epsilons – who would perform various managerial, industrial, and service roles in a strictly regimented society.

The details of Huxley's story are not important for our purposes. But he provided some backdrop for our consideration of citizenship "wherewithal" because he famously pointed his readers toward appreciating how citizens in the future might be molded, by the regime

---

Morano, *The Politically Incorrect Guide to Climate Change* (Washington, DC: Regnery, 2018). For the opposite view, informed by scientific research and weather reports, see Ross Gelbspan, *The Heat Is On: The Climate Crisis, the Cover-up, the Prescriptions* (Cambridge, MA: Perseus Books, 1998), and David Wallace-Wells, *The Uninhabitable Earth: A Story of the Future* (New York: Penguin, 2019).

[19] I wrote about American think tanks (and institutes) in David Ricci, *The Transformation of American Politics: The New Washington and the Rise of Think Tanks* (New Haven: Yale University Press, 1984). There, I described how they arose and what they do. Since then, many additional entities of this sort have been sponsored, but I have moved on to other research topics.

around them, to the point of not being able to exercise the vocation of citizenship at all. That is, they would be cogs in a stable and prosperous society, and they would perform useful tasks. But they would also be so lulled by alcohol, and by tranquillizers – which Huxley called "soma" – and by various powerful entertainments, including endless games and frequent sex, that they would not even want to choose new roles for themselves and express preferences adding up to electoral mandates that politicians would have to fulfill.

In other words, Huxley's story warned of the possibility of a society not ruled every day by vicious jackboots but by circumstances wherein residents may simply be unable to think for themselves and constructively. Which prepares us to notice that, in a way, and not always deliberately, such mindlessness may be emerging, before our eyes, from what I am discussing here as the information system.

Common Sense

Now, keeping both Orwell and Huxley in mind, let us observe that we usually notice what is inside, rather than outside, of the information system. That is, what is there is what we see, and therefore what we talk about. However, there are two things we do *not* see in the system, because they are very significantly *not* there. Those are "common sense" and "a new narrative." And each of those is so important as to warrant being considered here separately.

Let us begin, then, with common sense. As Postman said, the public conversation conducted on our various devices is actually going nowhere because it is a form of "show business," presenting first one thing and then another, in a "peek-a-boo" way punctuated by "now … this." In this process, typically expressed in television news, we find a staggering implication of what has gone wrong with the marketplace of ideas, and that is the gradual loss in America of "common sense."

What I mean by losing common sense is that on "platform" media entities – like newspapers and television, blogs and podcasts – every sort of opinion, on every sort of subject, no matter how smart or stupid, benign or dangerous, will be given time and space for expression. Everyone knows how it goes, Rachel Maddow and Greg Gutfeld, side by side.

Think about it. Orwell writes in *1984* that Winston Smith knows he is oppressed because he is forbidden to declare openly that two and two make four. And in Orwell's day, shortly after World War II, this was considered to be a keen insight.

Yet today, as Postman points out, every American is free to say two and two make four. The problem, then, is not that some people are suppressing this truism but that whoever says two and two make five will be given time on television (or social media) and interviewed by celebrity sages like Christiane Amanpour, Anderson Cooper, Bret Baier, Tucker Carlson, and Joe Rogan.

It is as if wacko opinions are worth discussing, as if common sense is irrelevant to life in the information system. And as if there are no "self-evident truths" like the ones Jefferson described when he justified what became mixed government and democracy in America.[20]

Again, think about it. Shared understandings rooted in common sense have been a vital, and maybe even irreplaceable, resource in modern society since the Enlightenment. They arise from the notion that men and women are capable of exercising Reason, of extending it into the practice of Science rather than Theology, which rests on Faith, and then of using the knowledge so gained to make the world a better place to live in.

In this scheme of things – although we sometimes forget it – common sense is, in fact, what you are left with after you sit down with other people, talk soberly about this and that, check out the facts if possible, and arrive, not always easily, at well-founded understandings which are widely shared and which tell us who the loonies and nasties are and why they should be ignored or opposed.

Going Nowhere

Now think about the never-ending conversation promoted by the information system, where "news items" follow one another endlessly but aimlessly. That conversation starts anywhere and ends, if at all, nowhere in particular.

---

[20] Robert F. Kennedy, Jr., Donald Trump's Secretary of Health and Human Services, who has insisted that inoculations cause autism, is a recent example of this phenomenon. Another is the state of Utah, which in 2025 banned fluoridation of public drinking water as a menace to public health.

Which means that there is no commitment to progress there, only to continuing to talk. That is, the point is not to illuminate, not to edify, not to educate, not to get to any specific place, but to keep the conversation going to provide space for advertisements. Gossip, blather, anecdotes, rumors, allegations, panic, facts, suspicions, conspiracies, hysteria, truth, lies, chest thumping, veracity, hypocrisy, and more: all are grist for this ever-present and all-embracing mill.[21]

It is, at best, an affair of needles (truth) hidden in haystacks (chaff). In the circumstances, how can listeners or viewers locate in all this stuff the common sense of our shared situation? How can we know together even what that situation is? And where are the gatekeepers who will guide us along the way?

After all, if no one in the system is responsible for excluding the junk, what we wind up with, as citizens of the same society, is perpetual confusion rather than principles and practices which we can regard as plainly important to our collective survival.

Remember Jefferson. If in 1776 he had been in such shapeless circumstances, in such an intellectual bog, he could not have written the Declaration of Independence. And, being in that situation today, his descendants are increasingly hard-pressed to remember and stand up together for truths that he wrote about at the age of 33.[22]

---

[21] Kathryn Crammer Brownell, *24/7 Politics: Cable Television & The Fragmenting of America from Watergate to Fox News* (Princeton: Princeton University Press, 2023) describes this situation as no longer serving to educate Americans but to entertain them. She provides the historical details (*passim*), but (pp. 310–311) attributes the original insight to Neil Postman's *Amusing Ourselves to Death: Public Discourse in the Age of Show Business* (New York: Penguin, 1985). See also Todd Gitlin, *Media Unlimited: How the Torrent of Images and Sounds Overwhelms Our Lives* (New York: Metropolitan Books, 2001), which criticizes the torrent and describes it as a consequence of capitalism's need to sell commodities.

[22] One of the great alternatives to Jefferson's radical Enlightenment convictions was suggested in his day by thinkers who promoted what we now call "nationalism." Whereas Jefferson believed that men in any society possess natural rights which are self-evident, and which governments everywhere should respect, nationalists believed that men were different from one nation to another, which implied that they should enjoy only rights appropriate for their own nations. This concept was expressed succinctly by Joseph de Maistre when he said in 1795 that "During my life I have seen Frenchmen, Italians, Russians, and so on. Thanks to Montesquieu I even know that one can be a Persian; but I must say that as for Man, I have never come across him anywhere." De Maistre is quoted in Jacques Barzun, *From Dawn to Decadence: 500 Years of Western Cultural Life, 1500 to the Present* (New York: Harper Perennial, 2001), p. 477.

Thomas Paine

We can approach the matter of going nowhere from an additional angle. Common sense is not much discussed by thinkers who worry about what they call the "epistemological dilemma."[23] That is their term for the situation, reflected in our modern information system, which is flooded by every sort of claim, whereby the evidence available is so contradictory and inconsistent that it does not point us toward any particular understanding of what is true or false. Consequently, we find it hard to get together, to agree on what we know, to propose shared courses of action, and to collectively fashion decisions on matters of great importance to the community.

Thomas Paine did not have this problem. In his great pro-democracy tract entitled *Common Sense* (1776), Paine announced, point blank, that "I offer nothing more than simple facts, plain arguments, and common sense; and have no other preliminaries to settle with the reader, than that he will divest himself of prejudice and prepossessions [traditional stories] and suffer his reason and his feelings to determine for themselves."[24]

He then proceeded to make the case. For example, "There is something exceedingly ridiculous in the composition of Monarchy; it first excludes a man from the means of information, yet empowers him to act in cases where the highest judgment is required." Moreover, "A French bastard landing with an armed Banditti and establishing himself king of England against the consent of the natives, is in plain terms a very paltry rascally original indeed. It certainly hath no divinity in it." Furthermore, who needs the monarchy? "In England a King hath little more to do than to make war and give away places; which, in plain terms, is to impoverish the nation and set it together by the ears. A pretty business indeed for a man to be

---

[23] Dictionaries define "epistemology" as the science of how we know, of how we distinguish truth from fiction, and of how we define knowledge as different from opinion.

[24] The Paine quotations in this section are from Howard Fast, "Common Sense," in *The Selected Work of Thomas Paine and Citizen Tom Paine* (New York: Modern Library, 1943, 1945), pp. 6–39. Fast was interrogated in 1950 by Senator Joseph McCarthy in the House Un-American Activities Committee, refused to "name names" of left-wing friends and associates, and consequently spent three months in prison for contempt of Congress. See https://lithub.com/the-unapologetic-politics-of-howard-fast/.

allowed eight hundred thousand sterling a year for, and worshipped into the bargain!"[25]

In short, said Paine, "A government of our own is our natural right: and when a man seriously reflects on the precariousness of human affairs, he will become convinced, that it is infinitely wiser and safer, to form a constitution of our own in a cool and deliberate manner, while we have it in our power, than to trust such an interesting event to time and chance."[26]

The Age of Reason

To recall such statements today is to notice that common sense was a crucial product of the Enlightenment defined as an Age of Reason, where hundreds of thousands of Americans read Paine's propositions or listened while other Americans, more literate, read them aloud. And about those propositions, they mainly thought: "of course," "obviously," "undoubtedly," "no question about it," and "who could think anything else?"

That is, these people shared with Paine certain crucial understandings about who they were and what they deserved from the leaders and institutions that dominated their public life.[27] And the same sort of consensual thinking, within most of the American community, showed up when Jefferson announced, in the Declaration of Independence, barely six months after Paine published *Common Sense*, that "we hold these truths to be self-evident," that people have natural rights which include the right "to alter or abolish" the government if it does not safeguard the "inalienable rights" of people over whom it rules.

The point is simple. Common sense truths can unite a community and inspire great and decent deeds.[28] Then Freud told us, more or less, that

---

[25] According to conversion formulas on the internet, it looks to me like 800,000 sterling in 1776 would be worth $288 million today.

[26] There are similar passages in *The Federalist*, where some of the articles explain why and how (the enabling factor here is common sense) ordinary people can break through tradition and precedent to create a new and workable government, which the Founders did.

[27] Not everyone agreed. Therefore, loyalists left the colonies or fell silent to avoid repression. But an entire community did agree, fought the war, and then rearranged its life on the basis of shared beliefs which it regarded as common sense.

[28] Surely, common sense is sometimes wrong, like when most people thought the Earth was flat. My critics may present that as a "gotcha" observation. However, the framework of what I am thinking of as an explanation will describe individual and also shared common sense. First, "Individual common sense" is a capacity for perspicacity, for understanding the

people are mostly incapable of common sense. And now, the information system, which generates much of what citizens think they know today, is nailing Freud's point home because, even if he was too pessimistic about our abilities, part of the "wherewithal" instruments for our thinking are for sure killing common sense as a shared resource. And that is because common sense – that is, a collection of reasonable understandings about a particular set of circumstances – requires a body of patent truths that struggles to evolve, or cannot evolve, in our marketplace of ideas.

Overload

Let's backtrack a moment. Mill, who admired the Age of Reason, knew that, on the whole, free speech would bring us closer, but not all the way, to truth. From this exercise, he thought, society might progress.[29] But he never saw a marketplace for ideas that had been massively corrupted by media entities like Meta, Instagram, Twitter, Reddit, YouTube, Snapchat, and more.[30]

---

world around us without the support of tradition or traditional "opinion leaders" such as famous philosophers. See Burke, *Reflections on the Revolution in France* (1790), Part VI, Book 1, who said, against Paine, who relied on common sense, that we must go by precedent, because we (individuals) "know that we have made no discoveries … in the great principles of government." See also Alexis de Tocqueville, *The Old Regime and the French Revolution* (orig., 1856; New York: Dover, 2010), Vol. 2, Bk. 2, Ch. 1, on how Americans pay "little attention to philosophy." Then came Freud and Daniel Kahneman, where the latter's work, perhaps unintentionally, reinforced some of the former's assumptions about pervasive irrationality. Second, "Shared common sense" depends on science (e.g., Copernicus, Galileo) and other discoveries, which cause us collectively to adjust from time to time what we know together. Tradition (unto revelation) still rejects this sort of common sense, however, such as when some pious preachers say that "believing is seeing" rather than "seeing is believing." Moreover, we mostly do not believe that sludge in the information system will be winnowed out by people widely accepted as gatekeepers. And there is a sense in which belief in scientific understandings is itself often based on faith, because most of us don't know first-hand how science's discoveries are made. Thus some of us, like Trump's Secretary of Health and Human Services in 2025, will believe that vaccinations cause autism. And I won't even try here to parse the things Trump said, starting in early 2025, to argue that his ideas and administration of government agencies add up to what he calls "common sense." But see this claim about common sense issued in an unsigned White House "article" at www.whitehouse.gov/articles/2025/03/president-trump-is-restoring-common-sense-to-government/. See also Scott Jennings, *A Revolution of Common Sense: How Donald Trump Stormed Washington and Fought for Western Civilization* (New York: William Morrow, 2025).

[29] Mill, *On Liberty*.
[30] On what such entities are really doing to us, see Jaron Lanier, *Ten Arguments for Deleting Your Social Media Accounts Right Now* (New York: Henry Holt, 2018). Lanier describes social media accounts as designed to perform "continual behavior modification on a titanic scale" (p. 6).

All of these entities, for the sake of profit, today promote entertainment rather than education, and encourage silos rather than shared values.[31] In fact, while paying only lip service to any principles of conscience or ethics, such entities transmit to us every day millions or even billions of assertions no matter how reasonable or nonsensical, decent or disgraceful, benign or deadly. It is as if all of those assertions are equal and deserve our attention to the same extent.

In the shuffle, however, widespread agreement on common-sense truths gets lost. America has not fallen apart. But demagogues like Donald Trump, who care little, and who understand less, about holding it together, may appear in America at any time, and the cliff is still there for the country to walk over and fall off.

Giving Up

Let me stipulate. Common sense propelled good citizenship during the American Revolution, which was one of the greatest political acts of the Enlightenment. Today, however, in our world of echo chambers, stubborn animosities, and identity politics, many thinkers believe that common sense is a delusion and cover story for power plays which enable some people to create and maintain inequality and thereby rule over others.

In the circumstances, not only is the very notion of common sense belittled by academics like Michel Foucault, Edward Said, Stanley Fish, Jacques Derrida, and their heirs. But identity activists, like those in Black Lives Matter (BLM), the National Organization of Women (NOW), the Tea Party, Occupy Wall Street, and the Federalist Society, who oppose other activists in the information system, may believe that, in it, common sense truths cannot be attained.[32]

---

[31] This point about entertainment before education was made by Roger Ailes, a successful right-wing political campaign consultant and later CEO of Fox News. See him quoted in Brian J. Karem, *Free the Press: The Death of American Journalism and How to Revive It* (Lanham: Prometheus Books, 2021), pp. 47–48: "If you have two guys on a stage and one guy says, 'I have a solution to the Middle East problem,' and the other guy falls in the orchestra pit, who do you think is going to be on the evening news?" Karem reports that Ailes called this insight, about what becomes news, "The Orchestra Pit Theory."

[32] Arguments along these lines do not say point blank that common sense cannot be achieved, but that it is impeded by powerful social and intellectual inertia. For example, on behalf of feminism, Betty Frieden, *The Feminine Mystique* (New York: Norton, 1963), argued that

In other words, we seem to know, and apparently accept, that the information system – a huge marketplace which facilitates the transmission and exchange of every sort of understanding and misunderstanding – does not produce common sense, which I would define as a set of shared truths about real circumstances in which a community finds itself.[33]

Worse, we have conceded that we are no longer even trying to communicate publicly with one another to achieve collective understandings, which is what Mill and his followers recommended doing. Instead, we continue to bombard one another, again and again, with every sort of allegation, aspersion, disdain, slur, rumor, and denunciation. In the circumstances, and without gatekeepers to straighten out the mess, nothing emerges but "sludge" and more sludge – endlessly.

Narratives

Switch concepts for a moment, though, because it can be helpful to frame the problem of common sense in terms of what scholars call "narratives" or "Stories." We know that the world is changing. But Republicans, promoting their culture war, are engaging that world via a MAGA (Make America Great Again) "narrative" that directs them to look backward. And other Americans, including ordinary citizens but also liberal thinkers, nowadays trust no one, assume that national narratives amount only to rationalizing, and have nothing with which to replace them.

Moderate Conservatives

This situation has elicited a great deal of conservative comment, some of which comes from Edmund Burke's moderate heirs rather than

---

the American culture of male dominance must make way for women who do not want to place only motherhood and housework at the center of their lives and thinking. And on behalf of race theory, Ta-Nehisi Coates, *Between the World and Me* (New York: Spiegel and Grau, 2015) argues that the dominant American culture of white identity must make room for people who are Black.

[33] Mill said that the marketplace for ideas must be open, calm, and tolerant. Instead, the information system is commercial, clamorous, and disparaging. Within it, common sense cannot win. Instead, as George Scialabba, *Slouching Toward Utopia: Essays and Reviews* (New York: Pressed Wafer, 2018), p. 47, said: "The system filters out the thoughtful and replaces them with the faithful." Which is exactly what Mill hoped to avoid.

partisan zealots like Ann Coulter, who writes books like *Treason: Liberal Treachery from the Cold War to the War on Terrorism* (2004), *Demonic: How the Liberal Mob is Endangering America* (2011), and *In Trump We Trust: E Pluribus Awesome* (2016).

Some moderate conservatives worry about mainstream Americans who used to regard capitalism, and now regard neoliberalism, as acceptable or even praiseworthy despite the fact that it entails a process of endless change, innovation, and disruption. To admire this side of American life is to sanction conditions of perpetual uncertainty and turmoil where not every transformation constitutes improvement, and not every change equals progress.[34]

From economics, Joseph Schumpeter described the process of unending transformation with his phrase "creative destruction." He thereby indicated that when one "creates" new commodities and services, one also "destroys" the value of old commodities, old services, old locations, old skills, and old facilities.[35] In which case, someone pays the bill.

For our purposes, two moderate conservatives highlighted this painful point admirably. First, Karl Polanyi proposed that

> Nowhere has liberal [post-Enlightenment] philosophy failed so conspicuously as in its understanding of the problem of change ... [As capitalism flourished in the nineteenth century]

---

[34] Religious conservatives are also wary of change, which they believe can lead Americans away from the Ten Commandments. And some economic conservatives worry as well, like when they scorn Lenin and Stalin for (reputedly) saying that if you want to make an omelet, you must break eggs. Nevertheless, most politicians and publicists on the modern Right usually praise capitalist innovation and entrepreneurship. Many of them seem confident that new technology will eventually halt the global warming which technology caused in the first place. Or maybe they don't believe that fossil fuels cause global warming at all. On that score, many Republicans, who regard Ronald Reagan as a great former president, probably don't know that, in 1986, he had workmen remove the solar heating panels that President Carter had installed on the White House's roof in 1979. Perhaps Carter, former commander of a nuclear submarine, understood better than Reagan, a former movie actor, the scientific issues at stake.

[35] For example, many longshoremen lost their jobs when shipping containers were invented and container terminals were constructed in major ports around the world. Mainstream economists may assume that workers so displaced will, sooner or later, find adequate new employment, in which case their pain and loss is only temporary. In David Ricci, *A Political Science Manifesto for the Age of Populism* (New York: Cambridge University Press, 2020), esp. pp. 107–109, I discussed this issue with reference to the potential creation of driverless cars while, in America today, an estimated 3.5 million people work as drivers.

elementary truths of political science and statecraft [for example, those that animated Burke] were first discredited, then, forgotten. It should need no elaboration that a process of undirected change ... should be slowed down, if possible, so as to safeguard the welfare of the community.[36]

More recently, Andrew Bacevich edited a collection of items written mainly by twentieth-century American conservatives and explained there why various thinkers on the Right have feared an uncritical intoxication with modernity and have, therefore, regarded the Left's enthusiasm for constant change as dangerous to the point where it should be tempered.[37]

Looking at the information system, we can say that, unintentionally, and without malice, its activity backs up these conservative apprehensions because its instruments certify constant change, random change, and unending change. And we can see its threat, on that score, in how it handles narratives.

Stories

The size of the constant-change problem is suggested by what Neil Postman said in his *Building a Bridge to the 18th Century* (1999), and which I repeated in *Post-Truth American Politics* (2023), about the importance of narratives, which he calls "stories":

> I mean by "narrative" a story. But not any kind of story. I refer to big stories – stories that are sufficiently profound and complex to offer explanations of the origins and future of a people;

---

[36] Karl Polanyi, *The Great Transformation: The Political and Economic Origins of Our Time* (orig., 1944; Boston: Beacon, 1957), p. 33. Polanyi extended this passage by saying that "Such household truths of traditional statesmanship, often ... reflecting the teachings of a social philosophy inherited from the ancients, were in the nineteenth century erased from the thoughts of the educated by the corrosive of a crude utilitarianism combined with an uncritical reliance on the alleged self-healing virtues of unconscious growth."

[37] Andrew J. Bacevich (ed.), "Introduction," in *American Conservatism: Reclaiming an Intellectual Tradition* (New York: Library of America, 2020), p. xiii. From this point of view, when Barack Obama campaigned by promising "Change We Can Believe In," he was participating in a charge by lemmings. On the other hand, not only Leftist Americans rhapsodize about change. Conservatives from Ronald Reagan to Margaret Thatcher, who enthuse about "unleashing" capitalism, do the same.

stories that construct ideals, prescribe rules of conduct, specify sources of authority, and, in doing all this, provide a sense of continuity and purpose ... What is important about stories is that people cannot live without them.[38]

That is, Postman did not mean stories like Tom Hanks saving Private Ryan, or Jean Valjean stealing the bishop's silver candlesticks, or why John McCain couldn't raise his arms to salute crowds, or how Donald Trump encouraged a right-wing mob to storm and occupy the Capitol Building in Washington.

Postman meant, rather, what we can call, for clarity's sake, "Stories" with a capital "S," which are large and fundamentally important narratives. And he said that Stories are a sociological necessity.

Much the same understanding of Stories, without using that term, appears in Yuval Harari's *Sapiens: A Brief History of Humankind*. There, Harari reminds us that "any large-scale human cooperation – whether a modern state, a medieval church, an ancient city or an archaic tribe – is rooted in common myths that exist only in people's collective imagination."[39]

Extending this insight into a wide-ranging account of human affairs, Harari observes that different eras, different peoples, different religions, different states, and more, all have their myths, that is, Stories. They justify living in certain ways and not others; they recommend dwelling with some neighbors and shunning the rest.

Yes, there are concrete devices, such as artificial irrigation, iron weapons, water wheels, stirrups, compasses, telescopes, steam engines, hypodermic needles, barbed wire, refrigerators, electric lights, telephones, and computers, which enable communities to endure and some even to prosper. But myths control the disposition of those devices, and Harari makes this point uncompromisingly. Without effective myths – that is, without religious, legal, national, financial, and other Stories – Harari says that things would fall apart, or, as Yeats feared, the center might not hold.[40]

---

[38] Neil Postman, *Building a Bridge to the Eighteenth Century* (New York: Vintage, 1999), p. 101.
[39] Yuval Harari, *Sapiens: A Brief History of Humankind* (London: Penguin, 2015), p. 30.
[40] W. B. Yeats, "The Second Coming" (1921). At www.poetryfoundation.org/poems/43290/the-second-coming.

Narratives or Stories in this sense may be religious and, if so, they may be maintained by "faith." But if faith does not sustain them in the modern world, they must be maintained by the common sense of people in the community. And on that point Postman insisted that Stories "provide a sense of continuity and purpose [therefore] ... What is important about stories is that people cannot live without them."

There is the bottom line to all this, bold but sensible. People cannot live without Stories. It is a patent fact of social life. But if that is really true, modern people are in terrible trouble. And that is because Stories of the necessary size and credibility, not merely short-term stories discussed in "the news cycle," will not be generated and certified by the current information system.

On the one hand, if the system does suggest Stories, it will suggest too many of them, in too many silos and echo chambers, via too many news feeds, for the audiences to agree on any one, or even a few, Stories in particular. In which case they won't be Stories but only stories.

On the other hand, if some powerful Stories already exist, say based on tradition and faith, then men and women in the information system, and among them energetic scholars, who are especially driven by Reason and Science, may undermine or destroy those Stories. Thus, as we have seen, these people are most likely to produce not Stories but "disenchantment."

8 COMMON SENSE

> The time has come, the Walrus said,
>   To talk of many things:
> Of shoes – and ships – and sealing wax –
>   Of cabbages and kings –
> Any why the sea is boiling hot –
>   And whether pigs have wings.
>   Lewis Carroll[1]

Lewis Carroll wrote a lot of entertaining nonsense. That much has long been obvious. What is less obvious is that he thereby provided a framework within which one can consider important aspects of American public life and Trump's successes within them. Until now, no one noticed that. For example, whether pigs have wings. What do winged pigs have to do with Donald Trump?

The link is that much of what Trump says and proposes, like what the Walrus and the Carpenter said to each other in Carroll's poem, is also nonsense and entertaining, at least politically speaking (I'll come back to that). That being the case, although such frolicking qualities rarely appear to such a degree in acts by presidents of the

---

[1] Lewis Carroll, *Through the Looking Glass* (1871), www.poetryfoundation.org/poems/43914/the-walrus-and-the-carpenter-56d222cbc80a9.

United States, let us discuss now some aspects of Trumpism whereby, as Carroll suggested, we shall talk of "many things" – which he called "cabbages and kings" – or, at least, unto "the Pied Piper" of Hamelin (more on that later).

This isn't easy to do, because the man from Trump Tower, from Mar-a-Lago, and from many Fox interviews and golf courses in between, seems vastly admirable to many millions of Americans who voted for him but equally dreadful to an only slightly smaller number of Americans who haven't slept well since he was elected for a second time in 2024. The latter are shocked that, while I wrote these lines, the president deployed to Los Angeles thousands of heavily armed California National Guardsmen and quickly supplemented them with additional hundreds of equally armed United States Marines. Against the most basic constitutional concept of American federalism, Trump sent all of these soldiers into LA's 50% Latino local community as a provocation opposed by California's elected governor, LA's elected mayor, and the democratically appointed chief of the Los Angeles Police Department (the famous LAPD).

Chapter Title

We may begin by stepping back for a moment. This book is about citizenship as a vocation. Therefore, when I began to write it, I expected that I would start winding it down, with appropriate observations and conclusions, under the heading of "Citizenship." After all, citizenship as a political role in modern society was my central concern. However, after writing most of the book, I decided to call this chapter "Common Sense."

What happened was that, using mainly American cases, I explored aspects of citizenship beyond the legal status which entitles a person to vote, to run for office and, if elected, to serve in that office. Then, unexpectedly, it struck me that, in order to do any of these things *well*, citizens must acquire and use "common sense." My suddenly noticing the need for common sense was not so much an analytic discovery as it was an observation of something important in life which we occasionally overlook because we are focused on other important things.

The sequence was as follows. Many thinkers have warned that democratic institutions in America aren't working well. I argued at the outset, however, in favor of changing the angle of analysis slightly, to say that the problem is not democracy itself but producing enough good citizenship to maintain and preserve that regime.

In other words, in some countries, democracy is not in great shape. But the underlying danger is that the vocation of citizenship may be delinquent, that its practice may not be *good* enough, because if citizenship is working *well*, democracy will follow and prosper.

That is why this book's title calls upon citizens to defend democracy. That is, they should stand up for government "by the many." In the modern world, most of us want to live in democratic states. Only voraciously power-hungry people, like Viktor Orban, Vladimir Putin, Marine Le Pen, Benjamin Netanyahu, and their supporters, don't.[2] Everyone else sees that democracy is a desirable aim of what sociologists call "modernity."

In Weber's terms, we know it won't hurt democracy if Scientists and Politicians will do their work well. Every bit, large or small, helps. But the ultimate defense of democracy depends on alert and ethically responsible Citizens. Historical examples of that imperative abound, especially from the 1920s and 1930s, when many European citizens permitted (but not intentionally) fascist regimes to arise because they, the citizens, were indifferent to, or too late in recognizing, this basic truth of modern political life.

Therefore, in my analysis, I reached a side step from democracy to citizenship on this point. But then I took another side step because I began to see, after exploring historical developments and what many thinkers have said about them, that effective (good) citizenship is unlikely to emerge under present conditions.

Impossible?

Along this line, I eventually concluded that, in today's circumstances, effective citizenship across the board may be an impossible goal for many people. Consequently, it is a non-starter which must be explained.

---

[2] I refrain from including Donald Trump in this list. I am not sure he would insist on living in a democratic state. Still, in his case, to be on or off the list here depends on how one defines democracy, and there is insufficient space to argue that point here.

To that end, we can see that, since the Enlightenment, there are Scientists, Politicians, and Citizens in modern society. All of these are necessary but, while the first two stand on their own by formulating fairly clear understandings of who they are and what they are supposed to do, the thinking of citizens, about who they are and how they should act, is muddled.

In the language of social science, I could describe the vocation of citizenship as a "dependent variable," where, in this case, good citizenship is dependent upon "common sense."[3] It does not matter much, though, which terms we use to make this point. In truth, whatever the vocabulary, good citizenship has always flowed from common sense.

A Dependent Variable

Why always? Because *good* citizenship has always looked different from country to country, starting, if you like, with Athens and Sparta, where good Athenians and good Spartans behaved differently. Both were fierce warriors on behalf of their city-states when necessary, in a dangerous neighborhood. But Athenians were more open-minded while Spartans were more military-minded.[4] Which means that good citizens in both places were made, not born.

To continue that thought, what is appropriate for America today is not necessarily appropriate, for example, in France or

---

[3] The common-sense requirement, described in other terms, but powerfully implicit, is a centerpiece of what Hannah Arendt posits as the good citizenship we need to save democracy. See Hannah Arendt, "Personal Responsibility under Dictatorship" (1964), in *Responsibility and Judgement* (New York: Schocken Books, 2003), pp. 17–48. The most reliable good citizens, she says, "will be the doubters and skeptics, not because skepticism is good or doubting wholesome, but because they are used to examine things and to make up their own minds." Furthermore, she says, "the precondition for this kind of judging is not a highly developed intelligence or sophistication in moral matters, but rather the disposition to live together explicitly with oneself, to have intercourse with oneself, that is, to be engaged in that silent dialogue between me and myself which, since Socrates and Plato, we usually call thinking." In which case, if information technology and today's marketplace for ideas both muddle our thinking, we are in very deep trouble.

[4] On Athens and Sparta, see Paul Rahe, *Republics Ancient and Modern*. Vol. I: *The Ancient Regime in Classical Greece* (Chapel Hill, NC: University of North Carolina Press, 1994). See also Peter Riesenberg, *Citizenship in the Western Tradition: Plato to Rousseau* (Chapel Hill, NC: University of North Carolina, 1992), esp. pp. 3–55.

Indonesia now, although there may be some overlap. In that sense, de Maistre was right when he said that he was acquainted with Frenchmen and Italians but not with "Man" as that person appears, abstractly, in Jefferson's proposition that "all men are created equal."[5]

Therefore, the practice of good citizenship requires commitment to common sense (based on "knowledge," not just "opinion") that relates to the distinctive needs of one's own country, and that may be irrelevant to the different needs of another country.

Or, ultimately, based on details recognized by common sense, good citizenship requires commitment to wide-ranging "Stories" in Postman's view, which may be appropriate for one's own community but not for others.

In Sum

We can rephrase that. The key "wherewithal" for good citizenship is common sense, which enables us to choose what is appropriate for ourselves and our neighbors, in the form of the right Story.[6]

But at the moment, we don't have the necessary common sense and we haven't built it into a serviceable Story.[7] And that is because, as we saw, "the information system" is dysfunctional to the point where it produces neither.

Cutting-edge scholars, sometimes using terms different from, but consistent with, those I am using in this essay, agree on that point. Thus Byung-Chul Han, in *The Crisis of Narratives*, concludes that too much digitalized information, transmitted to us via smartphones, amounts to a "heap" of "meaningless" facts that are too "transparent" and therefore cannot be shaped into "narratives" but foster "disenchantment" in the modern world.[8]

---

[5] See Chapter 7, n. 22.
[6] See Chapter 7, n. 28.
[7] Note that neither of these has to be right, correct, or accurate. Both simply have to be sensible and shared to produce a good effect. It annoys many thinkers, though, among them scholars and journalists, if common sense and large narratives are not right, not correct, and/or not accurate.
[8] Han offers a complete theory of large-scale narratives and storytelling based on the academic disciplines of art, philosophy, and literature, and especially citing Walter Benjamin, the German-Jewish cultural critic. See Byung-Chul Han, *The Crisis of Narratives* (New

Community

The matter is additionally complicated. Before extending these propositions about information, let us note that, if the point of good citizenship is to know what is good for the "community," Americans are paused today at a moment when it is not clear that there actually *is* an all-embracing community within the borders of the country known as the United States.[9]

Other writers will explore this matter thoroughly, but three of its dimensions are already obvious. First, in a sense, there is simply no overall community among nominally linked American citizens because the present economy is quite different from what preceded it. Thus, (a) it has favored with prosperity the technologically advanced cities of the East Coast, West Coast, and a small number of similarly advanced cities in between. And, (b) especially in the South and Midwest, it has stranded a "hinterland" of rural villages, towns, and small cities, (c) which are less profitable than the big cities within a world of long supply chains, often carried on container ships from port to port, and (d) which tend to suffer from backsliding because the hinterland's formerly

---

York: Polity, 2024), *passim*, but esp. p. 3: "The cause of the narrative crisis in modernity is deluge of information. The spirit of narrative is suffocated by the flood." See also p. 50: "Big data merely discloses *correlations* between things. Correlations ... do not allow us to understand anything." See also p. 62: "The narratives on which the neoliberal regime is based prevent the formation of community. The neoliberal narrative of performance turns every individual into an *entrepreneur of his own self* ... It does not produce a *we*." See also Kathryn Crammer Brownell, *24/7 Politics: Cable Television & The Fragmenting of America from Watergate to Fox News* (Princeton: Princeton University Press, 2023), esp. pp. 1–41, 305–311, where Brownell proposes that cable television stations "entertained rather than informed viewers," and "generated profits but not knowledge of public affairs."

[9] This is a point where, as I noted earlier, the information system acts as an ecology, in which everything is related to everything else. Thus the technology (medium) encourages people to dislike one another; this encourages what is called identity politics; and that sort of politics encourages insular groups (which make incompatible claims in politics and education) to arise and their members to pursue self-realization rather than community. Such links are the major theme in William Egginton, *The Splintering of the American Mind* (New York: Bloomsbury, 2018), *passim*. The same loss of community is described by Amy Chua, *Political Tribes: Group Instinct and the Fate of Nations* (New York: Penguin, 2018), which argues, *passim*, that there used to be a sense in America of national identity which transcended different groups, which she divides lately into tribes of Right and Left. Fierce political conflict between those tribes "is tearing the country apart ... [therefore] America is in danger of losing ... [a sense of] who we are" (p. 166).

successful factories have been hit hard by deindustrialization and the outsourcing of many good jobs to poorer countries.[10]

Therefore, in a way, economic circumstances have divided the United States into two sets of citizens who are not quite united. This is not as easy to see today as when a former division precipitated the Civil War. At that time, slave-owners were gathered in the South, while free citizens lived mainly (but not entirely) in the North and West. This time, the contiguity is mostly gone.

The second divisive factor is that sentiments of community and shared interests, to the extent that some or both still exist, are prevented from holding together, or bringing back together, the country's citizens because of the Electoral College. On this score, when a popular majority, scattered through all the states, is still available, it may not be able to express its preferences via the college and therefore may fail to gain control of the Executive Branch of government, with all the powers that follow.[11]

This second development has been aggravated by ideological fervor in the Republican Party, as we have seen. But it is also an institutional roadblock that cannot be overcome because thinly populated

---

[10] See Phil A. Neel, *Hinterland: America's New Landscape of Class and Conflict* (London: Reaktion Books, 2018). See also Wendell Berry, "Local Knowledge in the Age of Information," in *American Conservatism: Reclaiming an Intellectual Tradition*, ed. Andrew J. Bacevich (New York: Library of America, 2020), pp. 481–492. Using a vocabulary different from but complementary to that used by Neel, Berry describes "centers" and "peripheries," where urban centers based on science, finance, and long supply lines control rural peripheries to the point where local knowledge and protection of the land – in agriculture, mines, forestry, and fisheries – is disappearing and environmental disasters are multiplying. This while people from the centers and the peripheries are less and less likely to know each other personally and exchange ideas. Sometimes economists, too, use binaries to describe centers and peripheries within countries and/or within the world economy. For example, see discussions of "the Global North" exploiting "the Global South" in Grace Blakeley, *Vulture Capitalism: Corporate Crimes, Backdoor Bailouts, and the Death of Freedom* (New York: Astria, 2024), *passim*.
[11] Andrew S. Hacker and Paul Pierson, *American Amnesia: How the War on Government Led Us to Forget What Made America Prosper* (New York: Simon & Schuster, 2016). Hacker and Pierson argue, *passim*, that many Americans have forgotten how government action in previous generations fostered the creation and maintenance of prosperity in America. They believe (esp. pp. 256–259) that it can be restored, but only if the power of the Electoral College will not be used by rural Republicans to thwart a national majority – mostly city-based – capable of fixing the new economy so that it will distribute income and benefits more equally. (Hacker and Pierson are political scientists and do not use the term "hinterland," which is more deployed by geographers.)

states, pursuing power in Washington, are unwilling to permit enactment of a constitutional Amendment that would abolish the Electoral College and, while divided somewhat by mixed government, enable a national popular majority to invariably rule.

Third, a demagogue of extraordinary rhetorical talent named Donald Trump appeared in America. He assiduously nourishes cultural hostility between red and blue populations, praising the insularity of hinterland dwellers while condemning "the elites" and "the swamp" of more successful and sometimes more educated coastal and high-tech Americans, where "Make America Great Again" is Trump's way of praising the hinterland for what it once was and belittling people who want to look forward.[12]

Trump himself, for the moment, is an exceptional cross for his victims to bear. But there is also a matter of equivalence here. The Electoral College is (a) an *institution* which uses longstanding rules to hold back a potential reinvigoration of an American community, whereas Trump is (b) an *individual* who does the same thing by exercising his special talent for exploiting the information system – via trash talk, trolling, gaslighting, vulgar accusations, and social media snippets – to turn presidential elections into an entertaining reality show where the audience eventually votes for a survivor with little or no connection to reality outside the show.[13]

On this score, Kamala Harris clearly scorned Donald Trump's MAGA promises, which were about doing something that would transform America into what it once was. That is, what it will be "again."

---

[12] See Matt Grossman and David A. Hopkins, *Polarized by Degrees: How the Diploma Divide and the Cultural War Transformed American Politics* (New York: Cambridge University Press, 2024).

[13] During the 2024 election campaign, I thought Trump was enormously entertaining. You could watch him speak every night; his performance was exciting and never the same; he never stumbled; he had an answer for everything. His assistants could not get him to "stay on message." But not knowing what outrage he would promote, night after night, was, in a way, the major attraction. Now, compare Harris' appearances with those of Trump. If you heard one of her speeches, you heard them all. It was no contest in terms of entertainment. Her performance was a one-off. His was a continuing reality show. The two candidates were simply not in the same game. And, of course, Trump continued his entertainment game after the 2024 election, taking office with a daily barrage of outrageous statements and florid signing ceremonies which were picked up by news broadcasts, newspaper reporting, and internet messaging day after day. In fact, what Americans now receive and think of as "daily news" really amounts to a continual melodrama (or soap opera) that could be called "Trump's Life."

Instead, her campaign slogan insisted that "We're Not Going Back." That is, we, including Blacks and women, are not going *again* to where we *were*.

He replied to her, also clearly, with a figurative middle finger, calling her "a stupid person," "retarded," "lazy," and asking "Does she drink? Is she on drugs?"[14] And she, the Black and the woman, lost the 2024 election, for whatever that means.

Common Sense

Let's return to my claim that, presently, we cannot define good citizenship. Even apart from cultural and economic divisions, which divide the overall community that American citizens might admire, those citizens cannot know how to relate constructively to others if they do not know what the others are thinking and will support. Yet the information system, and especially social media and "news feeds," while relentlessly fragmenting and fracturing the nation, makes that all but impossible.

Remember, then, that I started this project by asking what we can know about the vocation of Citizenship, which Weber did not discuss after he wrote about the vocations of Politics and Science. Now I admit that I cannot completely carry out the mission.

It is not that I can't propose a philosophical answer to the original question of how citizens should behave.[15] It is that existing conditions, in the Post-Truth Society, make such an answer irrelevant. As Plato said, on the basis of philosophical *deduction*, we should choose to be ruled by philosopher kings. But, like Aristotle pointed out, on the basis of philosophical *induction*, there are no such kings available to serve us in the real world.[16]

---

[14] See https://apnews.com/article/trump-kamala-lazy-trope-stereotype-4c2ded1046e492c5d24c7382245d0f7b.

[15] I already did that, before smartphones were invented, in David Ricci, *Good Citizenship in America* (New York: Cambridge University Press, 2004), pp. 253–294.

[16] After the Greeks, the Ten Commandments told Westerners how to behave well. But even those excellent injunctions, widely praised as sublime moral principles backed up by divine authority, don't inspire enough citizens enough of the time. So, philosophy is also available – say, from Kant and Rawls, Burke and Goldwater, Reagan, Falwell, Gingrich, Irving Kristol, and George Will. But it is not, by itself, sufficiently effective, as Aristotle observed.

In short, more than 2,300 years ago, Aristotle knew that we need to use common sense (although maybe along with some philosophy) to organize a safe, stable, and decent regime based on widespread citizenship. Therefore, he recommended a "mixed government" which would fashion practical compromises between different classes of citizens.

To that end, America's Founders took his advice. As Madison said in Federalist Paper No. 51 on checks and balances, "If angels were to govern men, no government would be necessary." So much for Plato. Whereupon, also in No. 51, "Ambition must be made to counteract ambition." There we can hear echoes of Aristotle, Polybius, Locke, and Montesquieu.

Puzzles and Problems

If my original inquiry about citizenship cannot be completed satisfactorily, what should worriers do, since good citizenship today is a matter that is obviously and hugely important, even while the common sense that citizens need, to recognize its parameters, seems less and less available?

The situation looks intractable. So I suggest, first of all, that we will be frustrated less than we are presently, if we will decide that attaining good citizenship is a "problem" rather than a "puzzle." As I have explained in previous books, a puzzle is like when we open a box we just bought and which contains 1,000 jigsaw pieces of a picture of Donald Duck. We assume that the puzzle has a solution, even though it may be very hard to find. Consequently, we get to work.

But a problem is like when we try to fit together 1,000 jigsaw pieces from a Donald Duck box which we buy at a toy store and which mistakenly contains 500 pieces of Donald Duck and another 500 pieces of Mickey Mouse. We don't know that a mistake has been made. Therefore, we get to work and, no matter how hard we try to assemble the pieces, we achieve only frustration.

Eventually, we will discover why the pieces don't fit together, and we will understand that we are confronting not a "puzzle" but a "problem." A problem, however, has no solution. It is a difficult situation that we simply must live with, hard as that may be. Therefore, we should try to confront it as best we can and not make it worse.

The example may sound trite to some readers. I suggest, then, that they compare the information situation around us to when printing books started in a big way, around 1450, thereby enabling an enormous increase in the circulation of information, like today. Here was a "medium" (movable type in printing presses using paper) that began to change the world by generating millions of books, including vernacular Bibles, and thereby breaking the Catholic Church's power, long exercised in the name of true Christianity, over the thinking of most Western Europeans. Therefore, around 1560, to protect its place in society, the Church responded to stepped-up printing by establishing the Index (the *Index Librorum Prohibitorum* in Latin) which warned ordinary people against reading from a list of publications the Church thought were dangerous.[17]

That didn't work, and now an analogous challenge arises from smartphones (connected to the internet) because, like Gutenberg's printing presses, they convey to us unmanageable quantities of ideas, more and less sensible, and piles of information, or disinformation, which muddle our thinking and therefore impede our search for good citizenship.[18]

Accordingly, their presence in our society constitutes a "problem" and not a "puzzle." At the moment, regrettably, this problem seems to have no easy solution. The Church told people to stop looking at certain books. They didn't stop. Try telling your children or friends

---

[17] A few of the authors whose works, singly or in whole, were banned, included Machiavelli, Bruno, Grotius, Hobbes, Calvin, Descartes, Montaigne, Spinoza, Locke, Defoe, Montesquieu, Voltaire, Diderot, Hume, Rousseau, Gibbon, Condorcet, Kant, Bentham, Heine, and J. S. Mill.

[18] Daniel Levitin, *The Organized Mind: Thinking Straight in the Age of Information Overload* (New York: Dutton, 2016), p. 6, reminds us: "In 2011, Americans took in five times as much information every day as they did in 1986 – the equivalent of 175 newspapers. During our leisure time, not counting work, each of us processes 34 gigabytes or 100,000 [sic] words every day. The world's 21,274 television stations produce 85,000 hours of original programming every day as we watch an average of 5 hours of television each day, the equivalent of 20 gigabytes of audio video images. That's not counting YouTube, which uploads 6,000 hours of video every hour." Moreover, p. 15: "The amount of scientific information we've discovered in the last twenty years is more than all the discoveries up to that point, from the beginning of language. Five exabytes (5×10^{18}) of new data were produced in January 2012 alone – that's 50,000 times the number of words in the entire Library of Congress." Furthermore, p. 20: "Conflicting viewpoints are more readily available than ever, and in many cases, they are disseminated by people who have no regard for facts or truth. Many of us find that we don't know whom to believe, what is true, what has been modified, and what has been vetted."

to stop looking at their phones.[19] Most of them won't. We know that their addiction is going to change the world, maybe for the worse, if it has not done so already. Yet we cannot talk them out of looking.[20]

Show Business

Now, if there is a problem, we should consider, in the short run, that Weber's ethic of responsibility – which obliges us to check out what political actors are likely to do and what will happen as a result – is the key to confronting "problems." We want to live in democratic states, therefore we are going to have Politicians in our modern midst, said Weber. And some of those will be demagogues, like Donald Trump, who will woo citizens shamelessly in the Age of the Smartphone.

In this situation, Weber's advice was that, where Politicians of every sort are legitimate modern characters, we should calculate the consequences of voting for this or that candidate.[21] Such advice is eminently sensible, but we will have to expand on it considerably if we are to understand the significance of Donald Trump as an unprecedented sort of candidate within Weber's category of Politicians.

Causes

Remember, Weber thought of politicians as promoting "causes" related to current national circumstances. In his day, some of those causes were varieties of nationalism, imperialism, liberalism, socialism,

---

[19] If you need help on that, refer them to Jaron Lanier, *Ten Arguments for Deleting Your Social Media Accounts Right Now* (New York: Henry Holt, 2018).
[20] The size of this current problem is impossible to measure, but a sense of how much dislocation and confusion it is causing can be gained by considering how the Gutenberg Revolution upended so much of European life. See Elizabeth L. Eisenstein, *The Printing Press as an Agent of Change: Communications and Cultural Transformations in Early-Modern Europe* (Cambridge, UK: Cambridge University Press, 1982). Like in today's "information system," printing an endless flood of books caused established sources of information – like Aristotle, Galen, Ptolemy, the Catholic Church, and more – to clash with the ideas of new authors. In the circumstances, a great many people didn't know what to think.
[21] I already prescribed that ethic, more or less, in David M. Ricci, *Post-Truth American Politics: False Stories and Current Crises* (New York: Cambridge University Press, 2023). I also recommended it years ago in David M. Ricci, *The Tragedy of Political Science: Politics, Scholarship, and Democracy* (New Haven: Yale University Press, 1984).

communism, and so forth. And you could, presumably, talk at least somewhat sensibly about some of the likely results of those causes.

In the case of Trump, however, the candidate, (1) who was not originally a politician, (2) entered the political arena, and (3) performed there not as if it were an arena for "causes" but as if it were a place for doing "show business." That is, this candidate all along campaigned, very deliberately, as if he were starring in a reality show similar to his 14-year television bonanza called *The Apprentice*.

In short, Trump is present in Weber's category of Politicians but he has always been a "showman" in his work, which has always been designed to generate, over time, mostly a good deal of noise and excitement. Therefore, as a New Yorker, he would fit comfortably into the cast of *Guys and Dolls*, among flashy characters like Nathan Detroit, Sky Masterson, and Harry the Horse.[22]

I know, I know. To say that Trump belongs in *Guys and Dolls* is to exaggerate. But surely there is a sense in which Donald Trump, since descending the escalator, comes across as someone from fiction rather than reality, a leading man rather than a leader of men. And that is why pundits, such as Thomas Friedman and Paul Krugman, find it difficult, if not impossible, to grasp and describe exactly what Trump's "cause" is.[23] What does he really stand for? Who knows? David Bromwich expresses the research dilemma on this score when he observes that "Anything one says [about Trump] is sure to be displaced by some entirely unexpected thing the president does between writing and publication."[24]

---

[22] It is easy to see how Trump would blend in among the characters in *Guys and Dolls*. It is harder to see why 77 million Americans thought the country could be governed properly by someone like Harry the Horse, who appears in a Damon Runyon short story here: https://hackneybooks.co.uk/books/88/136/ButchMindsTheBaby.html.

[23] I am using Weber's term of "cause" here to observe that Trump does not seem to have one. American critics say the same thing in other terms, such as that Trump has presented no "coherent plan" that would explain how to "align America" with the "biggest trends in the world today" in order to "thrive" in the twenty-first century. See Thomas Friedman, "A Great Unraveling is Under Way," March 11, 2025, at www.nytimes.com/by/thomas-l-friedman. On Paul Krugman's inability to discern any rational explanation and/or consistent basis for Trump's promotion of variable tariff rates against imports from different countries into America, see Ezra Klein, "Paul Krugman on the 'Biggest Trade Shock in History,'" at www.nytimes.com/2025/04/05/opinion/ezra-klein-podcast-paul-krugman.html.

[24] David Bromwich, *American Breakdown: The Trump Years and How They Befell Us* (New York: Verso, 2019), p. 89.

Whatever it is, Trump's cause certainly does not resemble what earlier Republican presidents have said and done, although Ronald Reagan, long trained by Hollywood, also consciously acted on his way to the White House and after he got there.[25] Of course, Trump is nominally a Politician because he ran for office and won. But in his apparent dedication more to acting than to substance, he is also like no other Politician ever seen on America's political stage.

For example, unlike the Bushes, Clintons, McCain, Obama, Romney, Biden, and other modern candidates, Trump campaigned for the presidency without issuing position papers. The result is that it was never clear, by formal commitment, what he planned to do if elected. Therefore, trying to discern a "cause" in the sum total of his various promises, assurances, boasts, animosities, grunts, scowls, grimaces, squints, and tweets, has always required endless speculation without solid and reliable testimony.

Whatever he may have seemed to commit himself to, in written or spoken statements from time to time, was often contradicted as early as the next day, withdrawn, or simply ignored.[26] Which was not

---

[25] Ronald Reagan consciously performed as an actor in the role of American president. And some "supporting players" – such as Michael Deaver, Edwin Meese, and James Baker – latched on to him and his career and coached him, while they were in White House posts, to generate policy achievements depending on how well he played that role. See Bob Schieffer and Gary Paul Gates, *The Acting President: Ronald Reagan and the Supporting Players Who Helped Him Create the Illusion That Held America Spellbound* (New York: E. P. Dutton, 1989), *passim*, but esp. pp. 164–190.

[26] Difficulties on this score are endless. For example, on March 4, 2025, Trump told Congress that "it has been stated by many" that his presidency is "the most successful in the history of our nation," with George Washington trailing at second. He did not say who the "many" are. Then he observed that "government databases list 4.7 million Social Security numbers from people aged 100 to 109 years old. It [sic] lists 3.6 million people from ages 110 to 119. I don't know any of them ... I know some people that are rather elderly but not quite that elderly. 3.47 million people from ages 120 to 129, 3.9 million people from ages 130 to 139. 3.5 million people from ages 140 to 149. And money is being paid to many of them." What are the "databases" Trump is talking about? Do they simply list all people, alive or now dead, who have ever received Social Security? And if the implication is that the SSA is sending monthly checks to "many" of these people now, what is the breakdown by age? Like in the previous assertion linking Trump's name to George Washington, the term "many" has no exact relation to reality. But, in perfect Trumpist fashion, it makes no claim to literal truth but promotes a hint at wrongdoing, which cannot be faulted as a lie because, grammatically, it does not amount to a factual proposition. The bottom line here is that serious researchers find, in the archive of Donald Trump's self-advertisements, that there is little testimony to anything beyond hint, insinuation, aspersion, implication, innuendo, and the like. In which case, what is really there

surprising, because Trump was, in fact, always entertaining rather than educating.[27]

In the light of such muddling, to use our vocabulary, one journalist who interviewed Trump as a reality television actor and later as a retired president, concluded, shortly before the 2024 election, that Trump "is not a politician. There's no way to ask him about governing. He's not able to govern ... He doesn't care about the specifics of the plot during his time in the White House – he just wants to get renewed for another season."[28]

Charisma

We can see the same situation in terms of "charisma," which very much intrigued Weber, and which he credited with having the power to introduce new ideas, or new maneuvers, into established institutions and practices. Charisma may explain much of Trump's ability to win elections in the sense that, like Ronald Reagan, he personally charms his admirers.[29] But it still does not identity his "cause."

We can sharpen this point on charisma because, even without being able to consult Trumpist position papers, it is possible to describe many a rich American's outlook underlying what Trump says

resembles what Churchill said in 1941 about Russia being "a riddle wrapped in a mystery inside an enigma." Social science is hard pressed to investigate such a thing.

[27] Thus when he met Ukrainian president Volodymyr Zelensky in the Oval Office in February of 2025, there were important people and reporters in the room, whereupon, before conversation between the two presidents started, Trump remarked to the people present (and to their cameras) that the meeting "is going to be great television." That is, this would be a great opportunity to entertain viewers. See https://thehill.com/homenews/administration/5169464-trump-zelensky-great-television/. Of course, when Churchill and Roosevelt met to discuss military strategy during World War II, none of their discussions were broadcast.

[28] Ramin Setoodeh, *Apprentice in Wonderland: How Donald Trump and Mark Burnett Took America Through the Looking Glass* (New York: Harper, 2024), p. 220.

[29] Non-scholars rarely use academic words like "charisma" in everyday conversation. But here is a perfect description of charismatic action from Harrison Fields, Special Assistant to the President, in April 2025: "Traditional presidencies [like Obama, Biden] have failed to bring meaningful change to the ways of Washington, and the president [Trump] is committed to upending the entrenched bureaucracy." Which is exactly how Weber, in sociological terms, described the "charismatic" politician as capable of shattering the "iron cage" of bureaucracy. Fields is quoted in Michael S. Schmidt, "In Trump's Second Term: Retribution Comes in Many Forms," at www.nytimes.com/2025/04/07/us/politics/trump-biden-law-firms-revenge.html.

from time to time, but not coherently. Thus, if we argue that he promotes a pro-capitalist point of view – which is nowadays called neoliberalism – then his not being clear about that confirms what some economists have said about neoliberal tenets being vague.[30]

For example, Philip Mirowski in *Never Let a Serious Crisis Go to Waste: How Neoliberalism Survived the Financial Meltdown* found no formal catechism of those ideas, which together he called the "Neoliberal Thought Collective."[31] And James Kwak in *Economism: Bad Economics and the Rise of Inequality* claimed that pro-capitalist ideas, which he called "economism," are influential, especially because they reflect an "unspoken worldview."[32]

Nevertheless, what Trump's speeches show, over many years, is that he sees life as a Hobbesian war of all against all, wherein nations try mainly to gain security and economic success at the expense of other nations. That is one implication of his slogan "America First."[33] Therefore, so far at least, in 2025 he seems

---

[30] His appointees are sometimes (but not always) more intelligible than he is. For example, Secretary of Education Linda McMahon, previously CEO of World Wrestling Entertainment, Inc., was asked on CNBC about her department's dispute with Harvard University. She insisted that the case, which Harvard took to court, was about anti-Semitism on campus and therefore belonged in the category of a dispute over civil rights, which she seeks to maintain. As for the government's demand that Harvard will hire professors according to a government standard of "viewpoint diversity" or lose billions of dollars in government research grants, she insisted that the money issue was a matter of "negotiations." That is, she said explicitly that the government made a negotiating offer and expected Harvard to make a counter-offer, perhaps leading to smaller reductions of government grants. This is a common practice in the business world. One person makes a first offer, a second person responds, and then the two sides continue to haggle, like in a Middle East market or *souk* for oriental carpets. It has no proper place in one of the world's greatest research universities, where the institutional aim, after the Enlightenment and working on the basis of Reason and Science, is to approach the truth and not the cheapest rug price. On the Trump Administration's view of Harvard research grants, see www.cnbc.com/video/2025/04/22/education-secretary-mcmahon-on-harvard-lawsuit-this-is-about-civil-rights-not-freedom-of-speech.html. On the national importance of scientific research, in the Enlightenment tradition, at Harvard University, see www.nytimes.com/interactive/2025/06/22/upshot/harvard-funding-cuts.html.

[31] Philip Mirowski, *Never Let a Serious Crisis Go to Waste: How Neoliberalism Survived the Financial Meltdown* (London: Verso, 2013), pp. 27–88. Here, neoliberalism is described as a "Neoliberal Thought Collective" embracing a variety of principles and proponents.

[32] James Kwak, *Economism: Bad Economics and the Rise of Inequality* (New York: Vintage, 2021), pp. 6–17.

[33] The point of this slogan is not just "America" first, but exactly what *kind* of America should be first. There is a wide-ranging understanding among some right-wingers that

intent on achieving these gains (1) by raising tariff barriers behind which some Americans will be able to do business more profitably than today and (2) by reducing military alliance obligations so that some Americans will wind up paying lower taxes than they pay now to support the Pentagon.

Obfuscation

But Trump does not clearly and repeatedly describe the outcome he hopes to achieve as more "wealth" for the country. Perhaps that is because he does not want to discuss who will acquire large portions from "the nation" when it obtains additional wealth. After all, a redistribution of the country's *current* wealth – even without higher tariffs and while maintaining America's international alliances – could provide comfortable and safe lives for many poor and/or precarious citizens such as service workers and older Americans.[34] Meanwhile, it is mainly corporation shareholders who will benefit from higher tariffs and the already wealthy who are benefitting the most from Republican tax cuts.

Public discussion of such matters was last conducted intensively in America during the New Deal. And historians remind us that businessmen and McCarthyites worked hard, before and after World War II, to shut that discussion down.[35] People like Donald Trump and his associates, in or out of politics, are not keen to open

---

America is in decline because liberals have fostered atheism, big government and the "managerial elite." For example, see Auron MacIntyre, *The Total State: How Liberal Democracies Become Tyrannies* (New York: Regnery, 2024). MacIntyre enjoins us to learn from political philosophers like Bertrand de Jouvenel, Joseph de Maistre, Gaetano Mosca, and Carl Schmitt rather than the Founders. Together with them, MacIntyre regards the Enlightenment, based on science and reason, which inspired the Founders, as destroying the foundations – in family life, in religion, and in tradition – of a successful political regime. We do not know if Donald Trump reads such books, or any other books. But some of what he does, or tries to do – like punishing Columbia, Johns Hopkins, Harvard, and other universities because they are liberal flagships – fits comfortably into that "cause," or "vision," of what he does *not* want America to be.

[34] An argument along these lines can recommend improving the social and economic conditions in America which are described by Ezra Klein and Derek Thompson, *Abundance* (New York: Avid Reader Press, 2025).

[35] See Kim Phillips-Fine, *Invisible Hands: The Businessmen's Crusade against the New Deal* (New York: Norton, 2009).

it up again. But for invitations to renew exactly that debate, against the professional inclinations of many mainstream economists, see Thomas Piketty's *Capital in the 21st Century*, and Nat Dyer's *Ricardo's Dream: How Economists Forgot the Real World and Led Us Astray.*[36]

In this sense, Trump is a kind of politician whom Weber just did not foresee – not that I blame him – because (1) Trump is acclaimed, voluntarily, by a great many citizens even though, in a way, he is not leading them anywhere in particular because he doesn't believe in anything but applause and winning.[37] And because, (2) in a way, he operates in the political arena but does so chiefly to conduct a riveting spectacle rather than to pursue coherent policy aims.

And because (3) he is making sure that the show will go on rather than that it will arrive anywhere in particular, which we can see when (4) he occasionally announces policy goals – like building a wall between the United States and Mexico, or ending the Ukraine war even before he took office, or expelling more than two million Palestinians from Gaza and turning that territory into a tourist riviera or "freedom zone," or annexing Greenland – but does not move steadily and efficiently to achieve those goals.[38]

---

[36] Thomas Piketty, *Capital* (orig., 2014; Cambridge, MA: Harvard University Press, 2017) and Nat Dyer, *Ricardo's Dream* (Bristol: Bristol University Press, 2024). For professional economists who are not looking for a conversation about redistribution, see Robert Lucas, "Of the tendencies that are harmful to sound economics, the most seductive, and in my opinion the most poisonous, is to focus on questions of distribution." Lucas was awarded the Nobel Prize in Economics for 1995. He is quoted in Avner Offer and Gabriel Soderberg, *The Nobel Factor: The Prize in Economics, Social Democracy, and the Market Turn* (Princeton: Princeton University Press, 2016), p 36. See also, against redistribution, N. Gregory Mankiw, "Defending the One Percent," *Journal of Economic Perspectives*, 27(3) (2013): 21–34. Mankiw is a former head of the Harvard University Economics Department and a former Chairman of the Council of Economic Advisors to President George W. Bush.

[37] I leave aside his constant pursuit of personal enrichment while in office. He apparently does believe in that. But it is not exactly a public policy worth discussing here.

[38] If we assume that, in an important sense, Trump actually does "show business" rather than "politics," I am not expressing partisan political criticism when I observe that, in 2024, he promised voters that he will halve the price of energy within eighteen months of taking office and that he will also deport all illegal immigrants, whose number is now estimated at 11 million. These are highly unrealistic aims, given conditions on the ground, and it is not likely that any president can do either of these two things. On the other hand, scholars could argue that such aims were not really promoted as political intentions but as show business glitter.

A Tale of Woe

I have described how Weber's sociology suggests useful insights into a situation shaped by Scientists, Politicians, and Citizens in America today. But, with Donald Trump in the White House, we cannot recycle Weber's advice to make these three kinds of modern people fit together safely and prosperously by considering what he called "causes" and how to respond to them properly.

Nevertheless, with Trump continuing to bombard us with venomous tweets, and with Elon Musk waving a chain saw maniacally, we should think about where all this tri-partite modernity is taking us. America may produce faster computer chips than China, and it may invent more nimble artificial intelligence programs. But are those ultimate ends, in the sense of being inherently worthy? What about the quality of American life, which flows from how the nation's citizens interact among themselves, with other countries, and with the global environment that sustains us all?

The speculation we need on that score is not purely hypothetical but at least somewhat grounded on existing facts having to do with, as we have seen, the ever-growing demand for entertainment in our society. And to the extent that that demand takes center stage in public life, we can project our regret over it, and fear of what it is doing to us, by telling a tale.

Rachel Carson

Rachel Carson inspired me in this regard. As a biologist, she foresaw great danger in the country's extensive use of agricultural poisons. Therefore, she composed a tale in 1962 wherein she described a "Silent Spring" that will descend upon the land after birds like robin redbreasts and bald eagles will die off from heavy use of pesticides like DDT. With this tale, which she called a "fable," Carson warned that scientific agriculture, which had come to be regarded as a normal practice in American life, was on its way to producing a national disaster.[39]

---

[39] Rachel Carson, *Silent Spring* (Boston: Houghton Mifflin, 1962).

With Carson in mind, we can recall that the essay you are holding, as I explained in earlier chapters, projects not an academic "theory" but a collection of analytic "terms" that frame useful understandings of how democracy and citizenship developed in America. From that collection, a dark and foreboding tale about American democracy almost writes itself, starting with the fact that, for generations, various politicians have offered music, slogans, pamphlets, parades, yard signs, bumper stickers, and speeches to lead empowered citizens in this policy direction or that.

A New Pied Piper

We can regard these men – they were mostly men – as Pipers after the legendary thirteenth-century Pied Piper, who lured away from their parents the children of Hamelin, a small town in what is now Germany. This colorful and talented performer, who was a skilled rat catcher, was angry at some of Hamelin's parents who, behaving like medieval versions of Donald Trump, skipped paying his wages.[40] So he lured their children into leaving the town by *entertaining* them with music played on his "pipe," which was probably a flute.

Later, during and after the American Revolution, American Pipers (aka Weber's newly invented Politicians) did not *play* pipes but *talked* to other Americans. Thus James Madison's, Alexander Hamilton's, and John Jay's "Federalist Paper" newspaper articles (1787–1788), Andrew Jackson's "First Inaugural Address" (1833), Daniel Webster's Senate speech "The Constitution and the Union" (1850), John C. Calhoun's *A Disquisition on Government* (1851), and Illinois debates between Stephen Douglas and Abraham Lincoln (1858). The aim there was *education*, that is, to discuss with citizens what the political situation was and what the American Pipers proposed to do if elected to, or already serving in, public office.[41]

---

[40] On Trump not paying workmen and contractors, see www.usatoday.com/story/news/politics/elections/2016/06/09/donald-trump-unpaid-bills-republican-president-laswuits/85297274/.

[41] Politicians like Lincoln and Douglas were *also* entertaining, but their main objective was *education*, not entertainment.

Later still came the rise of advertising, public relations, and propaganda, whereby talk in many realms became increasingly distorted, where the practice of deliberately promoting only some facts, while framing them attractively and persuasively, entered American public life at the expense of candid, even if turbulent, political education.

The new work of selling, and of shifting commodity demand from people's *needs* to their *wants*, saved industrial capitalism from overproduction before World War II. Later, it validated "consumerism," which united most Republicans and many Democrats around the concept of economic growth, which is the process of constantly increasing commercial production so that, in the name of freedom of choice, the world of commodities will expand endlessly.[42]

Hence, marketing produced material gains for many people. Therefore, you can learn how to do it nowadays in prestigious business schools like Wharton at the University of Pennsylvania, which is Donald Trump's alma mater.[43] But the same marketing, which does not insist on truth and integrity, also contributed to how America slid into becoming a post-truth society.

In that society, Science and Reason, two pillars of the Enlightenment, are used to help many Pipers today – say via survey research and focus groups – to manipulate the thinking of millions of citizens. Furthermore, in post-truth society, politics is less about *education* than it is about *entertainment*, because everyone is competing to attract followers as effectively as the original Pied Piper enticed the children of Hamelin.

In the circumstances, an outstanding Piper named Donald Trump came down the escalator. He was a demagogue no less than

---

[42] The post-World War II justification for capitalism as freedom of choice appeared famously in Milton Friedman, *Capitalism and Freedom* (Chicago: University of Chicago Press, 1962). For historical perspective on this understanding of consumerism (as an American way of life characterized by freedom of choice), see Steve Fraser, *The Age of Conscience: The Life and Death of American Resistance to Organized Wealth and Power* (New York: Little Brown, 2015), pp. 302-323. See also Sarah Churchwell, *Behold America: The Entangled History of "America First" and "The American Dream"* (New York: Basic Books, 2018), esp. pp. 267-283, on the post-World War II shift of American politicians and thinkers from regarding American exceptionalism as maintaining democracy and equality to their championing it as providing growth and prosperity.

[43] The quality of Trump's academic performance at Penn is not known publicly. See www.phillymag.com/news/2019/09/14/donald-trump-at-wharton-university-of-pennsylvania/.

Alcibiades in Athens, and his ability to entertain citizens imbued him with considerable charisma, suggesting that we should recognize him as a Great Piper, who is truly something special.

One thing is certain, I think. He was exceptionally attractive to his followers because the behavior he displayed looked to them "amusing," in Neil Postman's term, even though, as a local-culture form of entertainment, it might not have enlisted many followers elsewhere, say in Norway or New Zealand.

The Democrats

In 2016, Hillary Clinton probably did not understand any of this about Donald Trump. Apparently, she thought that the presidential campaign in that year was still, as for so long, about education. If that were so, then she, as a policy wonk, would explain government services and capabilities with such *panache* as to defeat the man whom she regarded as a real-estate shyster from Manhattan, who offered not modern *knowledge* of anything but, at best, *opinions* on everything.[44]

Then came Kamala Harris. She and various prominent Democratic "strategists," like James Carville, David Plouffe, and David Axelrod, had eight years after 2016 to learn what Hillary Clinton had not known about Donald Trump. But her 2024 campaign, which attracted fewer Democratic votes than she and Joe Biden received in 2020, suggested that Harris and her colleagues had not learned enough.

What Is Amusement?

Now let us step outside the box of routine analysis. The new move is this: where more demagogues whose strong suit is entertainment are likely to appear in the future, a new question arises about the relations between democracy and citizenship. It appears while we don't know exactly what is unfolding in American public life, because we cannot

---

[44] On March 28, 2025, Clinton was still speaking publicly in the policy wonk mode. See her article entitled "How Much Dumber Will This Get," at www.nytimes.com/2025/03/28/opinion/trump-hegseth-signal-chat.html.

predict the future for sure. But we do know a good deal about what is already here.

On that score, in a time dominated by smartphones, we know that Donald Trump on Election Day in 2024 had 80 million "followers" on X, Snapchat, Facebook, Instagram, and other social media platforms.[45] We also know that Trump's MAGA proposal, a sort of "shock and awe" vision, received 77 million votes when many of those admirers went to the polls in November of that year.

We don't know if all of the people who voted for Trump were among his phone followers. Still, putting our terms together, we should ask, using Postman's vocabulary, what is it about Trump that "amused" those people? That is, if it is realistic to say that Trump is more a powerful entertainer than a serious thinker, what do his followers, many of whom probably *did* vote for him, find amusing about what he does?[46]

I repeat. To ask about Postman's concept of amusement – not just the Woody Allen kind – is to step outside the box. It is the sort of question that would arise if we were to ask who attends professional wrestling matches. And if we were to wonder why some of us watch "tribal councils" in endless episodes of *Survivor*. And if we were to notice that many viewers were intensely loyal to Donald Trump's long-running drama *The Apprentice*, which was no more real than the soap opera *General Hospital*.

In other words – and let's talk about this plainly – if you know that what you are looking at is fake (in wrestling, it is called "kayfabe")

---

[45] Depending on which websites they cite and when, internet sources differ on how many followers they think Trump has or had at any specific time. I am using the number of 80 million, which appears in some of the internet estimates, only to make an analytical point. Therefore, it does not matter here exactly how many followers Trump had in 2024.

[46] Using a variety of terms, Chris Hayes, Neil Postman, and I complement one another. Along this line of analysis, but highlighting Trump's talent for getting attention, see Chris Hayes, *The Sirens' Call: How Attention Became the World's Most Endangered Resource* (New York: Penguin Press, 2025), *passim*, but esp. pp. 209–231. Hayes uses the term "attentional regime" to refer to "some set of rules, norms, or structures" that govern how attention is acquired in this or that society. By violating those restraints, says Hayes – for example, by openly disparaging other people, by repeatedly interrupting competitors on national television, and by posting and re-posting every sort of conspiracy theory – Trump does not focus his public talk on anything to the point of engaging in debate, as we would expect from a normal politician. Instead, says Hayes (p. 217), the president does "shtick" (which is a Yiddish term for comic routine) and "Borscht Belt insult comedy."

why are you there? For the fun of it, presumably. And fun is legitimate and permitted in life. It is even recommended, for many reasons.[47]

Having Fun

But if you know (1) that, at press conferences, Trump ducks and weaves, often untruthfully, or (2) that he will appoint so-called "judges," unlike King Solomon, whose decisions are mainly predictable in advance,[48] and (3) that he has no idea of how to run a national government of over 4 million employees, (4) then why did you vote for him instead of trying to defend something precious and real, like democracy, with your vote? Is that vote also a matter of having fun?[49]

---

[47] I hope other writers will address the question of "what is amusing" in this sense. The subject is not simple. We sometimes know that something is fake but allow it to engage us anyway. It is like looking at a successful advertisement. There was no tiger in your car's tank even when a 1960s Esso ad said that there was. Nevertheless, some people responded to the ad by buying Esso gasoline. There are some very puzzling questions here, about our ability and/or willingness to hold two (or more) contradictory truths in mind at the same time. Some people knew that the tiger was false but also related to it as if it were somewhat true. For a discussion of this paradox, see Sut Jhally and Justin Lewis, "Television and Reality: How Real is The Cosby Show?" in *Enlightened Racism: The Cosby Show, Audiences, and the Myth of the American Dream* (Boulder, CO: Westview Press, 1992), pp. 15–33.

[48] The principle here is "first the verdict, then the trial." That is not verbatim what Alice's Queen of Hearts said in *Through the Looking Glass*, but it is what she meant.

[49] To some people, Trump is amusing. But when a consequential matter is to be discussed in Trump's vicinity, I am reminded that the Founders dealt with such matters very seriously. They sequestered themselves for four months at the Constitutional Convention in Philadelphia, kept no record of the proceedings, excluded the public, and did not report to the press on their discussions. That is, they maintained what they considered to be a suitable decorum for talking about a very consequential matter, and their way of doing that was light-years from the public behavior of Donald Trump. Michael Schudson, *The Good Citizen: A History of American Civic Life* (Cambridge, MA: Harvard University Press, 1998), p. 52, described what happened among the Founders as follows: "On Monday, the second day of the Convention, the committee on procedures 'reported back.' Among its proposed rules were that when one member of the meeting held the floor, other members should not talk with one another 'or read a book, pamphlet or paper, printed or manuscript.' No one could speak more than twice on the same question without special permissions and could speak the second time only if all others who wanted to speak had had a chance to do so ... The president [of the meeting, who was George Washington] could decide questions of order without appeal or debate." Trump, alternatively, suggested on June 17, 2025, that the Iranians should evacuate Teheran "immediately." Did he seriously consider the process and consequences of "immediately" moving roughly 9.7 million people out of that city? See www.pbs.org/newshour/world/trump-says-all-of-tehran-should-evacuate-immediately-amid-intensifying-conflict.

Or, if you regard yourself as patriotic, (5) what happened to your devotion to the "self-evident truths" of Jefferson and the Declaration of Independence? You voted for Trump. But how does he relate to such truths, now updated, when he announces that he is withdrawing Washington from the Paris Agreement on Climate Change and that he will encourage an increasing use of fossil fuels in America? Or, as he put it, "drill, baby, drill."[50]

Perhaps he believes that the findings of science, about human health, safety, and prosperity, which are among civilization's greatest achievements, are not self-evident but just another entertainment contestant, like *Dancing with the Stars*, or *House of Cards*.[51] Do you, too, believe that?[52]

And how are we to understand the appeal of a Piper who promotes himself (and his business entities) as a profitable *brand* instead of speaking to the public as a political *prophet* praising national traditions and values going back at least to Abraham Lincoln, who was the greatest Republican of all?[53]

America's public conversation still alludes to biblical and republican values and aspirations. But does this particular Piper, convicted fairly and squarely of multiple financial frauds, even know that George Washington reportedly set for all Americans an example by not lying about what he did to the cherry tree?

---

[50] He repeated this campaign promise in his second Inaugural Address. See www.whitehouse.gov/remarks/2025/01/the-inaugural-address/.
[51] In the name of several thousand scientists who work on environmental matters, the UN's Intergovernmental Panel on Climate Change (IPCC), established in 1988, issues periodic reports warning that the increase in global temperatures due to greenhouse gas emissions must be kept below 1.5 degrees centigrade. See the 2018 report at www.ipcc.ch/sr15/.
[52] What is the significance, then, of Trump appointing Linda McMahon, a former CEO of the professional wrestling organization (WWE), to head the Department of Education? Why choose an entertainer rather than an educator to head that department?
[53] David Bromwich, "Shakespeare, Lincoln, and Ambition," in *Moral Imagination: Essays* (Princeton: Princeton University Press, 2014), pp. 162–163, reminds us of how great a republican Lincoln was. In an 1838 speech at the Young Men's Lyceum of Springfield, Illinois, Lincoln talked about "men of ambition" who would look for new ways to shape events and public life. Such a man of "genius," said Lincoln, is a necessary part of politics but, in his enthusiasm, might seek to override earlier arrangements and agreements, that is, laws. In that case, "it will require the people to be united with each other, attached to the government and laws, and generally intelligent, to successfully frustrate his designs." In other words, even before Weberian terms were available, Lincoln warned us that, on behalf of democracy, men of "charisma" must be checked by "good citizenship."

Theatrical Imperatives

Here is an enormous threat to democracy and its citizens. Will modern communications technology produce not just Donald Trump but additional Pipers who are super entertainers? And, if so, will such people formulate "causes" consisting mainly of slogans, sound-bites, interviews, podcasts, press conferences, trial balloons, and other pseudo-events to the point where a great country will be guided by theatrical imperatives – America's president as P. T. Barnum – rather than by sensible thinking, even if not all the way to a national consensus?[54]

Irving Berlin wrote the famous song that jubilantly shouts out: "There's no business, like show business!"[55] Does that mean that, on behalf of coast-to-coast show business, American voters should electorally staff public offices on the basis of television ratings, internet followers, dopamine jolts, and click-bait accounting?[56]

---

[54] In a way, there is no Weberian "cause" in Trump's performance. There is, instead, an endless series of press conferences, social media blurts, shouted exchanges on the tarmac, exciting announcements, trial balloons, and "pseudo-events," where every day Trump says or posts things which do not contribute to a coherent program but are bits and pieces of sludge which he knows that media outlets will spread around in order to draw attention to their messages by borrowing his celebrity as an entertaining actor. In the exchange, profits are mutual. Trump gains financially from maintaining his name recognition in business and politics, and the media gain financially from selling their large and captivated audience to advertisers. Policy-wise, it doesn't usually matter exactly what Trump says because, in the days or weeks to come, he may say something very different or entirely the opposite.

[55] Berlin would have been horrified by Trump's constant trashing of immigrants. He was a Yiddish-speaking Jew (born Israel Beilin) who in childhood fled from pogroms in Russia and grew up in America, who loved his adopted country so fiercely that he wrote one of its most beloved Christmas songs ("White Christmas"), one of its most beloved Easter songs ("Easter Parade"), and, of course, its alternative national-anthem, "God Bless America."

[56] Political scientists can consider this possibility via their understanding of an analytic concept known as "the permanent campaign," whereby incumbents do not wait for an upcoming election to mount the stump but campaign constantly, every day, from election to election, to keep themselves visible to voters and maintain at least name recognition. Sidney Blumenthal, *The Permanent Campaign: Inside the World of Elite Political Operatives* (Boston: Beacon Press, 1980). In this sense, Trump's career and the business model for media entities match each other perfectly. Trump, campaigning permanently, wants elements of his theatrical performances to appear every day, and media entities, to stay profitable, will look at, and listen to, what he yammers ceaselessly on social media or elsewhere and turn it into headlines and discussion to fill up their pages and screens every day. He and they will continue – like Siamese twins of information and disinformation – at least until 2029, which means that television ratings and click-bait accounting are changing the way democracy has been conducted in America since the days of George Washington.

And if offices are so allocated, what would Berlin have thought of citizens being entertained, from *Slate* to *Breitbart News*, with one catchy headline after another – like renaming the Gulf of Mexico – that add up to daily episodes of a political soap opera, while familiar news anchors and presenters (but maybe not on Fox News) are proclaiming their outrage, and while media tycoons are smiling all the way to the bank?

Can Democracy Survive?

Most important, can American democracy survive by doing politics as if it were an activity no more intrinsically important than entertainment?[57] Trump's Inauguration displayed some of the Great Piper's billionaire allies – Elon Musk, Mark Zuckerberg, Tim Cook, Sundar Pichai, Jeff Bezos, Meriam Adelson, Sam Altman, and more – who paid millions of dollars (which was pocket change for them) to make his Inauguration especially splendid.

In fact, though, they were imitating the wealthy elites of America's late nineteenth-century Gilded Age, including Jacob Astor, Andrew Carnegie, Cornelius Vanderbilt, J. P. Morgan, John D. Rockefeller, Jay Cooke, James Duke, and Peter Widener. That is, they were turning themselves into "oligarchs" (long defined as "the few promoting their own interests") such as the rich and powerful men whom George Washington, Benjamin Franklin, James Madison, John Adams, Alexander Hamilton, and their colleagues feared when, in

---

[57] I believe that, as Postman suggested, Trump is a powerful entertainer. Someone closer to the discipline of psychology might approach Trump more as what used to be called a "con man" or "grifter," telling stories that encourage credulous people to believe that what he or she tells them makes sense of the world, resolves their anxieties caused by incoherent surroundings, and imputes meaning to puzzling events. This approach appears in Maria Konnikova, *The Confidence Game: Why We Fall for it… Every Time* (New York: Penguin, 2016). Penguin released Konnikova's book in January 2016. Perhaps she assumed that Donald Trump would not be elected later that year. Whatever, her book says nothing about him. His enriching himself in office then, and even more the second time around, probably did not surprise her. On psychological techniques in Trump's entertainment stories, see also Steven Hassan, *The Cult of Trump: A Leading Cult Expert Explains How the President Uses Mind Control* (New York: Free Press, 2019), for example, "The Persuasiveness of Trump," pp. 88–119, and esp. p. 89 on the use of shocking exaggeration, which Trump calls "useful hyperbole."

the Constitutional Convention, they established a mixed government regime.[58]

The upside of this striking inequality, as the new oligarchs and their retainers announce to whoever is willing to listen, in whatever forum, is that multi-millionaires and billionaires are grand for helping us to push up Gross National Product, Gross Domestic Product, and stock market indexes.[59] The downside, which they don't talk about, is that while they claim to be serving our *wants* endlessly (some of which they created), their market-based behavior is ignoring our *needs* – remember: "drill, baby, drill" – to the point of helping to destroy the world that we need in order to live in it.

That last point is large enough to fill up another book. But for that, readers don't need me, because they can see the terrifying predictions about global warming, coral bleaching, climate change, worldwide deforestation, species extinctions, spreading wildfires, rising seas, lethal pandemics, plastic contaminations, melting icebergs, fertilizer runoff, escalating hurricanes, and more, in David Wallace-Wells, *The Uninhabitable Earth: A Story for the Future*.[60]

---

[58] Tim Wu, *The Curse of Bigness: Antitrust in the New Gilded Age* (New York: Columbia Global Reports, 2018). See also Benjamin I. Page, Jason Seawright, and Mathew K. Lacombe, *Billionaires and Stealth Politics* (Chicago: University of Chicago Press, 2019).

[59] The rejoinder to this kind of talk promoting entrepreneurs and their talent for sometimes making money, is criticism based on the notion that prosperity and progress are not caused only by "shareholders" in highly profitable companies but also by the work and creativity of "stakeholders." A thorough defense of stakeholders appears in Mariana Mazzucato, *The Value of Everything: Making & Taking in the Global Economy* (New York: Public Affairs, 2018), *passim*.

[60] David Wallace-Wells, *The Uninhabitable Earth: A Story for the Future* (London: Penguin, 2019).

9 FIXING THE PHONES

I try to end books I write on an optimistic note. There's a puzzle? It can be solved. You have a problem? We'll deal with it. Meanwhile, here is my advice. Brace yourself. Chin up. Consider these options. Do things this way. Or that. Don't stay here. Go there. The nation might not line up. But at least my suggestions are reasonable.[1]

Freedom of Speech

Nevertheless, I am desperate this time. In Orwell's *1984*, Winston Smith worked in the Ministry of Truth, and its people lied constantly about life in Oceana. For example, from his desk in that ministry, Smith adjusted claims, coming from the Ministry of Plenty, that Oceana's factories had produced, in the previous quarter year, 62 million pairs of boots. He knew this was false because, among other reasons, he saw that "perhaps half the population of Oceana went barefoot."[2]

---

[1] A good example of reasonable advice about how to confront Donald Trump appeared in D. J. Dionne, Jr., Norman J. Ornstein, and Thomas E. Mann, *One Nation after Trump: A Guide for the Perplexed, the Disillusioned, the Desperate, and the Not-Yet Deported* (New York: St. Martin's Press, 2017). It was a case of three very savvy Washington think-tankers from the Brookings Institution and the American Enterprise Institute devoting almost half of their book (pp. 175–291) to dealing with "The Way Forward." Some of their advice may have helped in 2020. In 2024, nothing helped.

[2] George Orwell, *1984* (orig., 1949; London: Penguin, 2008), pp. 43–44.

In the circumstances, Winston believed that freedom is the right to step back from lies and say that two and two make four. He regarded that equation as expressing a scientific and incontrovertible fact. Something you can stub your toe on.

But here is what his insight means now. First, Smith, a sort of Everyman character, is free to declare his belief in what is true. Most modern democracies, thank heaven, still permit that.

But second, when surrounded by the epistemic crisis today, Everyman (or woman) often no longer knows *what* he believes. He is bombarded by various truth claims, as if two and two sometimes make five. These claims confuse him, and no authoritative watchdogs are available, at least not on his wavelength, to help him winnow out the disinformation. So, his thinking may be muddled.[3]

And, finally, if he ever *does* make up his mind, whatever he decides to say publicly will be drowned out by confident sponsors of every thesis, who are still in Plato's cave, and who promote every sort of "opinion" rather than "knowledge." In the circumstances, Mark Zuckerberg and his clones have decided to shut down their fact-checking as if, on our behalf, they will righteously oppose "censorship," which is bad, aimed against the exercise of "free speech," which is good. In reality, however, they will continue to pass around intellectual poison and lies, for which they will take no responsibility, as the *New York Times* once did.

For television, the same sort of indiscriminate trumpeting (no pun intended) appears in many major networks. For example, the CNN program *NewsNight*, which features the popular presenter Abby Phillips, is occasionally preceded by an announcement saying – proudly – that she "brings all sides to the table." For the sake of entertainment, we know that variety can be the spice of life. But if "all sides" means that CNN will occasionally invite guests who promote, in effect, 2+2=5, then this gigantic media corporation is endorsing, validating, and sanctioning the muddling capacity of an open marketplace for ideas.

---

[3] Philosophically minded readers might consider that, if the information system prevents many of us from thinking, that outcome suggests odd, if not grim, implications for the famous maxim of René Descartes, announced in his *Discourse on Method* (1637), that "I think, therefore I am." On that maxim, see www.britannica.com/topic/cogito-ergo-sum.

In other words, on behalf of free speech, which is one of civilization's great accomplishments, we are where Lenin said that, if you give capitalists enough rope, they will together hang themselves. It is a frightening scenario which, in present circumstances, looks increasingly likely to unfold.

And that is not a partisan prediction. On the Left, Center, and Right, we *all* know that something terrible has happened to talk in America, to what people say, to what they believe, to what they understand, and to whom they trust. Hence, what I am really proposing in this essay is that, if we will continue with more of the same, we will be on our way to the cliff together and that, when we will get there, trying to imitate Wile E. Coyote may not work.

Context

Meanwhile, there is always more to say about the subjects I have been discussing all along: democracy, citizenship, and common sense. And if we wait a few minutes, the president of the United States, and his loyalists like Scott Bessent, Steven Miller, Karoline Leavitt, Robert F. Kennedy, Jr., Linda McMahon, Marco Rubio, Howard Lutwick, Peter Navarro, and Pete Hegseth, will shock us into fresh anxieties about all of those things. Therefore, I want to comment on only one final matter, and that is the factor of "context," which has turned "freedom of speech" into a national nightmare.[4]

---

[4] Of course, I mean here freedom of speech without gatekeepers to keep out the "sludge," whose presence muddles our thinking. Donald Trump scorns universities precisely because, as a class of special institutions, their freedom of speech is moderated by gatekeepers (who rarely praise him). In fact, gatekeeping, against intellectual chaos, is the signature service provided to society by universities (and colleges) such as Harvard (and many others). Their professors, chosen for scientific and/or professional competence, perform gatekeeping in the sense that they help us to understand which books and articles in the library, or other items in the information system, are worth heeding. And if their students for any reason decide that a particular university's gatekeeping is onerous, those students are free to study elsewhere. It's a democracy, after all. On Trump's animus toward Harvard, see his demands against that university conveyed in a five-page letter, dated April 11 2025 and sent to Harvard's president and a "Lead Member" (and donor) of the Harvard Corporation. See www.nytimes.com/interactive/2025/04/14/us/trump-harvard-demands.html. The letter sent to Harvard was not signed by Trump himself but by several of his administrative people in federal departments. Among its demands was that "Every [Harvard] department or field found to lack viewpoint diversity must be reformed by hiring a critical mass within the

Failure

What I am thinking is this. Just before I finished the first draft of this essay, Donald Trump was elected president a second time. It was an unmistakable case of too many Americans choosing an autocratic demagogue who openly mocked civil service rules and safeguards, who gleefully promised to stomp on various "elites" who were "destroying America," who sourly announced that he would fire "persecutors" who accused him of committing felonies, groping women, and encouraging insurrection, who grimly assured his supporters that he would pack federal courts with loyal rather than impartial judges, and who clearly showed international statesmen that he knew more about 9-irons than what to do with nuclear weapons. And, for the moment, let's leave aside his delusions about fracking, world health, and climate change.

In other words, what happened on November 5, 2024 demonstrated historical ignorance, and historic irresponsibility, on the part of some American citizens – Gustave Le Bon might have called them a "crowd" – amounting to a popular plurality. They voted for Trump and thereby failed to defend their democracy, which only they can do adequately, and which I call for in this essay repeatedly.

It is not too early to discuss why this failure occurred, therefore many journalists, politicians, pundits, activists, "influencers," and ordinary citizens are talking about it non-stop. But full-scale research on what happened, and why, is not yet available and won't be for some time.[5]

---

department or field who will provide viewpoint diversity." A critic of Trump 2.0, with an eye on his ally Robert F. Kennedy, Jr., might interpret that concept as a requirement that the Harvard pharmacology department should hire a band of colleagues who will teach that vaccines cause autism. On April 18, the *NYT* reported that "a Trump official" from the White House called Harvard and said that the letter had not been "authorized," whatever that means.

[5] Here is one reason to wait for serious research results. Immediately after Trump's election in 2024, it seemed to some pundits that Trump won because, this time, they believed that he, rather than the Democrats, was at the center of American thinking and preferences. That argument, before research, assumed that, because Trump in his campaign boosted racism and misogyny (against his Black and female opponent), similar sentiments probably motivated the people who voted for Trump. I suspect, however, that many of such voters may have admired Trump less for his policy positions than because of his entertaining trash talk, which is sometimes described by pundits as his "authenticity." Which means, for us here, that, instead of making assumptions about why people voted, it is best to wait for careful research results based on asking citizens directly why they voted as they did.

Therefore, I did not make the 2024 election a centerpiece in this book. I did refer to it occasionally, but only as a large-scale confirmation for some of what I was prepared to say about democracy, good citizenship, and common sense.

An Alternative

Overall, then, this book is different from many that publishers will offer us in 2025 and beyond. Those others will be chiefly about how Donald Trump outran Kamala Harris, what he has already done since then, and what he is likely to do on any day in the future. That is, they will be mainly about the president.[6]

Fear and loathing of Trump drove me to write. And I have not changed my mind. But I want to emphasize that, unlike those other books, my project is not especially about him. It is, instead, about how American society, in various realms, made room for someone like Trump to appear and smash much of what many Democrats and Republicans have long admired as "a city on a hill."[7]

So, there is the matter of "context." That is, *Defending Democracy* highlights some of the institutions and practices – context – which surround Trump and invite him to behave rabidly. Put that another way. Trump is behaving like a bull in a china shop. It is part of what he *is*, having grown up as an arrogant and narcissistic rich kid. But it is also part of what he *does*, as a remarkably successful and full-time entertainer.

Other writers will discuss this Great Piper's egotism, his arrogance, his brutality, his vulgarity, his conceits, his petulance, and his paranoia. In newscasts, talk shows, and internet chattering, those traits will provide abundant material for some pundits and thinkers to praise Trump and others to scorn him, until his second term expires in January 2029. If he will agree to retire then.

---

[6] Past performance shows that there will be a great many of them. In 2020, Carlos Lozada had already reviewed 150 of such books as a sample of what had been published by then. See Carlos Lozada, *What Were They Thinking: A Brief Intellectual History of the Trump Era* (New York: Simon & Schuster, 2020).

[7] This is one description of American "exceptionalism," and the reference is to Jerusalem. On Ronald Reagan and the "City on a Hill," see www.reaganlibrary.gov/archives/speech/farewell-address-nation.

But that is not the only conversation we need to conduct. My view of Trump in this essay focuses more on *contextual* factors than on *personality* disorders.[8] Therefore, I have suggested for discussion the matter of how, over time, America set itself up for someone like Trump to operate as he does, and about how he is more the result than the cause of where we are today.

With these parameters in mind, I understand that most of Trump's critics will first and foremost address their audiences about how to repair the enormous damages to American principles, institutions, and practices that Trump has already produced or is going to produce.[9] For example, they are horrified by a presidential "deal-maker" who, in their names, proposes to sell, for immediate payment, American military assistance to a ravaged and debt-ridden Ukrainian democracy (1) which was attacked by Russian forces as reprehensibly as the United States was attacked by the Empire of Japan at Pearl Harbor, and (2) which is struggling desperately against heavily armed aggressors to survive as a free nation.[10] And they might believe that American presidents are, by constitutional law, forbidden to accept gift airplanes ("emoluments," according to the Constitution) worth $400 million from oil potentates in Qatar.[11]

---

[8] On Trump as emotionally disturbed, see www.huffpost.com/entry/psychologist-how-to-stop-trump-narcissist_n_682df1cae4b09b7e5013a586.

[9] Readers can peruse, for example, the Office of Management and Budget (OMB) memo (from January 27, 2025), which incorporates Trumpist ideas and suspends disbursements for all "financial assistance programs" of the federal government, on the grounds that they might waste taxpayers' dollars by advancing "Marxist equity, transgenderism, and green new deal social engineering policies." As the memo says, such spending "is a waste of taxpayer dollars that does not improve the day-to-day lives of those we serve." There is no estimate in the memo of how many billions of dollars will be suspended or how many millions of Americans will be deprived of benefits duly appropriated by the Legislative Branch of America's national government. See the memo at www.washingtonpost.com/documents/deb7af80-48b6-4b8a-8bfa-3d84fd7c3ec8.pdf?itid=lk_inline_manual_40.

[10] Trump obviously doesn't share FDR's determination to help a viciously assaulted neighbor. As Roosevelt put it in 1940 to justify the concept of Lend Lease, if your neighbor's house were on fire, and the fire could spread to your house, you would lend him a garden hose. See https://teachingamericanhistory.org/document/press-conference-on-lend-lease-policy/.

[11] See www.vox.com/politics/412901/trump-qatar-plane-gift-air-force-on. Readers can see how public reactions to gift events have evolved since the mid 1950s by comparing reactions to Trump's personal enrichment today to how President Eisenhower's chief of staff, former New Hampshire governor Sherman Adams, was pushed into resigning his job in 1958 for, among other reasons, accepting the gift of a vicuna cloth overcoat (worth perhaps $700) from a New England industrialist seeking favorable decisions from the Federal Trade Commission and Securities and Exchange Commission. On the Adams scandal, see www.latimes.com/archives/la-xpm-1986-10-28-mn-7917-story.html.

So far, I am not participating in that discussion, but I fully understand its immediate importance.

Our Mission

The bottom line is this. I am not suggesting that we will stop writing books about Trump but that we will add to them action against the circumstances in which he finds himself and which enable him to behave as he does.

First, one such possible action is obvious and conventional, therefore many frightened and angry citizens will surely adopt it. Millions upon millions of anti-Trump Americans, across the land, are going to turn out to vote against this man's allies in the federal elections to be held in November 2026. If Democrats at that time will gain majorities in the House and Senate, a great many of Trump's toxic policy proposals will be annulled, and that is something which we know that MAGA Republicans now in Congress are, so far, unwilling to do.

It is a project that will require billions of dollars of campaign money, thousands of paid workers, even more volunteers, demonstrators, parades, stickers, lapel pins, banners, billboards, lawn signs, parlor meetings, and a massive presence of attractive anti-Trumpers on television and social media. I have no doubt that all of these things will come forth, and that success in the 2026 elections, if achieved, will go far to neutralize at least some of Donald Trump's worst sins.[12]

That is, however, the relatively easy response to a Great Piper. We have also to prepare for doing something less familiar, more

---

[12] Because America mostly observes separation of church and state, there is not much public talk linking politicians to the theological concept of sin. However, using the seven deadly sins as one convenient standard for judging anyone's behavior, it is obvious that Trump is committing them all: pride, greed, lust, envy, gluttony, wrath, and sloth. It is also obvious that he doesn't exercise the virtues which stand against them: humility, charity, chastity, gratitude, temperance, patience, and diligence. See www.britannica.com/topic/seven-deadly-sins. Trump's evangelical supporters might consider his relationship to St. Paul's "Epistle to the Galatians," 5:14 (KJV): "For all the law is fulfilled in one word, even in this; Thou shalt love thy neighbor as thyself." Trump is not big on treating his non-similar-identity neighbors – including women, minorities, LGBTs, and immigrants – with love. At Charlie Kirk's memorial on September 21, 2025, Trump declared that he hates his opponents. See his remarks at www.nytimes.com/2025/09/22/us/politics/trump-kirk-memorial-hate.html.

difficult, and more aimed at the long run. The imperative there is that, as I observed earlier, if the country doesn't try to close up the space it created for Trump in the first place, more entertainers like him may step into that breach, with terrible consequences.[13]

Second, in the circumstances, what prescription comes to mind? In fact – and here is the hard truth – national success in preventing additional Great Pipers from emerging and continuing to sow chaos in American public life will depend on figuring out a way to turn smartphones into benign tools. This is what democracy needs rather than what the phones do now, which is to offer a standing invitation to barbarians who don't care if, by entertaining us via such instruments, they will destroy much of civilization, and maybe even the Earth that we live on.[14]

It is not that we don't know what needs to be done. We know. But to actually do it will be uniquely difficult, because what is called for is not an ordinary exercise of day-to-day political activism – half a loaf here, half a loaf there, put up another sign, stuff another envelope, make and show another YouTube video. In fact, even to propose defeating such a stubborn and usually pleasant addiction may strike some readers as unrealistic to the point of being ridiculous.[15]

---

[13] On someone who might be regarded as a new Piper but not, in my opinion, as noxious as Donald Trump, see Chris Hayes and Ezra Klein discussing Zohran Mamdani's New York City mayoralty primary election victory in June of 2025 at www.nytimes.com/2025/06/28/opinion/ezra-klein-show-chris-hayes.html. Mamdani defeated former New York governor Andrew Cuomo by using mainly social media videos (via smartphones) rather than television ads to promote himself and his candidacy. In other words, he is a young Piper, 33 years old, who stepped into the political space now dominated by Donald Trump and who is operating there, perhaps joining additional Pipers possessing his talent for attracting modern attention on the Right, such as Charlie Kirk, who was murdered in September of 2025. Klein argues that older Democrats, like Cuomo, Nancy Pelosi, and Chuck Schumer, are skillful at bargaining, which enables them to hold numerous Democratic Party factions together. Based on that talent, they rose to power in the past. But since they rarely use social media in their own lives, they have little or no feel for how to use phones to gain attention for themselves or their party. The same might be said for Kamala Harris and her campaign of 2024.

[14] From early impressions, it seems that both Harris and Trump conducted much of their 2024 campaigns on social media, via smartphones, through podcasters and influencers. And that Trump, supremely talented at this sort of communication, was more successful than Harris. When more research results are available, we will know more. Meanwhile, see www.wired.com/story/donald-trump-online-campaign-era/.

[15] We need not provide here illustrative numbers from research into the addictive power of smartphones. But readers can find such numbers and discussion of their consequences in

Let's not forget, though, that smartphones are for Donald Trump an Achilles heel. If he is attacked there, he will lose the instruments which, while used without restraint, overload a marketplace of ideas, foster intellectual muddling, vitiate common sense, and enhance his entertainment power. Therefore, in spring 2025 as I was composing this call for government regulation of phones, the president of the United States, without consulting me, ordered the US Customs and Border Protection Bureau of the Department of Homeland Security to declare that smartphones imported into America from all over the world, including China, would not be subject to tariff increases and thereby made more expensive.[16]

We do not know exactly why Trump ordered this exemption. As so often, he didn't explain. But we can understand keeping down the price of smartphones as, among other things, maintaining the "wherewithal" (a) that helped Trump to receive 77 million votes in the election of November 2024, and (b) that continues to maintain his "base" today.

The Trump Test

Paying attention to Mark Thompson might help us to stand up to the stunning power of phones in our public life. Thompson was the director general of the BBC and also the CEO of the New York Times Company, therefore he is a man of exceptional messaging experience. We should listen to him, then, when he argues that we must fix our rhetoric so that it will pass what he calls a "Trump test."

By such a test he means that our "public language ... must enable ordinary citizens to distinguish at once between matters of fact and those of opinion, between grown-up political discourse and outright nonsense."[17] If not, he fears that we are doomed.

Adam Gazzaley and Larry D. Rosen, *The Distracted Mind: Ancient Brains in a High-Tech World* (Cambridge, MA: MIT Press, 2016), *passim*, but esp. pp. 101–157.

[16] China makes probably 80% of the world's smartphones, and supplies around 70% of those imported into America. On the tariff exemption order, see www.washingtonpost.com/business/2025/04/12/trump-tariff-exemptions-smartphones-computers/.

[17] Mark Thompson, *Enough Said: What's Gone Wrong with the Language of Politics?* (New York: St. Martin's Griffin, 2017), p. 295, but also pp. 295–301.

Fixing the Language

Currently, says Thompson, "public language" in America, Britain, and some other Western countries, is not passing the Trump test. While observing that failure, he uses his terms, not mine. But he is actually describing the "epistemic crisis" of information overload, the "muddled thinking" it generates, the "marketplace of ideas" choked by examples of 2+2=5, and, at bottom, the painful shortage of "common sense" which now plagues human understanding itself.

Then Thompson goes on, not optimistically, to discuss how public talk might slowly be improved by new forms of rhetoric, by new subjects for discussion, and by new leading practitioners (influencers, presenters, communicators), as we go forward. I won't discuss his recommendations here, because even he doesn't put much stock in them for the near future.

I will observe, instead, that, if what he calls our public language is not working well for us, we can react in two ways: we can try to fix the language itself, as Thompson recommends but not very hopefully; or, we can try to block some of the technology which projects that sort of talk, disastrously, into modern societies.

Fixing the Phones

What I suggest is to leave how to fix our talk with Mark Thompson. If repair will eventually be achieved, as he hopes, vast and lasting damage will probably already have been done. Therefore, instead of waiting for that, we should go directly to the second option. The way there is clear, but not easy to walk, and taking it would constitute serious progress toward resolving, or at least mitigating, this crisis.

To that end, and while recognizing how the "medium" is sending us indigestible or unwholesome "messages," we must decide that we will rein in the phones which, for now at least, all the way down to children, fracture us and our thinking.[18]

---

[18] Current surveys show that many parents are unhappy about how their children use smartphones and how they are hurt by them. See the extent of parental anxieties in www.nytimes.com/2025/06/18/opinion/parents-smartphones-tiktok-facebook.html. It is not clear, though, that the same parents understand that they, too, while older than their

It is a move that can emerge only from "good citizenship." Which means that, no matter what our differences may be on other issues in various forums, democrats from every party must get together as voters to elect officials who will instruct government workers, by law, to regulate smartphones and how they are used. This even though such regulation will require us to limit some precious First Amendment freedoms of speech and association.

To make this happen, it will help immensely if we will refuse to assume that easier solutions will arise but will instead hold fast to the fact, plain and simple, that this is the *only* way to seriously confront the context problem. Wishful thinking won't help. Individual acts of resistance, such as boycotting or firebombing Tesla cars, may be personally gratifying but are likely to deliver only marginal social gains. And foot dragging over years, by many of the most powerful and wealthy people in America, shows that nobody else, such as Bill Gates, Elon Musk, Mark Zuckerberg, Warren Buffet, George Soros, Michael Bloomberg, and the rest, will do a decisive job for us.[19]

Defending Democracy

In short, an immense and resolute project of *defending democracy* is required. Within the terms that appeared in this essay, we can regard the need for action to that end as a project to un-muddle much of our thinking and maintain enough common sense to inspire us to insist on democratic principles, institutions, and practices.

The need for action on this score is a staggering challenge to the vocation of citizenship in America. Moreover, at first glance, I

---

children, are probably equally addicted and equally unable to deal with the way those phones fracture their own thinking and identities.

[19] On some of the rich slackers, we should note that Orwell was brilliant but also, in a way, wrong. Big Brother today – in the future society that has already arrived – is not looking at *us* via what Orwell called the Leader's "telescreens." Rather, we are condemned to looking at *him* on *our* screens, because he has turned himself into an entertaining television show and the information system, much of which is owned by extraordinarily wealthy people, publicizes *him* every day to increase *their* wealth. On this point, see Robert W. McChesney and John Nichols, "Down the News Hole," in *Will the Last Reporter Please Turn out the Lights*, ed. Robert McChesney and Victor Pickard (New York: Free Press, 2011), p. 103.

admit, history suggests we are not likely to complete such a project. Remember, the Catholic Church in sixteenth-century Europe faced a sudden change in the marketplace of ideas when it found itself facing an enormous overload of books. Consequently, it tried with the Index to limit its congregants' access to some of those books. It was a move that failed. The people went right on reading whatever they wanted to read.

But we should remember, too, that for the Church to establish an Index was not a democratic project, because it did not involve full-fledged citizens addressing a dangerous situation by working constructively with their elected representatives. The Index was, instead, a case of an elite imposing its vision on the rank and file.

In that sense, to agitate widely for a regulation of phones, and to succeed, would be, in fact, to perform a legitimate, democratic, and responsible act of majority understanding and rule. Moreover, such regulation would not have to cancel the right of free speech. It would only have to limit it, within the framework of longstanding judicial warnings against "clear and present dangers," on behalf of the public interest.[20]

Inspiration

Some readers may feel that what I am recommending is as far-fetched as proposing to cut down the telegraph lines and revive the Pony Express. And I will concede, but not happily, that asking the public to limit the use of smartphones would be extremely difficult politically. I am convinced, however, that some measure of regulation is worth trying to achieve because, directly or indirectly, these instruments massively degrade the health and happiness of a great many people in modern society.

Therefore, let us regard this sort of oversight as a worthy democratic project. That is, let us regard it not as democratic in the sense

---

[20] The precedent here was set by Justice Oliver Wendell Holmes, Jr., when he wrote the 9–0 majority opinion in *Schenck v. United States* (1919). In that case, he ruled that, yes, freedom of speech is constitutionally *protected*. It is also *limited*, though, because, for example, it does not permit citizens to shout "Fire!" (thereby endangering other citizens) in a crowded theater (unless there is a fire).

of Democratic Party propositions but as a non-partisan challenge to good citizens from both major parties, that they will work to improve America's quality of life.

Many obvious reasons may inspire worriers to join such a project. For example, their fears may be stoked by patently awful results flowing from voters already electing someone like Donald Trump. Among others, these will include climate change, environmental destruction, disruption of governmental programs, dismemberment of essential agencies, unemployment in public and private services, lowering of standards in Medicare, Medicaid, and Social Security, assaults on higher education and research, intensification of identity clashes, and perpetuation of the culture war.[21]

In addition, however, those who are reading this book may follow Neil Postman and find quieter inspiration for a revolt against phones – girding up our historical loins, so to speak – in the Age of Print.[22] Our inheritance from that Age can still spur us to action, because its best writers understood so well the importance of straight thinking and astute formulations.[23]

---

[21] Such policy results emerge from Trump's determination to change the nature of American government which until now has functioned as a "mixed regime." Thus, see a short discussion of Trump 2.0's moves to tyranny in Anne Applebaum, *Autocracy, Inc: The Dictators Who Want to Run the World* (New York: Doubleday, 2025), pp. xiv–xx. See also a longer discussion, from the liberal point of view, of how what Trump 2.0 is doing, by shattering constitutional "guardrails," adds up to an "imperial presidency" in www.americanprogress.org/article/trumps-first-100-days-creating-an-imperial-presidency-that-harms-americans/. This report, without using the term "French temptation," nevertheless describes how Trump, his lawyers, and his colleagues, such as Vice President J. D. Vance, subscribe to the notion that the American president is elected by the nation as a whole and therefore possesses a mandate, via Article II of the Constitution, to rule without checks and balances which rest on congressional or judicial powers according to Articles I and III.

[22] See Neil Postman, *Building a Bridge to the Eighteenth Century* (New York: Vintage, 1999).

[23] We don't always remember how often, in the Age of Print, many ordinary people – not only those who were writing specialists – learned to express themselves more clearly and impressively than the same sort of people today. An outstanding example is the letter which General William Tecumseh Sherman sent to local government officials in Atlanta explaining his intention, as the commander of a Northern army, to drive all rebel civilians out of that Southern city late in 1864. Recently, news broadcasts have featured many retired generals commenting on wars such as those in Ukraine, Gaza, Syria, the Sudan, and the Congo. They know a good deal about making war. But almost none of those who I saw spoke as precisely and powerfully as Sherman wrote. See his now-remarkable letter at http://carolmelton.com/sherman_atlanta.pdf.

Shakespeare

Shakespeare, for example, is always worth consulting. In this case, that is especially so for what he said about ancient Rome. Accordingly, we may remember, from high school English classes, that Julius Caesar came to Shakespeare's attention because Caesar had wielded exceptional power in Rome and therefore was in a position to overthrow the Roman republic (mixed government) centered on that city.[24]

Therefore, in his play entitled *Julius Caesar* (1599), Shakespeare had the conspirator Cassius powerfully describe this sort of large-scale threat to the citizens (well, to the senators) of Rome: "Why, man, he [Caesar] doth bestride the narrow world like a colossus, and we petty men walk under his huge legs and peep about ... The **fault, dear Brutus**, is not in our stars, but in ourselves, that we are underlings."[25]

The message is clear. Not in our stars, but in ourselves. Not as underlings, but on our own behalf. Or, as I just described, via a democratic project pitched to achieve majority consent.

Whichever, we must begin to repeal at least some of the conditions that enable Trump and his wrecking-ball allies to lay waste to crucial parts of modern America. The challenge is enormous, but the job is ours and belongs to no one else.

Back to Paine

On this score, Ronald Reagan probably assumed, if he thought about it at all, that English actors like Vanessa Redgrave, Laurence Olivier, John Gielgud, and Emma Thompson would keep Shakespeare alive in the minds of Americans. He was not an especially cerebral Hollywood personality.

He had it exactly right, though, when he reminded us of what Thomas Paine, rather than Shakespeare, wrote. The 37-year-old former

---

[24] In *Amusing Ourselves to Death: Public Discourse in the Age of Show Business* (New York: Penguin, 1985), Neil Postman suggested that, when much that people learn today about life comes from frothy television broadcasts, Shakespeare's works are in danger of becoming a dead letter. I continue to hope that education can overcome a significant amount of that sort of indifference.

[25] William Shakespeare, *Julius Caesar*, Act I, Scene 2.

stay-maker from Thetford, England, with a recommendation from Benjamin Franklin in his pocket, sailed from London to Philadelphia in 1774 and quickly joined the Revolution against Parliament and King George III. Then, in *Common Sense* (1776), he declared, and Reagan quoted him on this many times, that "We have it in our power to begin the world over again."[26]

So he did, and so do we.[27]

---

[26] In his acceptance speech to the 1980 Republican nominating convention, and on many other occasions, Reagan quoted Paine about our power to remake the world. I am for some remaking in principle but not necessarily for the particular remake that Ronald Reagan had in mind. On his version, see www.reaganlibrary.gov/archives/speech/republican-national-convention-acceptance-speech-1980.

[27] Thomas Paine really had an extraordinary way with words. Thus he observed, in the first "Crisis Paper" (1776), that "These are the times that try men's souls. The summer soldier and the sunshine patriot will, in this crisis, shrink from the service of his country; but he that stands it now, deserves the love and thanks of man and woman. Tyranny, like hell, is not easily conquered; yet we have this consolation with us, that the harder the conflict, the more glorious the triumph." It is no wonder that George Washington ordered Paine's words to be read aloud to American troops at Valley Forge. In translation, the Allies parachuted the same words into occupied Europe during World War II.

INDEX

abortion, 4, 18, 97, 98, 121
  unborn, rights of the, 97
Abrams, Jacob, 67
absolute convictions, 45–46, 52
Adams, John, 3, 56, 57, 179
Adams, Sherman, 186
Adelson, Meriam, 17, 130, 179
ADHD (Attention deficit hyperactivity disorder), 101
advertising, 70, 71, 108, 110, 112, 115, 117, 121, 125, 126, 131, 135, 143
  modern, 110
  political parties and, 110–111
affirmative action, 137
Affordable Care Act (2010), 89
African Americans, 11
Age of Post-Truth, 133. *See also* post-truth society
Age of Print, 124, 126, 193
Age of Reason, 145–146
Agency for International Development, 1
agricultural subsidies, 13
Ailes, Roger, 147
air pollution, 17
Alcibiades, 25, 49, 174
Alito, Samuel, 4, 94
Allen, Woody, 129, 175

Altman, Sam, 179
Amanpour, Christiane, 126, 142
Amazon, 80, 130
America First campaign, 168
America PAC, 96
American adoptions, 67–68
American Association of University Professors (AAUP), 67, 132
  Declaration of Principles, 67
American Civil Liberties Union, 68
American Dream, 15
American Enterprise Institute, 181
American Legion, 65
American Revolution, 29–30, 147, 172
amusement
  concept of, 175
  definition of, 174–180
  having fun, 176–177
Amway, 100
anarchy, 18, 23, 35, 36
Anderson, Carol, 91, 93
Anderson, Kurt, 135
anti-ballistic-missile defense system, 88
anti-federalists, 58
anti-pluralism, 15, 21
anti-Semitism, 168
apartheid, 59

Apprentice, The (TV show), 165, 175
Aquinas, Thomas, 26
Arctic National Wildlife Refuge, 17
Arendt, Hannah, 24, 78, 156
   The Origins of Totalitarianism
      (1951), 78
aristocracy, 23, 24, 35, 103
   France, 28
Aristotle, 24, 25, 58, 74, 161, 162, 164
   natural law, concept of, 26
   Politics (c.350 BC), 23
Arlington, Earl of, 56
armed forces, 13
Armour (meatpacking), 111
arms manufacturing, 113
arms, right to bear, 59, 96, 97. *See also* gun rights
artificial intelligence (AI), 119, 171
Astor, Jacob, 179
atheism, 26, 169
Athenians, 156
attention
   fracturing, 133–134
   means of, 139–141
   society, 125, 131, 134
attentional regime, 175
audiences, business of selling, 125
Augustus, 25
Austria, 113
authenticity, 184
authoritarianism, 72, 77
autism, 142, 146, 184
autocracy, 1
automation, 119
automobiles, 123, 149
Axelrod, David, 174

Bacevich, Andrew, 150
Bacon, Francis, 41
bad news, 108, 127, 128, 131
Baier, Bret, 142
Baker, James, 166
Baldwin, Roger, 68

Baltimore Sun, 64
bankruptcy, 110
banks, 98
Barber, Benjamin, 135
bargaining, 188
Barnum, P. T., 178
Barrett, Amy, 4
Barry, W. T., 56
Baumeister, Roy F., 128
BBC (British Broadcasting
      Corporation), 189
Beard, Charles A., 58
Bell, Daniel, 80
Bellah, Robert, 115, 116, 117
Benjamin, Walter, 157
Bennett, William J., 89
Bentham, Jeremy, 163
Berlin, Irving, 178, 179
Bernays, Edward
   Propaganda (1928), 115
Berry, Wendell, 159
Bessent, Scott, 183
Bezos, Jeff, 16, 130, 179
Bible
   Old Testament *Book of Exodus*, 28
   Ten Commandments, 126, 149, 161
Biden, Joe, 2, 8, 9, 166, 167, 174
Bill and Melinda Gates Foundation, 101
Bill of Rights, 32
Black Americans, 4, 31, 60
Black Lives Matter (BLM), 147
Bloomberg, Michael, 17, 95, 191
Bodin, Jean
   Six Books of the Republic (1576), 27
Bok, Sissela, 133
Boorstin, Daniel, 6, 80
   The Genius of American Politics
      (1953), 80
border patrolling, 13
'born free' 30–31
Boston Public Library, 63
boycotting, 191
Brandeis, Louis, 67, 68, 132

brands, 177
Breitbart News, 179
Bridget Jones movies, 124
Brinkley, David, 104
British Empire, 30, 59
Bromwich, David, 165
Brookings Institutions, 181
Brown, Wendy, 16, 39
Brownell, Kathryn Crammer, 158
Bruno, Giordano, 163
Brzezinski, Zbigniew
  Totalitarianism, Dictatorship, and Autocracy (1956), 78
Buchanan, Pat, 93, 97
Buckingham, Duke of, 56
Buffet, Warren, 191
bureaucracy, 44, 48, 51, 167
Burke, Edmund, 33, 82, 108, 146, 148, 150, 161
Bush family, 103, 166
Bush, George H.W., 93, 95, 98
Bush, George W., 93, 94, 95, 99
Bush, Jeb, 93
business
  entities, 121
  model, 128, 140
Butler, May, 86
butterfly ballots, 93

cabals, 56
Calhoun, John C.
  A Disquisition on Government (1851), 172
California National Guardsmen, 154
Calvin, John, 163
Capa, Robert, 126
capitalism, 70, 79, 96, 109, 110, 129, 143, 149, 150, 173, 183
  capitalist philanthropy, 16
Capitol Building riots (2021), 8, 151
Carlson, Tucker, 105, 142
Carnegie, Andrew, 63, 179
Carroll, Lewis, 153-154

Carson, Rachel, 171-172
Carter, Jimmy, 149
Carville, James, 174
Casals, Pablo, 17
Catholic Church, 28, 100, 163, 164, 192. *See also* Christianity
Cats (musical), 128
causes, 164-167
CBS, 104
censorship, 182
Channing, William Ellery, 61
Chaplin, Charlie
  Modern Times (1936), 81
charisma, 44-45, 49, 51, 75, 167-169, 177
Charles II, king of England, 56
checks and balances, 2, 3, 18
Chicago Tribune, 64
China, 39, 78, 80, 88, 171, 189
Christianity, 47, 163. *See also* Catholic Church
  conversions to, 26
  evangelical, 19
Chua, Amy, 158
Churchill, Winston, 167
citizenship, 9-10, 22, 50-53. *See also* good citizenship
  beyond legal status, 154
  democracy and, 8, 10, 18-19
  democratic, 112
  dependent variable, as a, 156
  duties of citizens, 19
  political role of, 154
  practice of, 48, 110
  problem of, 19
  rights, 5
  third vocation, as a, 47-49
  vocation of, 10, 132, 154, 161
civil rights, 3, 20, 59, 60, 168
Civil Rights Act (1964), 86, 92
Civil War (1861-1865), 35, 54, 57, 58, 61, 68, 84, 90, 130, 159
civilization, 188

Index

class wars, 79
click-bait accounting, 178
Clifford, Thomas, 56
climate change, 25, 139, 180, 184, 193
   denialism, 139
Clinton, Bill, 89, 135
   family, 166
   impeachment of, 89
Clinton, Hillary, 174
CNBC, 168
CNN, 104, 105, 133
Coates, Ta-Nehisi, 148
Colbert, Stephen, 105
Cold War, 77–81, 83, 84, 98
   ideology, end of, 79–81
comedy, 175, 176
Committee on Public Information (CPI), 113, 115
commodities, 115
common sense, 144, 146, 147, 152, 153–180, 185, 189, 190
   individual, 145
   shared, 146
   truths, 145, 147
communications, 131
communism, 5, 39, 72, 79, 80, 84, 164
community, 157–161
competition, 46
concentration camps, 79
concepts, entities *vs*, 21
Condorcet, Marquis de, 163
confirmation, 134–137
   thesis, 135
Congo, 194
Congress, contempt of, 144
consent, engineering of, 115, 131
conservatism, 83
conservatives, 148
conspiracy theories, 138
Constantine the Great, 26
Constitution of the United States (1787), 116, 133, 186
   amendments to. *See* constitutional amendments
   Article I, 59
   political parties, 56
   ratification, 32, 34
   sovereignty, 34
   theory of, 68
constitutional amendments, 32
   First Amendment, 96, 114, 191
   Fourteenth Amendment, 94
   Nineteenth Amendment, 4, 11, 60, 86
   Thirteenth to Fifteenth Amendments, 4, 60
   Twenty-Fourth Amendment, 60, 92
   Twenty-Sixth Amendment, 4, 60
Constitutional Convention, 3, 32, 176, 179
constitutionalism, 37
Consumer Financial Protection Bureau, 2
consumer society, 46
consumer sovereignty, 120, 131, 135
consumerism, 131, 173
contextual factors, 186
contract enforcement, 109
contractors, 172
convictions. *See* absolute convictions
Cook, Tim, 179
Cooke, Jay, 179
Cooper, Anderson, 142
Cooper, Ashley, 56
Copernicus, Nicolaus, 41
coral bleaching, 180
Cornwallis, Lord Charles, 30
Coulter, Ann, 137, 149
Council on Foreign Relations, 102
counterculture, 88
courts of first instance, 92
creative destruction, 149
Creel Committee (Committee on Public Information), 73, 114
Creel, George, 114
Croesus, 23
Cronkite, Walter, 104

Crossen, Cynthia, 118
crowds, 184
　mental unity of, 71
Cruz, Ted, 12
culture war, 96–99, 100, 121–122, 138, 193
Cuomo, Andrew, 188
Curie, Marie, 42
currency regulation, 13
cyclical history, 35
Cyrus, 23

Dahl, Robert A., 58
Dancing with the Stars (TV show), 177
Daniels, Stormy, 8
Dante Alighieri
　De Monarchia (1213), 26
Darwin, Charles, 42
　Origin of the Species (1859), 67
De Jouvenel, Bertrand, 169
De Maistre, Joseph, 143, 157, 169
De Tocqueville, Alexis, 31, 108, 116, 146
Deaver, Michael, 166
Debs, Eugene, 113
decency, 21
Declaration of Independence (1776), 3, 61, 81, 82, 116, 143, 145, 177
Declaration on the Rights of Man and the Citizen (1789), 28, 29, 43
Defoe, Daniel, 163
deforestation, 180
deindustrialization, 159
demagogues, 21, 25, 35, 49–50
　rise of, 71–72
democracy, 4–5, 21, 22, 24, 35, 53–76
　arsenal of, 76
　challenges to, 35
　citizenship and, 8, 10, 19
　crisis of, 8
　defending, 19–20, 191–195
　definition of, 155
　democratic arena, 66–68

democratic commitment, 54–56
　economic theory of, 120, 131
　functions of, 55–56
　good, 23
　institutions of, 11
　policy-making, 16
　survival of, 179–180
Democratic National Convention (2024), 106
Democratic Party, 2, 84, 86, 90, 136, 137, 174, 188, 193
　presidential primary elections (2020), 95
Democratic Republican Party, 57, 64
demos, 43, 50, 24, 131
Department of Education, 2
derangement, 99
deregulation, 98
Derrida, Jacques, 147
DeSantis, Ron, 2, 100
Descartes, Rene, 41, 163
　Discourse on Method (1637), 182
despotism, 18
DeVos, Betsy, 100
Dewey, John, 46, 73, 74, 75, 101, 115, 130, 132
　The Public and Its Problems (1927), 74
dictatorship, 78
Diderot, Denis, 163
digital surveillance, 98
dignity, 21
diplomacy, 13
Dirksen, Everett, 86
disenchantment, 6, 41, 42, 46, 51, 69, 108, 117, 118, 152, 157, 163, 178
　promotion of, 118
Disney, 134
disposable diapers, 129
diversity viewpoint, 168
division of labor, 109
Dixiecrats, 59
doctor's duty, 47
dog whistles, 87

doublespeak, 140
doubts, rise of, 68–75
Douglas, Michael, 129
Douglas, Stephen, 172
Dow Chemical, 125
'drill, baby, drill' 177, 180
Duke, James, 179
dysfunction, 8, 132–152

E. H. Harrimans (bank), 98
echo chambers, 127, 131, 152
economic equality, 98
economic exploitation, 79
economic growth, 97
  concept of, 173
economism, 168
edification, 123
education, 60–63, 67, 99–103, 106,
    132, 135, 172, 173, 177
  charter schools, 100, 101
  higher, 61, 193
  literacy rates, 61
  private schools, 100
  privatization of, 100–102
  public college funding, 103
  public schools, 61–62, 101
  rising costs of, 102–103
  SATs, 101
  scholarships, 102
  standards, 13
  student aid, 102
  student debt, 102
  tuition rates, 102
Egginton, William, 158
Einstein, Albert, 42, 119
Eisenhower, Dwight D., 9, 186
Election Day, 3, 93, 175
elections, frequency of, 11
Electoral College, 18, 19, 32, 35, 37,
    59, 159, 160
  as an institution, 160
elitism, 21
Elks, 65

emoluments, 186
employment, 149
Engels, Friedrich, 79
Enlightenment era, 10, 22–35, 36, 39, 41,
    50, 75, 109, 112, 115, 116, 118, 124,
    142, 143, 145, 147, 156, 168, 169
  boxes, matrix of, 24–25
  cyclical history, 23–35
  philosophers, 62
Enron, 98
entertainment, 123, 124–130, 131, 135,
    160, 172, 173, 174, 177, 189
entrepreneurship, 149, 180
environmental issues
  damage, 129
  destruction, 25, 193
  protection, 13
Environmental Protection Agency, 1
epidemics, 128
epistemic crisis, 190
epistemology, 144
  epistemological dilemma, 144
equality, 4, 21, 97, 102, 173
  'all men are created equal' 157
  economic, 98
  educational, 61
  political right of, 10, 21
  principle of, 28
escalator event, 10, 76, 165, 173
Espionage Act (1917), 114
essays, 5
Esso, 176
Estee Lauder (cosmetics brand), 134
ethics, 147
ethnic minorities, 187
European Union (EU), 37
exceptionalism, 173, 185
exclusion, 90, 93
Executive Branch, 13, 159
Executive Orders, 113
expertise, 72–75
experts, role of, 73, 74
extremism, 49, 86, 97

Facebook, 125, 127, 130, 134, 135, 175
fact checkers, 13
factions, 84, 90
factories, 110
  jobs, 88
fair trial, 11
fake news, 139
false consciousness, 48, 52, 79
false stories, 54
Falwell, Jerry, 161
Fama, Eugene, 129
fascism, 1, 2, 5, 72, 128, 155
  anti-fascists, 79
Fast, Howard, 144
federal budget deficit, 95
Federal Depository Library Program (1813), 62
Federal Trade Commission (FTC), 186
federalism, 21, 154
  principles of, 92
Federalist Paper, 33, 172
  No. 1, 33
  No. 10, 58
  No. 14, 33, 133
  No. 51, 161
Federalist Party, 57
Federalist Society, 147
Federalist, The (1788), 22, 33, 57, 145
federalists, 58
Feldman, Noah, 11
felonious activity, 8
feminism, 137, 143
  radical, 97
fertility crisis, 119. See also population decline
fertilizers, 180
feudal system, 30
Fields, Harrison, 167
filibustering, 19, 89
filter bubbles, 127, 131
financial assistance programs, 186
firebombing, 191
Fish, Stanley, 147

'fixing the phones' 195
  alternatives, 185–187
  context, 183–189
  failure, 184–185
  mission, 187–189
Floyd, George, 20
focus groups, 173
Food and Drug Administration, 2
food and drug safety, 13
footnotes, 6–8
Ford corporation, 80
Ford, Henry, 123
  Model T, 109, 110
forest fires, 127, 128, 139
format, 39–40
fossil fuels, 177
Foster, John Bellamy, 13
Foucault, Michel, 147
Founding Fathers, 3, 11, 22, 32, 34, 36, 37, 54, 116, 130, 145, 161, 169, 176
Fox News, 88, 134, 147, 154, 179
fracking, 184
France, 14, 27, 55, 156
  aristocracy, 28
  constitution of, 29
  monarchy, 28
  old regime, 62
  sovereignty, 43
  The Terror, 29, 35
franchise issue, 59, 60
Franco, Francisco, 72
Frank, Thomas, 98–99, 122
Franklin, Benjamin, 3, 56, 116, 179, 195
  Autobiography, 116
fraternity, 29
fraud, 92, 98. See also voters, fraud
free marketplace, 129
free riding, 5
free speech, 66. See also freedom of speech
Free Student Alliance, 40, 42
freedom, 27

freedom from fear, 136
freedom from want, 136
freedom of association, 191
freedom of choice, 173
freedom of expression, 137
freedom of religion, 11, 16, 136
freedom of speech, 11, 66, 67, 68, 114, 136, 146, 181–183, 191, 192
French and Indian War, 30
French Revolution, 28–29, 57, 62
French temptation, 34, 35
Freud, Sigmund, 39, 70, 72, 73, 145, 146
 ego/id/super-ego, 69
 Group Psychology and the Analysis of Ego (1922), 71
Frieden, Betty, 143
Friedman, Milton, 15, 129, 130
Friedman, Thomas, 165
Friedman, Vanessa, 106
Friedrich, Carl, 78

Galbraith, John Kenneth, 121
Galen, 164
Galilei, Galileo, 41
gated communities, 127
gatekeepers, 129, 143, 146, 183
Gates, Bill, 16, 191
Gaza, 170, 193
Gazzaley, Adam, 189
General Hospital (TV show), 175
General Motors, 80, 120, 125, 134
George III, king of England, 194
Germany, 113
 Nazi, 54, 78
Gibbon, Edward, 163
Gielgud, John, 194
gifts, 186
Gilded Age, 179
Gingrich, Newt, 88, 89, 95, 161
givenness, 80
'giving up' 147–148
Global North, 159
Global South, 159

global warming, 129, 139, 149, 180
'going nowhere' 142–143
Goldman, Emma, 113
Goldwater, Barry, 85, 86, 87, 89, 161
good citizenship, 10, 20, 21, 34, 35, 55, 59, 75, 86, 103, 108, 114, 131, 132, 147, 156, 157, 163, 177, 185, 191
 community and, 158
 practice of, 157
Google, 125
Gore, Al, 93
Gorsuch, Neil, 4, 32, 90
government
 bonds, 95
 choice of, 55
 representation by, 55
Graham, Lindsay, 2
Grant, Ulysses S., 122
Greece, classic, 156, 161
 origins of democracy, 36, 38
green new deal, 186
greenhouse gas emissions, 177
Greenland, 170
Gresham's law, 135
Griffin, Kenneth, 17
Gross Domestic Product (GDP), 180
Gross National Product (GNP), 180
Grossman, Matt, 90
Grotius, Hugo, 163
group thinking, 71
gun rights, 97, 98. *See also* arms, right to bear
Gutenberg Revolution, 163, 164
Gutfield, Greg, 141
Guys and Dolls, 165

Habits of the Heart (1985), 115–116, 117
Hacker, Andrew S., 159
Hacker, Jacob, 85
Hamas, 113
Hamilton (musical), 128
Hamilton, Alexander, 3, 23, 33, 57, 58, 172, 179

Hamilton, James T., 106
Han, Byung-Chul, 157
Hanks, Tom, 151
Hannity, Sean, 105, 126, 140
happiness, 119
Harari, Yuval, 151
Harris, Kamala, 2, 9, 93, 160, 174, 185, 188
Harrison, Benjamin, 58
Hartz, Louis, 30, 31
Harvard University, 168
Hassan, Steven, 179
Hayek, Friedrich, 15, 129
Hayes, Chris, 175, 187
health, 18
  global, 184
  insurance, 13
Hearst, William Randolph, 64
Hedges, Chris, 124
Hegel, Friedrich, 39
Hegseth, Pete, 183
Heine, Heinrich, 163
Henry, Jules, 118
Henry, Patrick, 3
herd instinct, 71
Heritage Foundation, 2, 32
Herodotus, 23
  Histories (c.430 BC), 22
hinterland, 159, 160
Hippocratic Oath, 47
Hiroshima, 117
Hitler, Adolf, 29, 53, 72, 78
  Mein Kampf (1925), 54, 72
  Third Reich, 5
Hobbes, Thomas, 163, 168
  Leviathan (1652), 27
Hofstadter, Richard, 58
Hollywood, 166, 194
  casting, 129
Hollywood Screen Actors Guild, 15
Holmes, Oliver Wendell, 67, 68, 114, 132, 192
Hopkins, David A., 87
House of Cards (TV show), 177

housing, 18
humanities, 41
Hume, David, 163
Hungary, 14
hurricanes, 180
  Hurricane Matilda, 124
Huxley, Aldous, 139, 140–141
  Brave New World (1931), 140
hyperbole, 179

icebergs, melting, 180
ID documents, 91, 92
identity politics, 99
ideology
  communist, 79
  end of, 79
imbalance, 17–18
immigration, 50, 100, 113, 121, 178, 187
  illegal, 170
impeachment, 89
imperialism, 164
inalienable rights, 145
inclusion, 59–60, 90–99, 106, 132
  neoliberalism, 94–96
  rigging the rules, 93–94
  techniques, 91–93
independent expenditures, 96
Index Librorum Prohibitorum, 163, 192
India, 39
individualism, 116–117, 136
  utilitarian, 116
individuals, problem of, 69–71
Indonesia, 88, 157
industrial capitalism, 173
industrial pollution, 13
Industrial Revolution, 109, 110, 117
influencers, 184, 188, 190
  opinion, 114
information, 108–131
  overload, 190
  system, 39, 108, 111, 122, 150, 157, 158, 160, 164
  technology, 117, 156
Inhofe, James, 139

inspiration, 192–193
Instagram, 127, 130, 146, 175
institutional imbalance, 18
Intergovernmental Panel on Climate Change (IPCC), 139, 177
International Harvester, 120
Iran, 39, 176
iron cage, 75, 167
Israel, Jonathan I., 28
Israel, 90, 113
Israel Today, 130

J. P. Morgan (bank), 98
Jackson, Andrew
   "First Inaugural Address" (1833), 172
Jacksonian Democrats, 58
Jacoby, Susan, 126
James I, king of England
   The Divine Rights of Kings (1610), 23, 27
James, William, 46
Japan, 186
Javits, Eric, 106
Javits, Jacob, 86
Jay, John, 23, 172
Jefferson, Thomas, 3, 57, 58, 116, 142, 143, 145, 157, 177
Jewish community, 28
Jim Crow segregation, 54, 86, 90
John Lewis Voting Rights Act (2021), 89
Johnson, Lyndon, 86
journalism, 63–65, 67, 75, 103–106, 124, 132
   click-bait, 65, 108, 131
   gatekeeping, 104–106
Judeo-Christian values, 97
Julius Caesar, 194
Julius Caesar (Shakespeare play, 1599), 194
justice, 21

Kabaservice, Geoffrey, 84
Kafka, Franz, 24
Kahneman, Daniel, 146
Kant, Immanuel, 39, 161, 163
Kavanaugh, Brett, 4
kayfabe, 175. *See also* wrestling, professional
Kennedy, Anthony, 94
Kennedy, Robert F. Jr., 142, 184
Kennedys (political family), 103
Kimmel, Jimmy, 140
King, Martin Luther
   Letter from Birmingham Jail (1963), 116
King, Martin Luther, Jr., 133
kings, divine right of, 111
kingship, 26
Klein, Ezra, 169, 187
Knights of Columbus, 65
knowledge, 81, 126, 182
   scientific, 99
Koch brothers, 17
Koestler, Arthur, 79
Konnikova, Maria, 179
Kristol, Irving, 161
Krugman, Paul, 165
Kwak, James, 168

Laffer, Arthur, 87
language, 109–117
   biblical, 115, 131
   fixing, 190
   fourth language, 117–122
   individualistic, 115, 131
   origins, 163
   persuasive, 131
   political, 21
   public, 190
   republican, 115, 131
Lanier, Jaron, 146, 164
Larson, Erik, 135
Latino community, 154
Lauderdale, Duke of, 56
law and order, maintenance of, 60
Lazarus, Emma
   "The New Colossus" 69

Le Bon, Gustave, 73, 184
  The Crowd (1895), 71, 111
Le Pen, Marine, 14, 155
Leavitt, Karoline, 183
Lee, Ivy, 111, 112
Lee, Robert E., 122
legality, 51
Legislative Branch, 186
legitimacy, 43–44, 52
  charisma, 44
  legality, 44
  sources of, 43
  tradition, 43
Leibniz, Gottfried, 41
Leipzig, battle of, 29
Lend Lease, concept of, 186
Lenin, Vladimir, 149, 183, 188
Leninism, 48
Lessig, Lawrence, 95
Levin, Mark, 137
Levitin, Daniel, 163
Levitsky, Steven, 12, 18
Lewinsky, Monica, 89
LGBT rights, 187
liberal democracy, 18, 37, 53, 57
liberal tradition, 31–32, 35
liberalism, 15, 39, 88, 164. *See also* neoliberalism
  scope of, 54
liberty, 28
libraries, 62, 63, 99
Library of Congress, 63, 163
Lincoln, Abraham, 9, 172, 177
  bedroom of, 17
  First Inaugural Address, 18
  Gettysburg Address (1864), 116
  physical appearance, 129
  Republicans, 58
Lippes, Adam, 106
Lippman, Walter, 73, 75, 104, 114, 115, 130
  Public Opinion (1922), 73
  The Plantom Public (1925), 73

Lipset, Seymour Martin, 80
literacy tests, 91
Locke, John, 31, 41, 162, 163
  The Second Treatise on Government (1690), 23, 27, 31
logic, 41
Los Angeles Police Department (LAPD), 154
Los Angeles Times, 64
Louis XV, king of France, 34
Louis XVI, king of France, 29, 31
Lozada, Carlos, 185
Lubbell, Samuel, 84
Lucas, Robert, 16, 129, 170
Ludendorff, Erich, 72
Ludlow Massacre, 111
Luther, Martin, 45
Lutwick, Howard, 183
Luvs (diaper brand), 129

Machiavelli, Niccolo, 163
  The Prince (1532), 22, 26
MacIntyre, Auron, 169
Macron, Emmanuel, 29
Macy's (department store), 110
Maddow, Rachel, 105, 141
Madison, James, 2, 3, 23, 31, 33, 53, 56, 58, 133, 162, 172, 179
MAGA (Make America Great Again), 2, 54, 148, 160, 175, 187
Maistre, Joseph de, 34
majority rule, 21
Mamdani, Zohran, 188
Mamma Mia, 128
managerial elite, 169
Mankiw, Georg, 16, 129, 170
Mann, Horace, 61
Mann, Thomas, 106
Marathon, battle of, 23
marketing, 118, 173
marketplace for ideas, 66, 75, 105, 130–131, 132, 137, 138, 146, 190, 192

Marshall Field (department store), 110
Marshall, Alfred, 70
Marx, Karl, 39, 79
Marxian ideas, 79
   dialectics, notion of, 79
   social theory, 48
Marxism, 186
Mazzucato, Mariana, 180
McCain, John, 151, 166
McCarthy Era (1947-1954), 15
McCarthy, Joseph, 144
McCarthyism, 68, 169
McConnell, Mitch, 2, 90, 138
McGuffey Readers, 62, 100
McLuhan, Marshall, 122, 123
   Understanding Media (1964), 123
McMahon, Linda, 168, 177, 183
Medicaid, 193
Medicare, 95, 193
medicine, 46
medieval European societies, 42
'medium is the message' 122, 123
Meese, Edwin, 166
mega donors, 17
Mellon, Timothy, 17
meritocracy, 103
   opponents of, 103
   proponents of, 103
Meta, 135, 146
Mexico, 88, 170
   Gulf of, 179
middle classes, 14, 15
Middle East military interventions, 136
military alliance obligations, 169
military service, 60
Mill, John Stuart, 66, 67, 132, 137, 138, 139, 146, 148, 163
   On Liberty (1859), 66, 67, 137
Miller, Arthur, 15
Miller, Steven, 183
Milner, Henry, 66
minority rule, 21
Mirowski, Philip, 168

misogyny, 18, 85, 184
mixed government, 35, 90, 133, 142, 162, 180, 194
   concept of, 22, 26, 32
mob rule, 24, 35, 36
modernity, 37-38, 39, 40, 42, 46, 51, 53, 62, 155, 171
   narrative crisis in, 158
monarchy, 22, 23, 24, 35, 144
   France, 28
monopolistic competition, 118-121, 131
Monroe, Marilyn, 15
Montaigne, Michel de, 163
Montesquieu, Baron de, 31, 143, 162, 163
   The Spirit of the Laws (1748), 23, 31
morality, 97
   moral character, 91
   moral rights, 19
   moral values, 39
Morgan, J. P., 179
Morrill Land Grant Acts (1862 and, 1890), 62
mortgage relief, 17
Mosca, Gaetano, 169
motherhood, 148
Mounk, Yascha, 36
muckraking, 99
muddling, 77-108, 137-139, 190
Muller, Jan-Werner, 15
Murrow, Edward R., 104, 130
Musk, Elon, 2, 16, 17, 20, 94, 96, 130, 171, 179, 191
Mussolini, Benito, 2, 72
My Fair Lady, 128
Myanmar, 134
myths, 151

Nadal, Rafael, 126
Nagasaki, 117
Napoleon Bonaparte, General, 29, 35
narratives, 35, 148-150
NASA, 17
nation, 35

national defense, 13
national forests, 13
National Gazette, 64
national identity, 158
National Institute of Health, 1
National Intelligencer, 64
National Labor Relations Board, 1
National Organization of Women (NOW), 147
National Voter Registration Act (1993), 92
nationalism, 28, 39, 143, 164
nationality, 29
Native Americans, 4, 11, 31
natural law, 43
  concept of, 26
natural rights, 31, 145
natural sciences, 41
Navarro, Peter, 183
negotiations, 168
Neoliberal Thought Collective, 168
neoliberalism, 15–17, 21, 88, 97, 98, 100, 125, 130, 158, 168
  characteristics of, 16
  definition of, 16
  inclusion, 94–96
Netanyahu, Benjamin, 130, 155
New Deal, 8, 80, 88, 97, 169
New World, 80
New York Evening Post, 64
New York Herald, 64
New York Sun, 64
New York Times, 64, 105, 106, 182, 183
  International Edition, 106
New York Times Company, 189
New Zealand, 174
news cycle, 128, 131, 152
news feeds, 127, 131, 161
news items, 142
newspapers, 99, 104, 141, 163, 172
newspeak, 140
Newton, Isaac, 41
Niebuhr, Reinhold, 76
Nielson boxes, 126

Nietzsche, Friedrich, 39
Nixon, Richard, 14
Nobel Prize in Economics, 119, 170
Norris, Frank, 111
Norway, 174
nuclear stand-offs, 25
nuclear weapons, 184

O'Connor, Sandra Day, 94
Oakeshott, Michael, 36–37
Obama, Barack, 32, 90, 150, 166, 167
Obama, Michelle, 106
Obamacare, 89
obfuscation, 169–170
objectivity, 70
Occupy Wall Street, 147
October 7, 2023, attacks, 113
Office of Management and Budget (OMB), 186
oil
  companies, 129
  resources, 135
Olasky, Marvin, 138
oligarchy, 23, 24, 35, 179, 180, 74
Olivier, Lawrence, 194
Olympic Games, 129
op-ed article submissions, 130
Open Secrets research group, 121
opinion leaders, 146
Orban, Viktor, 14, 155
Orchestra Pit Theory, 147
Orenstein, Norman, 106
Orwell, George, 120, 139–140, 141, 142
  1984 73, 140, 142, 181
  Animal Farm, 59
Ottoman Empire, 42
outrage, 137
overload, 146–148

PAC, 121
paganism, 26
Paine, Thomas, 82, 118, 143–146, 194–195

"Crisis Paper" (1776), 195
Common Sense (1776), 33, 144, 145, 195
Palestine, 170
  pro-Palestinian groups, 90
Pampers, 129
pamphlets, anti-war, 67
pandemics, 180
Paris Agreement on Climate Change, 177
Parks, Rosa, 132
parties. *See* political parties
party activity, 132
party press, 63–64
Pasteur, Louis, 42
patriotism, 114, 177
peace and prosperity, 11
Pearl Harbor, 186
Pelosi, Nancy, 2, 188
Pence, Mike, 8
Pennsylvania Railroad, 120
Pentagon, 169
permanent campaign, 178
personality disorders, 186
pesticides, 171
Phantom of the Opera, 128
philanthropy, 63
philosophy
  deduction, 161
  induction, 161
  key thinkers, 161
Pichai, Sundar, 179
piecemeal social reform, 79
Pied Piper, 172–174
Pierson, Paul, 85, 159
Piketty, Thomas, 170
plastic contaminations, 180
Platea, battle of, 23
Plato, 25, 126, 156, 161, 182
  Republic (c.375 BC), 22, 81
Plouffe, David, 174
pluralism, 21
  anti-pluralism, 15
podcasts, 188
Polanyi, Karl, 149–150

polarization, 136
police
  states, 79
  violence, 140
political parties, 56–59, 84–90, 110, 120
  advertising and, 110–111
  dissimilar, 89–90
  factions, 57–59
  new alliances, 87–88
  representation, 57
  right-wing, 85–86
  severe polarization, 88–89
political prophets, 177
politics, 22
poll tax, 92
Polybius, 24, 25, 26, 32, 162
  The Histories, 23
Popper, Karl, 75, 79
popular sovereignty, concept of, 28, 34, 35, 43
population decline, 119
populism, 8, 14–15, 17, 21, 54, 99
  age of, 53
pornography, 49, 97
Posner, Richard A., 89
post-truth society, 161, 173
Postman, Neil, 123, 124, 125, 126, 128, 129, 141, 142, 143, 150, 151, 152, 157, 174, 175, 179, 193
poverty, 100, 109
pragmatism, 46
preference formation, 120
prejudices, 82, 116
presidential election (2024), 128
press conferences, 178
Preston, Ivan L., 118
Price, Richard, 82
printing press, 163, 164. *See also* Gutenberg Revolution
privatization, 98
  opponents of, 101
pro-market economists, 129

problems, 164
Procter & Gamble, 129
product differentiation, 118, 131
professionalism, 64–65
propaganda, 73, 108, 112–115, 117, 131
　techniques, 115
property
　private, 109
　rights, 46, 86
prosperity, 159, 180
Protestantism, 47
pseudo-events, 178
psychology, 131, 179
Ptolemy, 164
public good, 101
public health, 142
public relations, 108, 111, 115, 117, 131
　growth of, 111
public schools, 101
Pulitzer, Joseph, 64
Puritanism, 47
Putin, Vladimir, 155
Putnam, Robert, 65
puzzles and problems, 162–164

Qatar, 186

race theory, 148
racial segregation, 59, 132, 133
racism, 4, 18, 85, 91, 136, 184
Radical Enlightenment, 28
　opponents of, 28
Rampton, Sheldon, 105
rationality
　functional, 44, 51, 83
　substantive, 44, 52
Rawls, John, 161
Reagan, Ronald, 15, 87, 88, 89, 94, 98, 135, 136, 149, 150, 161, 166, 167, 185, 194, 195
reason, 41, 62, 67, 69, 70, 72, 73, 75, 81, 112, 115, 118, 124, 131, 142, 152, 168, 169, 173

Reddit, 146
Redgrave, Vanessa, 194
redistribution, 170
Reformation period, 27
Rehnquist, William, 94
religion. *See also* freedom of religion
　biblical wisdom, 116
　church and state, separation of, 187
　faith, 17, 142, 152
　religiosity, 42
　schools, 98
reports, 5–6
republic (*res publica*), 26, 35
Republican Party, 84, 86, 87, 94, 95, 97, 121, 131, 159
Republican virtue, 35, 98, 116
republicanism, 88, 117
republics, 25–26
reputation management, 118
research institutes, 105
resentment, 21
rhetoric, 190
rights, 21
robber barons, 114
Roberts, John, 4
Rockefeller family, 111–112, 135
Rockefeller, John D., 179
Rockefeller, Nelson, 85
Rogan, Joe, 142
Roman Empire, 25, 26, 36, 194
　plebs, 15
Romanticism, 28
Romney, Mitt, 166
Roosevelt, Franklin, 76, 136, 167, 186
　Four Freedoms Speech (1941), 116, 136
Roosevelt, Theodore, 9
Rosen, Larry D., 189
Rousseau, Jean Jacques, 28, 163
　The Social Contract (1762), 27
Rubio, Marco, 183
rule-by-many, 29
rule-by-one, 26–27, 29
rule of law, 89

Runyon, Damon, 165
Russia, 80, 167
  Ukrainian war, 186

Said, Edward, 147
Salk, Jonas, 42
Scalia, Antonin, 138
Schenk, Charles, 114
Schlafly, Phyllis, 137
Schmitt, Carl, 169
school shootings, 128
schools. *See* education
Schudson, Michael, 11, 63, 176
Schumer, Chuck, 2, 188
Schumpeter, Joseph, 120–121, 149
Scialabba, George, 148
science, 46, 62, 66, 67, 69, 109, 124, 131, 142, 146, 152, 168, 169, 173
  knowledge, 99
  methods, 74
  models, 75
  scientific research, 13
Scranton, William, 85
sea levels, 180
Second Circuit Court of Appeals, 17
Securities and Exchange Commission (SEC), 186
Sedition Act (1918), 67, 114
self-evident truths, 81, 82, 142, 145, 177
selling/sales, 109–110
Senate, 18
separation of powers, 2, 3, 31
Seven Years War, 30
Shakespeare, William, 123, 124, 194
shareholders, 180
Shelbourne, David, 19
Sherman, William Tecumseh, 193
show business, 164–170
shtick (comic routine), 175
Silent Spring, 171
silos, 152
  silo thinking, 108, 127, 131

Simmel, Georg, 39
Simpsons, The, 124
sin, theological concept of, 187
Sinclair, Upton, 111
Slate Magazine, 127, 179
slavery, 35, 159
sludge, 105, 138, 148, 183
slum neighbourhoods, 100
smallest public office, 21, 51
smartphones, 108, 117, 123, 131, 138, 157, 161, 164, 175, 188, 189, 190, 192, 193
Smith, Adam, 109
Smith, Winston, 139, 142
Snapchat, 146, 175
social balance, 121
social capital, 65–66
social contract theory, 35, 27
social media, 8, 123, 146, 160, 161, 175, 178, 188
  algorithms, 130, 135, 138
social psychology, 109
social sciences, 41, 167
social security, 13, 95, 88, 166, 193
social studies, 81
social welfare, 83, 94
socialism, 39, 113, 164
society
  purposes of, 42
  shape of, 42
sociology, 48, 171
Socrates, 156
soma, 141
Sombart, Werner, 39
Somme, battle of the (1916), 113
Soros, George, 191
Southern Strategy, 87
sovereignty, 34–35
  concept of, 34, 35
  sovereign power, 27, 35
Soviet Union, 79. *See also* Union of Soviet Socialist Republics (USSR)
Spanish American War (1898), 64

Spanish Civil War, 126
Spanish flu, 49
Spartans, 156
special people, 48–49
species extinction, 180
Spinoza, Baruch, 163
spoils system, 44
stakeholders, 180
Stalin, Joseph, 72, 149
Stalinism, 48
Standard Oil, 120, 135
Stauber, John, 105
stereotypes, 73, 115
stock market indexes, 180
stories, 35, 150–152
Strategic Air Command, 80
strategic intelligence, 13
strategists, 112
students, 102. *See also* education
subjectivity, 70
Sudan, 193
super Political Action Committees (super PACs), 96
supply-side economics, 87, 94
Supreme Court of the United States (SCOTUS), 18, 49, 68, 96
  Abrams vs. United States (1919), 67
  Browder v. Gayle (1956), 133
  Buckley v. Valeo (1976), 95
  Citizens United v. FEC (2010), 20, 95, 138
  Crawford v. Marion County Election Board (2008), 92
  gay marriage rights, 16
  justices, 4, 67, 93, 94, 138
  McCutcheon et al. v. FEC (2014), 95, 138
  Schenck v. United States (1919), 114, 192
  Shelby County v. Holder (2013), 92
surveillance, 140
survey research, 173
Survivor (TV show), 175

syndicalism, 39
Syria, 193
'system', the, 136

tale of woe, 170–174
Tarbell, Ida, 111
target, 10–11
tariffs, 17, 165, 169, 189
taxation, 87, 94, 97, 119, 186
Taylor, Frederick Winslow, 80
Tea Party, 147
technology, 109, 122–130
telegraph, 122
television, 123–124, 125, 126, 131, 138, 141, 158, 163, 165, 167, 178, 187, 194
terms, 20–21, 35
Tesla, 130, 191
Thatcher, Margaret, 150
theatre
  imperatives, 178–179
  performance, 178
Theology, 41, 142
Thermopylae, battle of, 23
think tanks, 105, 140, 181
Thomas, Clarence, 4, 94, 137
Thompson, Derek, 169
Thompson, Emma, 194
Thompson, Mark, 13, 189, 190
Thucydides, 25, 49
  History of the Peloponnesian War (c. 411 BC), 22, 23
Thurmond, Strom, 85, 86
Tierney, John, 128
Times, The, 64
tobacco companies, 129
totalitarianism, 5, 78
trade associations, 105
trade unions, 98
Tragedy Syndrome, 80–84
transgenderism, 186
transportation, 18
trash talk, 184

Treasury notes, 95
trickle-down economics, 97
Troeltsch, Ernest, 39
Trump, Donald J., 6, 9, 13, 46, 66, 95, 103, 147, 153, 166, 167, 168, 169, 171, 172, 173, 175, 177, 178, 179, 181, 183, 184, 185, 186, 187, 188, 189, 192. *See also* escalator event; MAGA (Make America Great Again)
   academic performance, 173
   administration, 119, 168
   Age of Trump, 46, 103
   anti-Trump Americans, 187
   appointments, 177
   autism claims, 142
   Capitol Building riots, 151
   cause(s), 165, 166
   'crooked' nature of, 1, 2–3, 4, 5
   culture war, 138
   democracy and citizenship, 19, 20, 29
   Elon Musk, relations with, 94, 96
   family, 103
   followers, 175
   foreign policy, 170
   gender ideology, 35
   honors and awards, 87
   inauguration of, 179
   individual characteristics, 160
   Iran, view on, 176
   Israel, relations with, 113
   leadership style, 4
   military deployments, 154
   modernity, 37
   neoliberalism, 17
   nominations, 32, 90, 100
   personality, 12, 13
   populism, 14
   prejudices of, 4
   presidential elections, 1–2, 7, 8, 9, 10, 37, 54, 85, 90, 129, 133, 166, 167, 174, 175, 184, 189
   Republican Party, 89
   showmanship, 4, 160, 164–165, 170, 175, 176, 178
   sovereignty, 34
   speeches, 168
   tariff rates, 165
   television personality, 12, 167
   trends, 66
   Trump test, 189–191
   Trump shock, 11–13
   Trumpism, 55, 153, 167, 186
   truth, 12
   universities, 183
Trump, Melania, 9, 106
trust, decline of, 129
truth, 12, 114, 115, 118. *See also* Age of Post-Truth; post-truth society; self-evident truths
tsunamis, 128
'turning point' 75–76
Tussman, Joseph, 19
Twitter, 127, 130, 146. *See also* X
tyranny, 24, 26, 35, 47
   of the majority, 19

Uihlein, Elizabeth, 17
Uihlein, Richard, 17
Ukraine, 193
   democracy, 186
   war, 170
Ulysses
   The Odyssey, 134
unemployment, 193
Union of Soviet Socialist Republics (USSR), 78
United Nations (UN), 139, 177
United States Customs and Border Protection Bureau of the Department of Homeland Security, 189
United States Marines, 154
United States Steel Corporation, 111, 125
universal suffrage, 11

universalist principles, 28
urban centers, 159
USS Maine battleship, 64
utilitarianism, 150
utility, 119

vaccinations, 146, 184
Valjean, Jean, 151
Vance, J. D., 2
Vanderbilt, Cornelius, 179
veterans' benefits, 95
Vietnam, 88
  War, 14, 60, 88, 104
viewpoint diversity, 168
virtue, 187
vocation, 36–53
Voltaire, 163
von Bismarck, Otto, 48
von Mises, Ludwig, 129
voters
  behavior, 85
  dilution, 91
  fraud, 92
  ID laws, 91, 92
  roll purges, 91
  sentiment, 85
voting. *See also* universal suffrage
  rights, 60, 86
  studies, 70
Voting Rights Act (1965), 91

Wallace, George, 88
Wallace-Wells, David, 180
Walmart, 80, 99
Walton Family Foundation, 101
war mongering, 140
Washington, George, 3, 32, 56, 166, 176, 177, 178, 179, 195
  Farewell Address, 56
Washington Advertiser, 64
Washington Post, 64, 130
water, drinking, 142
Waterloo, battle of (1814), 29

wealth
  national, 169
  of nations, 109
Weber, Max, 10, 38, 39, 46, 40–46, 52, 53, 62, 75, 81, 121, 130, 155, 164, 167, 170, 177
  cause(s), 45, 46, 165, 166, 171, 178
  charisma, 167
  ethic of responsibility, 45, 46, 49, 52, 82, 164
  intellectual work as a vocation, 40
  politics, 161
  Politics as a Vocation lecture (1919), 38–39, 42–43, 45, 47, 48, 68
  science, 161
  Science as a Vocation lecture (1917), 38–39, 40, 41–42, 47, 48, 67
  scientists, 70
  two vocations, 46–47
  Weberian politicians, 60, 70, 165
Webster, Daniel
  "The Constitution and the Union" (1850), 172
Weimar Republic, 42
Wellington, Duke of, 29
wherewithal, 55, 59, 66, 68, 106, 108, 131, 146, 157, 189
  economic, 110
Whig Party, 58
White House concerts, 17
Whitman, Walt, 117
  Leaves of Grass, 116
Widener, Peter, 179
wildfires, 180
Wilentz, 58
Wilhelm, Kaiser, 42
Wilhelm II, Kaiser, 48
Will, George F., 58, 161
Wilson, Woodrow, 113
  administration, 68
Winfrey, Oprah, 130
Winthrop, John, 116
Wolfe, Alan, 20

women, 4, 11, 31, 187
  suffrage, 11, 86
Woodrow Wilson Foundation Award, 84
work ethic, 46
workers' safety, 13
workmen, 172
World War I, 40, 42, 72, 73, 113
  human costs of, 113
World War II, 4, 58, 65, 72, 73, 75, 76, 77, 81, 142, 167, 169, 173, 195
WorldCom, 98
wrestling, professional, 175. *See also* kayfabe
WWE, 177
Wright, Richard, 79

wrongdoing, 166
Wu, Tim, 125

X, 127, 175. *See also* Twitter

Yeats, William Butler, 151
  "The Second Coming" (1920), 54
yellow press, 64
Young Men's Lyceum, 177
YouTube, 146, 163, 188

Zelensky, Volodymyr, 167
Ziblatt, Daniel, 12, 18
Zuckerberg, Mark, 16, 130, 134, 135, 179, 182, 191

For EU product safety concerns, contact us at Calle de José Abascal, 56–1°,
28003 Madrid, Spain or eugpsr@cambridge.org.

www.ingramcontent.com/pod-product-compliance
Ingram Content Group UK Ltd.
Pitfield, Milton Keynes, MK11 3LW, UK
UKHW042107150326
469019UK00013B/1300